A Journey to Alaska

THE AUTHOR, 1923.

A Journey to Alaska
in the year 1868 :
being a diary of the late
Emil Teichmann

Edited with an Introduction
by his son Oskar

With a Foreword by Ernest Gruening

ARGOSY-ANTIQUARIAN LTD.
New York • 1963

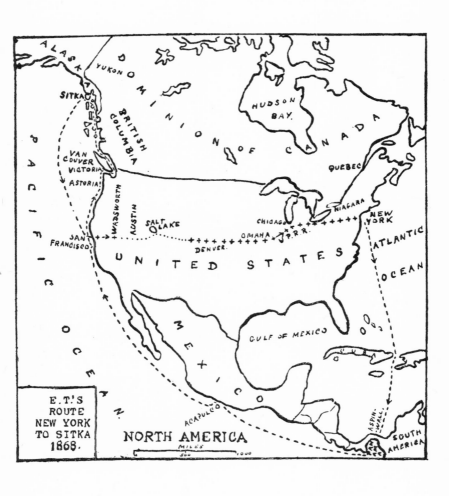

ALASKA

YUKON

DOMINION

SITKA

BRITISH
COLUMBIA

VAN
COUVER
VICTORIA

ASTORIA

WADSWORTH

AUSTIN

SALT
LAKE

HUDSON
BAY.

OF CANADA

QUEBEC

NIAGARA

CHICAGO

NEW
YORK

PACIFIC

SAN
FRANCISCO

DENVER

OMAHA
U.P.R.R.

UNITED   STATES

ATLANTIC

OCEAN

OCEAN

MEXICO

GULF OF MEXICO

E.T.'S
ROUTE
NEW YORK
TO SITKA
1868.

ACAPULCO

NORTH AMERICA

MILES
500   1000

ASPIN-
WALL.

SOUTH
AMERICA

Trans. Ham. Mr 71

51

FOREWORD

This unusual volume is another contribution to the self-
evident but nevertheless striking and intriguing revelation
of how much has happened in this world of ours in less than
a century.

When 21-year old Emil Teichmann's story begins, Alaska
was still "Russian America". To reach it from London the
author of the diary needed, of course, to cross the Atlantic
but could not conveniently continue his journey by land
across the United States. For although the race to span the
continent between the competing Union Pacific and Central
Pacific railways was "on", their construction had barely
reached the Rockies.

So he took a steamer from New York on February 12,
1868 to Colon, on the Atlantic side of the Isthmus of Panama,
crossed it by train, and resumed his journey northward along
the Pacific coast by another steamer. He had left New York
two years after the assassination of Lincoln, and arrived at
Mexico's port of Acapulco one year after the execution by
the Mexican patriot, Benito Juarez, of the ill-fated self-
imposed "Emperor" Maximilian. It took Teichmann thirteen
more days to reach the riotous frontier town of San
Francisco, where he stayed three weeks; and on April 4th,
he proceeded by steamer to Victoria in what just the previous year had ceased to be the territory of the Hudson's Bay
Company and had become the Dominion of Canada.

At Victoria only a one-masted sailing vessel, a sloop, was
available for charter to Sitka, Teichmann's objective in behalf
of his employers, who hoped to retain their hold on the
Alaskan fur trade. He and five others decided to engage this
frail craft. She was but 20 feet long, of 8-foot beam, with
one cabin 12 x 6 feet in length and breadth, and 4 feet in

height, which was to shelter the six passengers, two seamen, their luggage, as well as two large dogs. The cost of the charter was $240, but the passengers were to supply their food and blankets.

They sailed on April 21st and arrived May 17th, and in the course of their 987-mile journey of 26 days, landing somewhere almost nightly for fuel and for additional food, they experienced virtually every conceivable hardship and adventure, including encounters with unfriendly aborigines, narrowly escaping death repeatedly by acts of God and man. They traveled through regions known to few civilized men and previously described by even fewer.

In Alaska Teichmann was one of the first to see in process of establishment the ephemeral United States military posts of Fort Tongass and Fort Wrangell.

The diarist's six weeks in Sitka, until he had successfully accomplished his mission, furnish the fullest, most vivid, and virtually the only eyewitness account of life in the ancient Russian capital during the first year of U.S. occupancy. It is by no means a flattering picture of the habits and practices of the approximately 50 American newcomers —settlers and adventurers—, of the 250-man U.S. garrison, and of the some 500 temporarily remaining Russians, Creoles and others.

There is also much that is valuable about the customs of the Indian inhabitants of Sitka and surroundings which were then little known to the outside world despite the descriptions in the voyages of the early explorers, Vancouver, Portlock, Dixon, La Perouse, and others.

Teichmann was an intelligent observer, a facile writer and an accurate sketcher. As only a very few copies of his experiences were printed for private circulation, the reissuance of his Diary by ARGOSY-ANTIQUARIAN LTD. is a valuable contribution to the historic infancy of Alaska as part of the United States.

ERNEST GRUENING

PREFACE.

In 1866 the Author of this diary, then 21 years of age, entered the New York branch of Messrs. J. M. Oppenheim & Co., the leading fur merchants of London, with branches at Leipzig, St. Petersburg and Moscow. This firm, for many years before, had a contract with the Russian American Company of St. Petersburg for the purchase of the entire yearly catch of Alaskan fur seals, and consequently enjoyed an absolute monopoly in this fur, which could be dressed and dyed in London only.

When in 1867 Alaska and the Aleutian Islands were purchased by the United States from Russia, Messrs. Oppenheim's contract expired, and it became necessary for a representative to proceed to Alaska in order to safeguard the interests of the firm. The Author was selected for this mission, and in order to save time, owing to a gap of 1,000 miles existing between the termini of the Union Pacific and Central Pacific Railways, he travelled by steamer to Aspinwall, and crossing the Isthmus of Panama (the canal had at that time not been constructed) eventually reached Victoria, Vancouver Island, after staying a few weeks at San Francisco en route. In the absence of steam communication between Victoria and Sitka (Alaska), he had to charter a small sailing-sloop, and after a perilous journey through the uncharted so-called inland passage reached Sitka in the early summer 1868.

After spending some time at Sitka, he returned to San Francisco, and travelling overland by railway and stage coach to New York eventually reached London towards the end of 1868. During the whole of this time Emil Teichmann kept a most detailed diary; the original of the latter is written in a very fine and small hand in a pocket book; in January, 1869, the Author amplified this and translated it into German for the benefit of his parents, and it is from this MS., together with the original English version, that the contents of this book are taken. The original diary may be divided into four parts :—

1. New York to San Francisco via Panama. As this narrative is too lengthy to incorporate in a book and deals chiefly with the geographical, political and economic conditions of the localities described, the Editor has condensed it into a brief synopsis.

2. San Francisco to Sitka. In this portion a very lengthy description of San Francisco and Victoria have been omitted, but otherwise the MS. is quoted practically verbatim.

3. Residence at Sitka and return to San Francisco. In this part there are no omissions.

4. San Francisco to London via overland route and New York. This was considered by the Author to be of no interest, was never transcribed, and consists of a few daily notes in the original English version ; the Editor has amplified this in order to make the book complete.

The illustrations are reproduced from sketches made by the Author at the time.

The Editor is greatly indebted to Mrs. Ashley for the excellent translation of the German MS., and to his old friend Philip Gosse for his useful advice in producing this book.

The following is quoted from an appreciation of the late Emil Teichmann in " The Fur World " (April, 1924). " His advice and assistance in trade matters were repeatedly sought, not only by private individuals and public companies, but also by various Governments, to whom he rendered valuable aid. It is not too much to say that throughout the fur trade of the world there was no name more highly known or one more highly respected and esteemed—he was a great personality, he played the game, and endeared himself to all."   O. T.

THE AUTHOR, 1867.

CONTENTS.

PART I.

New York to San Francisco Via Panama. . 19

PART II.

Alaska, Formerly Russian America. . . . 23
Its position and extent, its discovery by Russian
seafarers in the eighteenth century, foundation of the
Russian-American Fur Company. Terra incognita.
The American-Asiatic Telegraph. Its purchase by
the United States ; motives and consequences. Pros
and cons ; enthusiasm for Alaska in San Francisco.

From San Francisco to the North. . . . 29
Communications with Alaska via Oregon and Vancouver
Island. Departure. On board one of the Californian,
Oregon and Mexican Steamship Company's vessels.
Foggy weather. Review of the passengers. Life of
the miners. History of three gold-diggers. Portu-
guese whale-fishers. Irishmen, Britons, German
adventurers, Chinese. An unexpected plunge-bath.

The Columbia River. 35
The Columbia in sight, its source, course and estuary.
Sandy shoals and dangerous entrance. Pilot's signals.
Disappointment. Two days at mouth of river in a
rough sea. Dearth of provisions and coal. Pilot boat
in sight. Entrance. Coast defences. Astoria and its
sights. Its foundation by John Jacob Astor. Original
inhabitants. Excursion on the Lower Columbia.
Settlements. St. Helens. The Williamette River.

The Town of Portland, Oregon and its Surroundings. 41
Size and inhabitants. Excursion to the Cascade
Mountains on the Upper Columbia. The military
station of Vancouver. The Cascade Range. River
scenery. Cape Horn. A miniature railway. The
return journey. Dangerous landings. Primitive
postal delivery. Two rainy days in Portland. News
from Sitka.

From Portland to Vancouver Island. . . 47
At last we leave. Astoria once more. A deputation
of Indians from Eastern Oregon to Washington.
Anecdotes of the last Oregon Indian war. At sea once
more. The "Race Rock" lighthouse. A prompt
pilot. Entrance to the harbour of Victoria.

Preparations for a Sailing Expedition. . . . 49
A bad disappointment. Travellers to Alaska meet and
charter the *Ocean Queen*. Purchase of provisions. My
own preparations. Departure. Maritime routes to
Alaska. Bad prospects. Choice of the "Inner
Passage."

On Board the "Ocean Queen"—I. . . . 54
Comfort on board the *Ocean Queen*, its size and arrange-
ment. The start. Dog overboard. The first night.
Reflections. The Island of San Juan, story of the
quarrel for it between Great Britain and the United
States. Scenery.

On Board the "Ocean Queen"—II. . . . 57
Scenery during the day. Lying at anchor. Fishing.
Excursion to an uninhabited island. Gulf of Trin-
comali and its surroundings. "Dodd's Narrows," a
dangerous passage. Against the stream. Critical
moments. Entering the Gulf of Georgia and arrival
at Nanaimo.

Nanaimo—I. 60
Reception. Agreement with the captain of the
Oriflamme. History of the town. Coal mines and their

working. Inhabitants. Indian camp of the "Flatheads." Their appearance. Canoes. Skilled manage-
ment of them by the coast Indians.

NANAIMO—II. 64
Conjuring entertainment with a very mixed audience.
Unpleasant meetings and moral character of the
natives. Purchases. Loss of our life-boat. Preparations for continuance of journey, we part with
two of our shipmates. A late visit and well-meant
advice. Fenian panic. Suspicion.

TOWED BY THE "ORIFLAMME." 67
An unpleasant awakening. Transferring the centre
of gravity. A nightmare journey. Lengthening the
tow rope. Half under water. Useless signals of
distress. Critical moments. Sailor's heroic courage
and the captain's cowardice. Cutting the tow line.
Saved. Parting from the *Oriflamme*. Feelings of
thankfulness. At the pumps. Afloat again.

SEYMOUR'S NARROWS AND JOHNSTONE'S STRAITS. . 72
Continuance of journey. Recollections of danger
undergone. Practical comfort. Cape Mudge. A
disturbed night. Through Seymour's Narrows.
Rudderless amid the tossing waters. Again in quiet
waters. Wonderful scenery. The Norway of America.
Becalmed and a landing. A deserted camp fire.
Canoes in sight. A night journey. Fort Rupert.
Of the Hudson Bay Company. Morality amongst
the Indians.

A VISIT TO THE NUKLETAH INDIANS. . . . 77
A calm. A little island realm. The entrance. Meeting
a canoe. A safe anchorage. Idyllic position of the
"Raucherie." Difficult landing. Hospitable reception. In the chief's house. Indian customs. Subordination of the squaws. Importunate visitors.

QUEEN CHARLOTTE SOUND. 82
Adverse wind. Entrance to the Nervitty Bay. The

encampment. Reception of the Indians. Distrust. Sketching under difficulties. The night watch. Barter. An Indian prophecy. At last under sail. The storm in the Sound. Canoe in sight. In Fitzhugh Sound. Wild scenery. Night journey decided on.

OUR LAST NIGHT JOURNEY. 88
Darkness falls. Fog. By chart and compass. Square sail overboard. Hurricane begins. With reefed sail. Driving on the shore. A mistake discovered in time. Tempestuous sea. Dog overboard. A desperate resolution.

FROM FITZHUGH SOUND TO MILBANK SOUND. . 91
Unexpected rescue. A disturbed night. Damage done by the storm. Preparations to continue journey. 100 miles in 18 hours. The Bella Bella Channel and encampment. A night with the Kokai Indians. Devastating diseases and Indian remedies. Chief Charley Hamsched. Hospitality. Unpleasant news.

THE FINLAYSON CHANNEL. 95
In Milbank Sound. Change of course. Loss of time. Through the Klemtoo Passage. Into the Finlayson Channel. Monte Diavolo and Monte Christi. Wonderful scenery. Disadvantages of the Inner Passage. Meeting with the *Red Rover*. History of a Californian adventurer. His followers. A valuable hound. Snow on the 3rd May. A calm. With the tide. A pleasant landing place. Traces of silver quartz. A race. A wolf in sight. A calm. On board the *Red Rover*.

THROUGH THE GRENVILLE CHANNEL TO FORT SIMPSON. 101
Across the Nipean Sound. Collision. Off the mouth of the Salmon River. Through the Grenville Channel. The Kittkatl encampment. Rain on shore. An Alpine landscape. Mountain sheep. In Chatham Sound. Parting from the *Red Rover*. Uncomfortable journey. Arrival at Fort Simpson.

FORT SIMPSON—I. 104
Foundation. Position. Appearance. Surroundings.
Landing. Hospitable reception. Visit to the Fort.
The Factor's house. Unusual luxury. Dinner.
Description of our host. Inspection of the Fort.
Warehouse. Fur goods. Barter on the north-west
coast. The sale room. Houses.

FORT SIMPSON—II. 110
Means of defence and fortifications. A modest kitchen
garden. Burial place. Former garrison and relations
with the Indians. Domestic circumstances of the
Factor. Offspring of mixed marriages. Subordination
of the Indian women. P. Legaic, chief of the Methlakatla Indians. Indian population of the settlement.
The Nass River fisheries. Disputes. Death of two
chiefs. Lamentation. Widow of the slain chief.
Return on board. Sounds of lamentation. Proposal
to take a pilot. A disturbed breakfast. Purchase of
supplies. Bad behaviour of the white men. Their
influence on the Indians. An episode in the life of
our sailor.

FORT SIMPSON—III. 114
Failure to engage a pilot. Purchase of a canoe. Visit
to the Indian settlement. Exterior of the houses.
Wooden carvings. Residence of the Methlakatla
chief. Sketches. Appearance of the Fort Simpson
Indians. Clothing and ornaments. Children. Depar-
ture of Legaic. Mission to the Methlakatla Indians.
Civilising influence. Mission on the Nass River.
The Tshimpsean language. Examples from a dictionary.

FORT TONGASS—I. 120
Across Chatham Sound. Good weather. Collision
with Clement City canoe. Arrival off Tongass Island.
The guard-ship. Appearance of the pilot. Camp
watch fire. Position of the military station. Accident
to our pilot. Landing and friendly reception. Garrison.

Tents. Primitive conditions. Breakfast with the officers. An interesting doctor. Details of the garrison. Discipline. Indian camp out of bounds. Recreations. Means of communication. Health conditions.

FORT TONGASS—II. 125

Relations of the military officials to the Indians. The doctor's practice. Disease among the Indians. State of war. Domestic feuds. Uselessness of Fort Tongass as a military station. English coast defence. Abandonment of the fort. Toasts. Medicinal brandy. Hospitality returned on *Ocean Queen*. Reminiscences of the *Oriflamme*. Formal engagement of the pilot. His name and rank. Personal appearance. Knowledge of languages. Modest luggage.

FROM FORT TONGASS TO FORT WRANGEL. . . 129

Departure from Tongass. Stormy weather. Cape Fox. Increasing violence of storm. Collapse of our square sail. Pilot's sense of locality. Longed for place of refuge. Island in Gravina group. Stormy night. Journey continued. Arrival in Ernest Sound. Prince of Wales and Revillegigedo Islands. Fort Stewart. Schooner in sight. Rising wind. Under reefed sails. Canoe passage to the Stikeen and Etoline Islands. Anchorage. Effect of storm.

FORT WRANGEL. 133

Position of the Fort. Surroundings. Stikeen River. Changed course. Signal shots. Customs canoe. Visit of an officer. Misunderstanding cleared up. Conditions in the military camp. Smuggling trade. News of loss of the *Growler*. News of our former travelling companions. Sailor's threats. Charley's uncertainty. Return of the canoe.

WRANGEL CANOE PASSAGE. 138

Shallow channel. Routes to Frederick Sound. An unpleasant discovery. Canoe passage chosen. Bad times for the pilot. Unsafe anchorage. Finding the passage. Becalmed. Scenery. Water-fowl. Welcome captures. Uninvited guests. Barter. Unrevealed secret. Deception and flight. At entrance to Frederick Sound.

FREDERICK SOUND. 143
Position and extent of Sound. Surroundings. Kuprianoff Island. Wonderful scenery on Admiralty Island. Glaciers. Well-earned anchorage. Neglectful captain. Renewal of voyage. Angry sea. Dangerous position. Visited by a canoe. Rejected invitation. Reaching the shore. Repairs. Kaigh Indians. A ramble. Unpleasant thoughts. Return of the hunters. Their spoils. Strict watch.

A STORMY JOURNEY. 148
Unpleasant awakening. Stormy weather. Cape Fairweather. In Christian Sound. Angry channel. Approach of the storm. Preparations. Hatchway closed. Shut in. Beginning of the hurricane. Feelings of the prisoners. Unpleasant company. Moments of despair. Under water. Welcome sounds. Saved.

LOST. 153
Renewal of dispute. Finding our way. Search for north-west passage. Surrounded by land. Scouting. Vain attempts. Wild region. Disappointment and bewilderment. Canoe in sight. The proper route. Fresh proposals as to pilot. Hostility of the sailors. Departure of the Chuznus.

A NIGHT ATTACK. 157
Awakened from sleep. Grave apprehension. Boarded by the Chuznus. Invasion of the cabin. Critical position. Decisive moments. Prepared to fight. Skilful negotiator. Friendly turn. Squaw and papoose. Forced liberality. Importunate guests. Indian watch. Fall of snow. Engagement of a pilot. Barter. An interrupted sketch. Towed by canoes. Departure of the Chuznus.

FROM THE PERIL STRAITS TO SITKA. . . . 164
Good weather. Indian fisherman. Entrance to the
Peril Straits. Pilot's testimonials. Chuznus. A calm.
Rain. Driven back. Shallow water. Water fowl.
Seals. Water plants. The Narrows. Sitka Indians.
Adverse wind. Lonely fishing hut. Continuous rain.
Rowing. Mount Edgcumbe in sight. Impatience.
Intolerable conditions. Sitka in sight. Customs
official. Landing.

PART III.

SITKA—I. 172
Position of town and surroundings. Population and
nationalities. A primitive hotel. Its equipment.
Lodgings for the night. Sitka Indians and Aleutians,
their origin. Character. Occupations. Hunting and
fishing. Summer and winter. Emigration.

SITKA—II. 178
My mission. An important contract. Loss of the
monopoly. Breach of contract. Authorised robbery.
Instructions for journey. Attempt to open relations.
Obstacles. Alteration in strategy. Jesuitical
friendliness.

SITKA—III 183
Incognito. Attempts to approach me. A rejected
invitation. Espionage. Temperature and climate.
Their influence on health. Illnesses. Russians in
Sitka, their mode of living. Piety. Clergy. The Com-
pany's officials. Workpeople. Dwellings. Immorality.
Drunkenness. Russian women.

SITKA—IV. 188
American population. Army officers. Loose discipline. Drunkenness of soldiers. Civilians : (i)
officials, etc. (ii) Jewish traders (iii) adventurers,
gold diggers, sailors, hunters and desperadoes. Criminal
cases. Administration of justice. An important
meeting. Engagement of a Russian spy.

SITKA—V. 193
The Indian village. Boundary defences. Exterior of
the houses. Their situation. Life on the shore.
Number of inhabitants. Division of races. Physical
characteristics. Clothing. Decoration. Morality.
State of health. Language.

SITKA—VI. 198
A Russian vapour bath. Its equipment. Procedure.
An unusual ceremony. Russian church service.
Arrival of a Government steamer. Increased espionage.
A disturbed night. Search for a dwelling. Sunday
in Sitka. The American church. Return of the
Ocean Queen. A sea trip at night.

SITKA—VII. 204
Change of abode. Russian block-house. Furniture.
My house-mates. Unwelcome visitors. Primitive
toilet arrangements. Eating house. Famine in
prospect.

SITKA—VIII. 207
Captain F. His personality and past. Collection of
curiosities. Dangerous surveying in Indian territory.
Desecration of graves. Critical situation. Fortunate
escape.

SITKA—IX. 212
A medicine man without conscience. A go-between
and bargainer. Protracted method of business. Visit
to the Indian village. The captain as guide. Market.
Indian haggling. Gambling to pass the time. Visit
to the huts. An unfortunate hunter. A rapid cure.
Gratitude.

SITKA—X. 217
Renewed espionage. Inexplicable refusal of a passage.
Bribery and corruption. Fine weather. Excursions
and picnics. Evening entertainments of the Russians.
Discovery of gold on the Tacon River. Departure of

gold prospectors. Murder and fate of the murderer. Mysterious disappearance of the other gold prospectors. Discovery of a coal deposit. Trade in furs. Good business. Imprudence.

SITKA—XI. 222
Arrival of a suspicious sailing-boat. Camp on the Indian river. Explanation. Expedition of the *Louisa Downes*. Experiences of the gold prospectors. A mythical story. Experiences at sea. Fenian suspicions in Victoria. Arrival at the Tacon River. Bitter disappointment. Lynch law by the infuriated adventurers. Return to Sitka. An old story.

SITKA—XII. 227
Expedition into the interior. Life in Sitka in the early morning. Toilsome journey through the virgin forest. Fallen forests. Wading through the mountain stream. Tumble of our leader. Supposed copper deposits. Siesta. Camp fire. Forest fire. Uneasy conscience. Prairie tactics.

SITKA—XIII. 231
Illness. Poisonous thorn. Rainy weather. Depression. Documentary evidence. Putting together the proofs. My legal house-mate. Celebrated " Property lawsuit " of Sitka. A valuable document. A disturbed night. Request refused. Daily events in the town. An unfortunate fellow.

SITKA—XIV. 234
Death of an Indian prince. The body lying in state. Strange watcher of the dead. Arrival of strange Indians. Indian funeral rites and election of a new prince, weird spectacle. Safely outside again.

SITKA—XV. 239
Greek Catholic funeral rites. Procession to the burial place. Christian burial. Digging up and burning the

body. A victim saved. Rising in Indian camp. War-
like demonstration. Negotiations. Blockade of Indian
camp. A blockade runner destroyed. Vendetta of
the Indians.

SITKA—XVI. 243
Arrival of war-ship *Saginaw*. News of shipwrecked
Growler. Squaw's deposition. Arrival of coaling
vessel, *Black Diamond*, from Nanaimo. Passage
engaged for the south. Violent scene with my
informant. Pressure brought to bear. Signing of the
deposition. Price of treachery. Legal confirmation.
Departure from Sitka and start on the *Black Diamond*.

ON BOARD THE " BLACK DIAMOND "—I. . . 247
Crew and condition of our ship. Food and comfort.
Sleeping accommodation. Uninvited guests. Our
passengers. Experiences of a gold prospector. Storm.
Heroic crew. Reward. Feelings of thankfulness.

ON BOARD THE " BLACK DIAMOND "—II. . . 255
Becalmed. Albatrosses. Seals. Whales. Scarcity
of drinking water. Small rations. Welcome breeze.
Uncertainty as to course. Land in sight. Fog. An
uncomfortable night. Again becalmed. Ocean
currents. Arrival in harbour of Victoria.

THE RETURN JOURNEY TO SAN FRANCISCO. . . 260
A long telegram. Believed to be lost. Attacks by
Indians. Destruction of the *Red Rover*. Attack on
the *Thornton*. Attempt on the *Black Diamond*. On
the steamer. Parting from the gold prospectors.
Arrival at San Francisco.

PART IV.

SAN FRANCISCO. 266
Overland stage. Salt Lake City. New York.
Southampton.

PART I.

NEW YORK TO SAN FRANCISCO VIA PANAMA.

Synopsis.

The Author left New York on February 12th, 1868, and arrived at Colon eight days later.

E.T. 1868

ASPINWALL, (COLON).

After crossing the Isthmus by train (the canal had not been made in those days), he arrived at Panama where a day was spent in visiting the old town.

E.T. 1868

PANAMA WITH ANCON HILL.

Six days later the steamer arrived at Acapulco and the Author set foot on Mexican soil for the first time : it was scarcely a year since the ill-fated Maximilian had met his death at the hands of this nation.

ENTRANCE TO ACAPULCO HARBOUR.

E.T. 1868

ACAPULCO BAY.

E.T. 1868

ACAPULCO.

E.T. 1868

20

ACAPULCO.   E.T. 1868

CHURCH, ACAPULCO.   E.T. 1868

RUINED CONVENT, ACAPULCO.   E.T. 1868

21

After thirteen days steaming up the coast of Mexico and California, the Golden Gate and harbour of San Francisco were eventually reached, the total journey from New York having taken 22 days and 6 hours.

E.T. 1868

SAN MARGARITA ISLAND, LOWER CALIFORNIA.

PART II.

ALASKA, FORMERLY RUSSIAN AMERICA.

After a stay of three weeks in San Francisco, on the 4th April, 1868, I received despatches which compelled me to go still further north.

E.T. 1868

SEAL ROCKS AND CLIFFHOUSE, SAN FRANCISCO.

The goal of my new journey was *Sitka* or New Archangel, the chief settlement in the extensive territory formerly known as Russian America, which was ceded by the Russian Government to the United States in March, 1867, for a payment of 7,000,000 dollars in gold, and formally passed into the possession of the United States in October of that year.

That territory, which since its acquisition by the Americans is called Alaska (after the peninsula which forms

23

its western portion), comprises some 500,000 square miles and forms a great peninsula on the north-west corner of America. It is bounded on the north by the Arctic Ocean, on the east by the territory of the Hudson Bay Company (which has long been regarded as a British possession), and on the south by the Pacific Ocean ; in the extreme west it is separated from Asia by the Behring Strait. The numerous islands along the coast, on one of which the port of Sitka is situated, and including a group called the Aleutian Islands which stretch westward to the neighbourhood of Kamtchatka, were included in the purchase.

E.T. 1868

MEXICAN CHURCH, SAN FRANCISCO.

The credit of the first discovery of the Behring Strait and the west coast of America must be ascribed to Russian seamen who, after the founding of Eastern Siberia and the discovery of the Kamtchatkan peninsula at the instigation of Peter the Great and the Empress Catherine, carried their explorations still further east. Behring and his lieutenant, Tschirikoff, landed in 1741 at various places on the mainland but then lost a large number of their crew, partly through conflicts with the natives and partly through scurvy—that plague of all travellers in the Far North—and were compelled to return hastily to Asia. Tschirikoff was fortunate enough to reach the coast of Siberia, but

24

Behring, whose weakened crew was not able to handle the ship, was wrecked on the island which had been named after him, and there with his fellow sufferers fell a victim to scurvy resulting from utter want.

The search for the North-West Passage (from the Atlantic to the Pacific Ocean) which was so much discussed at that time, impelled other bold explorers, Cooke, La Perouse, Van Couver, Kotzebue and others to complete the discoveries already made, and the reports brought to Siberia by Tschirikoff as to the newly discovered territory's wealth in furs led to the formation of a company for the purpose of exploring the fur products of the west coast of America.

In the year 1799 this company, formed by Siberian merchants under the name of the Russian American Company, received from the Russian Government the chartered rights of a trade monopoly and the independent administration of their territory, just as similar rights on the eastern coast of North America had been given to an English trading company—the Hudson Bay Company—in the reign of Charles II. towards the end of the seventeenth century.

In the year 1800 a Siberian merchant named Baranoff, who was then at the head of the Russian company, established numerous " Forts " or trading stations among which Sitka, being a harbour, was the most strongly fortified and provided with a small garrison. Some years later, when Baranoff chanced to be absent, the new station was attacked by an overwhelming force of Indians and the occupants were massacred ; only one Aleutian managed to escape and carried the news of the disaster to Baranoff. Through the latter's influence a Russian squadron appeared before Sitka where the Indians who were provided with firearms, had entrenched themselves ; there was severe fighting for several days till at last lack of ammunition forced the dogged Indians to surrender. A fort was erected, the residences of the Russians were surrounded with palisades, and a larger garrison was stationed there. The Indians made many attempts later on, even after the beginning of the 'fifties, to capture Sitka, but were repelled on each occasion with heavy loss by the Russians, who were much better armed.

After that time the Russian American Company enjoyed for many years a complete monopoly of trade on the north-west coast, although during the Crimean War even this remote possession of Russia was not altogether unaffected, since the port of Sitka was blockaded for some time by a British squadron.

Meanwhile great changes had taken place on the west coast of North America. Since the discovery of gold in California in the year 1849, whole populations had streamed towards the vaunted West and within a few years new states had been founded by free American citizens. California, Oregon and Washington Territory (this last separated from the Russian possessions only by a narrow strip of land under British rule) had developed with amazing rapidity, and the American pioneers who had now reached the extreme west and were prevented from going further by the Pacific Ocean, turned their gaze to the north-west where unknown lands of boundless extent offered themselves as a field for exploration.

The jealously guarded monopoly of the Russian company and the consequent isolation from the rest of the world gave the country in the eyes of the Americans all the attractiveness of the unknown, and made them more and more eager for its acquisition.

In the year 1865 permission was given for an expedition sent out by the American Telegraph Union to enter the Russian territory in order to erect a telegraph line to the Behring Strait, whilst on the Asiatic side a second expedition was engaged in erecting a line to the Strait. The intention was to connect the two terminal stations by a submarine cable and so place America in telegraphic communication with Europe via Siberia.

This remarkable American scheme was warmly encouraged by the Russian Government. The work was begun at both ends at once with the customary American energy and after innumerable difficulties due to the nature of the country, the severity of the climate, the hostility of the natives, etc., had been partly overcome, there was reason to believe that this vast undertaking would be carried out successfully, when in July, 1867, the completion of the transatlantic cable solved the problem of placing America in telegraphic communication with the Old World. The Russian-American line, on which three million dollars had already been expended, suddenly became unnecessary and the work on both sides of the Strait was brought to a standstill.

The only gain derived from these unfortunate expeditions was the accumulation of important scientific data relating to a country hitherto regarded as " terra incognita," and the acquisition of the first really authentic information as to the geographical and climatic conditions and the products of the territory which, as already remarked, passed into the ownership of the United States in March, 1867.

It is difficult to determine the reasons which induced the Russian Government to give up its possessions in America. Some think that the cession must be regarded as a hostile demonstration against England and intended to expose that country's American dominions more and more to the disintegrating influence of the United States. Others contend that Russia was influenced in taking this step simply by the large price offered to her.

The main reason is probably to be found in the tendency of the Czar's Empire to extend its power in the Pacific over the southern lands of the Mongols, to bring China and Japan within its sphere of influence, and with that object to consolidate its position rather than let it be weakened by the existence of isolated possessions in America. In these circumstances it is not surprising that the Czar should not let slip the opportunity of divesting himself, on satisfactory terms, of a territory which in the event of war would have neither the inclination nor the ability to hold out for any length of time.

Quite different was the secret motive of Seward, the United States Secretary of State, in supporting President Johnson's policy of purchase ; to him it was a step towards the realisation of the Monroe Doctrine—" America for the Americans, from the Arctic to the Tropics ! "

It was indeed a *European* Power which by this withdrawal lost the right to intervene in future in American affairs, and in this way a kind of warning was given to England also.

The British Colonies, bounded on the north and south by American territory and confined to a narrow strip of coast and the regions behind it, would find their position more and more untenable, and would have great difficulty in escaping absorption into the United States as their ultimate destiny.

As the American people are always inclined to injure Great Britain and to revenge themselves for the British recognition of the Southern rebels, the Seward purchase gave rise to considerable anxiety.

Two parties were immediately formed, one in favour of, and the other opposed to, the acquisition of the territory. To judge from the statements made by the former, Alaska must be an " El Dorado," whose healthy climate and abundance of furs, fish and wild animals, coal, silver and gold they were never tired of proclaiming—in short, a land which needed only the touch of the creative hands of the Yankees to become forthwith a veritable gold mine. On the other hand, the opponents poured the bitterest scorn upon a country whose climate they described as arctic in the north and as perpetually rainy and foggy in the south, with a population consisting only of Indians and Eskimos, who could never be civilised. " Have we not," cried this party with that fervour which the Americans bring into all political matters, " have we not hundreds of thousands of acres of the most promising agricultural land, and shall we part with our good money for icebergs ? "

There were stormy scenes in Congress at Washington. The purchase proposal was nearly rejected by the House of Representatives and it was only at the last moment, by the exercise of the utmost pressure and appeals to the Monroe Doctrine, that a majority was obtained, the proposal sanctioned and the money voted.

Meantime on the 18th October, 1867, in Sitka, the United States had taken possession of Russian America or Alaska ; two companies of artillery with their guns had been stationed there as a garrison ; and the Russian Fur Company had undertaken to evacuate the town and district completely within a year.

In San Francisco, as throughout the whole western coast, popular opinion was unanimously in favour of the purchase, since certain advantages would naturally accrue therefrom to the neighbouring States. One needs to know the character of the Californians to realise the delight with which old and young alike greeted the news of the increase of territory. Despite constant and bitter disappointments in mining matters the Californian is always full of excitement when he hears of any new discovery. Fabulous stories of the wealth of Alaska's resources spread abroad ; no one knew their origin, but everybody believed them none the less ; and in the spring of 1868 the whole of San Francisco was in a state of feverish excitement.

In the windows of the furriers were to be seen nothing but Alaskan pelts ; the confectioners sold Alaskan ice ; the money changers had samples of Alaskan gold and silver ores. Views of Sitka, some imaginary, others based on old Russian pictures, appeared by the side of Russian dictionaries in the booksellers' windows. In short, Alaska was the only topic.

Many enterprising merchants fitted out vessels and waited only for the commencement of the milder weather to send them to sea.

This was the position when, as I stated at the beginning, business connected with the winding-up of the Russian American Fur Company called me myself to Sitka.

FROM SAN FRANCISCO TO THE NORTH.

It was on one of those fine and incomparably beautiful April days, following as a rule on the rainy season which extends over many months, that I went to the office of the Californian Oregon and Mexican Steamship Company to make enquiries as to a passage to Alaska. Communication with Alaska was then, and so far as I know is still, irregular and confined to occasional conveyance of supplies for the troops stationed there; and moreover the season was not yet sufficiently advanced for there to be any considerable traffic. There was no possibility of getting a steamer or sailing ship to Sitka, but I might have the chance of a ship from Victoria (Vancouver Island), since the official gave me to understand with an air of great mystery that the Government had chartered one of his company's steamers for the purpose of carrying troops and supplies to Alaska, and that it would call at Victoria to coal.

In order not to lose any time I resolved to take the course suggested. Victoria was at least 600 miles nearer to Alaska and a steamer was clearing for that port that very evening.

The most important requisites for the journey I managed to obtain despite the lateness of the hour (it was a Saturday); the remainder of my letter of credit I transferred by telegraph to be available for me at Victoria; and, leaving part of my luggage at the hotel in order to be somewhat less burdened, I betook myself at 4 o'clock in the afternoon on board the small steamer " Active," a vessel which had formerly been employed by the Government on coast survey work and only later fitted for the carriage of passengers. In consequence of this the so-called " Saloon " was dark and stuffy, and the sleeping cabins, which were small and inconvenient, held out little hope of comfort.

After the usual turmoil before departure, the final signal was given, the last rope cast off and our journey began.

The trip across San Francisco Bay is always one of the most interesting in the neighbourhood and on that evening, thanks to the last rays of the setting sun, the famous exit appeared as a veritable " Golden Gate." Scarcely, however, had we passed through the Gate, when suddenly the sky grew darker and we were caught in one of the thickest of the thick fogs which sweep up from the sea regularly every evening like a cloud over the Bay. A fog at sea is always rather disquieting, and involuntarily the traveller thinks of collisions and of sunken rocks. It is not possible to stay on deck without getting wet through, and consequently in such weather the passengers assemble in the saloon, not in the best of tempers, relying on the steersman who, with the look-out man in the bows, is responsible for their safety. When an accident does occur, the collision usually follows almost immediately upon the alarm being given, and unhappily collisions are only too numerous in foggy weather in the neighbourhood of a much-frequented port.

At dinner I had an opportunity of passing my fellow passengers in review. At the top sat our captain, a quite young man who had just retired from the navy, son of a Minister of the Southern States and himself heart and soul a Southerner. On his right and left sat two ship's officers, and on both sides of the very sparsely occupied table, waited on by untidy waiters, chiefly Irish, were seated about a dozen rough-looking bearded fellows, whose coloured woollen shirts proclaimed them to be miners. These were the élite of the passengers—the so-called " first-cabin " travellers,—whilst in the fore-cabin the second-class passengers, some thirty men in more or less tattered garments, were encamped on old woollen blankets. My first impression of these was that they belonged to the outcasts of society and were adventurers of the most dangerous kind. The first group of passengers, despite their uncouth appearance, had at least decent clothes and new blankets, and their guns—each carried one—were in leather cases. The between-decks passengers were not only insufficiently clad, but carried their murderous-looking revolvers and bowie knives quite openly in a way which was very disturbing to nervous people.

As I gradually found out, most of the miners on board worked in the northern mining districts of British Columbia —the so-called Cariboo—and had spent the winter, when mining is impossible, in San Francisco, where they had squandered their hard-earned half-year's wages on the

31

pleasures of the town, and were now returning with empty pockets to resume their adventurous life in the Far North. There must be some very powerful attraction which draws these men again into the wilderness, away from the alluring attractions of the great city. Amongst those in our cabin with whom I became more closely acquainted were two Italians and one Frenchman; the former came from Genoa and the latter from Languedoc. All three of them seemed to have received originally a good education. The two former were involved in the revolutions of 1848, were compelled to flee from their country, and after twenty years wandering in South, Central and North America, found their way to the remote mines of the extreme North-West. Though several times on the road to prosperity, if not to wealth, they never knew how to seize the right moment for exchanging their adventurous life for European civilisation; they found themselves always remorselessly set back and forced to begin anew. Now they spoke often with longing about their return, one day, to their native land, to which they would go back only as successful men. Will these people ever attain their desire, or are they fated in their struggle for existence to fall victims to the snows, the wild animals and the Indians of the northern regions?

The reasons which drove the Frenchman to emigrate were altogether different. His history is quite a romance, the scene being his native place. He found himself scorned by the object of his love, a rich young girl who preferred one of his rivals. The result was a duel in which the despised lover had wounded, and possibly killed, his more fortunate rival. He fled to the coast, enlisted as a sailor, sailed apparently all round the world, was a gold-miner in Australia, a slave-owner in Brazil, a merchant in Central America, and now for many years had spent the summer in the mines of the North-West. He had nevertheless in his heart a longing for " la belle France," though he would not admit it openly.

Often in the evening from the fore-part of the ship there were heard strains of music, softly breathing a yearning for southern climes ; these were sung by the sons of Italy, whose rough exterior belied their tender hearts.

Those engaged in occupations which bring them into close contact with nature—such as seamen, mountaineers, fishermen, hunters, trappers, etc.—are generally characterised by good humour, straight-forwardness, and honesty : and so amongst the miners there are often to be found fine characters, thoroughly original, and anyone who wins their confidence discovers them to be as a rule reliable comrades, always ready to help by word and deed. I, too, found amongst my shipmates many a good fellow. These included some Portuguese whalers, men of the true stamp, who had often been caught in the ice in the North and had wintered there. Once, as they told me, they had made 2,000 dollars in a twenty months' campaign against the monsters of the deep. Now, enticed by the call of the golden treasure of Cariboo, they intended to spend a season in the mines there. These three seemed always to work together whether by sea or land.

Another group was made up of sons of the green isle of Erin, and they also were admirable specimens of that good-natured but excitable island race, whom to make contented is mighty England's most difficult task.

An English seaman, a regular John Bull, who was on his way to join his ship in Victoria, and a young Scotchman travelling to join his relatives at the same place, represented the interests of Old England. To these must be added an old, bent, shabby-looking Jew, who professed to have come from London and was now at an advanced age anxious to go to the mines : he seemed to know most of them, and in reply to my enquiries I learned that for many years the old man had frequented the mining districts, sometimes as a trader, sometimes as a digger. If one could trust his statements, he had occasionally been well-to-do, but had now fallen into poverty again.

There were also a number of German adventurers ; I am ashamed to say that they were by far the most wretched and ragged in appearance of the whole body of passengers and their low cunning and shiftiness could be read in their faces. Their speech was a jargon of German and English, and they seemed to know only the most unpleasant words of each language.

Finally, we must not omit a party of Greeks, from whom one can never escape on the West Coast ; they spent the greater part of the day cowering in a corner, and sought to relieve the long monotony of the voyage with the pleasures of opium.

The first three days passed with little incident, and quietly so far as the miserable cooking and other arrangements allowed. The sea was rather choppy and the sky cloudy, the weather cold and rainy. Although our course lay along the coast land was seldom in sight, and it was only occasionally that we had glimpses of the snow-covered mountains of the mainland in the far distance. A slight accident which befell me did not tend to raise my spirits. One night, in order to get rid of the oppressive smell of my freshly-painted cabin, I imprudently left the port-hole open : the sea appeared to be moderately smooth, so I breathed the fresh air with delight and fell sound asleep. But the awakening was unpleasant. The wind on our course had altered in the night ; the waves beat against my cabin, and about 6 o'clock in the morning I was awakened to my dismay by a torrent of water which burst through the window, flooded my berth, and threatened to swamp the cabin. To spring up and close the port-hole was the work of a moment, but already there was a great mess ; my clothes and luggage were floating about in the most appalling confusion as the water rose and fell with the movement of the ship. To make my situation still worse, I could not find my keys, which had no doubt been swept under the berth, and consequently I had to wait from 6 till 10 o'clock in my dripping garments until at last one of the stewards who had been told to help in the search brought the keys to me.

Such a soaking one would expect to be followed by a very heavy cold ; but I found by experience on this occasion, as on others, that salt water never has that result.

THE COLUMBIA RIVER.

Meanwhile our gallant ship was well on its way, and on the morning of the fourth day we approached the coast opposite the mouth of the River Columbia, whose lime-impregnated waters give the ocean a yellow tinge for ten miles from where it enters the sea. The Columbia is the largest river on the west coast of North America ; it rises in a small lake on the western slope of the Rocky Mountains and flows with many windings for a distance of 1,200 miles into the Pacific, its western course forming the boundary between the State of Oregon and the Washington Territory. In its upper stretches the Columbia is a rushing stream which has forced its way irresistibly through rocky gorges, and with many falls and rapids pours down to the lower stretches, and towards the mouth widens out into broads four to seven miles across. Navigation, which is practicable for the largest ships for a distance of 140 miles upstream, is at that point checked by a series of great rapids ; after those are passed the river is navigable again for a considerable distance.

As is generally the case with the estuaries of large rivers, there has been formed at the mouth of the Columbia a line of dangerous sandbanks whose constant shiftings makes the approach extremely difficult. Vessels venture on the passage of the sandbanks only under the guidance of an experienced pilot stationed there, since it is well known that deviation from the narrow channels by even a foot's breadth would result in running aground, and this, owing to the nature of the so-called " quicksands," would entail a complete loss. The extent of the danger attending this passage can be realised from the fact that it is practicable for big ships only at certain stages of the tide and when the sea is calm.

As out steamer was not going direct to Vancouver Island, but had to discharge goods and passengers at Portland, Oregon, which is situated on a tributary of the

Columbia, about a hundred miles from the mouth, we ourselves had occasion to make this notorious passage.

After a stormy and rainy night, we could, in the early morning, distinguish with the naked eye the coast at the point where the Columbia mingles its mighty waters with the Ocean. Against the dark background of pine woods we could pick out with our telescopes, the white lighthouse and the fortifications placed on a height above the mouth of the river. As we steamed up and down at half-speed the pilot signal was hoisted and the warning gun fired from our forecastle sounded faintly, being carried away by the wind and the roar of the sea. Although the sea was very rough, no one of us—not even the captain himself, who was making this particular voyage for the first time—had the slightest doubt that a pilot-boat would put out from the shore and provide us with a pilot. Eagerly we looked across the white foam that surged over the sandbanks to the coast some eight English miles away ; but what we thought to be a sail always proved to our disappointment to be a rock on the shore or a white-capped wave. A second and third signal shot was fired : 12 o'clock struck, but no pilot boat, no sail was to be seen near or far.

Lunch time passed in silence, and the passengers became more and more depressed at being so close to port and yet unable to reach it. It was early in April, the days were short, and at dusk we had to abandon hope for that day. Towards evening the wind increased perceptibly in violence, blowing up from the west and driving us towards the land, so that to avoid the dangerous shallows we were compelled to stand out to sea against the wind and waves.

The next morning, the fifth since our departure from San Francisco, we were on the high seas, out of sight of land, and mercilessly tossed about by the raging waves ; our stock of provisions, sufficient only for five days—and not even abundant for that period—began to give out, the meat was turning bad, and though there was no danger of absolute starvation no one quite knew what would happen.

In addition to this the coal supply began to run short, so that in order to be prepared for any contingency the engines had to be run only at half-speed, and we could move but slowly. Apparently we must have gone further away from the coast during the night than was necessary, for after steaming eastward during the whole of that day and the following night at half our normal speed we found ourselves at 10 o'clock in the morning of the sixth day back again at the point from which we had been compelled to move two days previously. This time, happily, the weather was fine and the sea quite calm, and towards noon we had the satisfaction of seeing our signals answered by the appearance of a sail, which from its number we recognised to be that of a pilot-boat. Like a swan it glided coquettishly over the water, rising and falling with the waves ; the swelling sails seemed to make the shapely, rounded boat even more diminutive than it was. We stopped, and after it had circled round us several times, there was a conversation between our captain and the pilot, the upshot of which was that for some reason or other the pilot refused to come on board, but was willing to precede us in his boat and show the way. The offer was accepted and our steamer followed closely on the track of the skilfully-guided sailing-boat. Though dangerous surges beat on both sides over treacherous shallows, though wild floods and raging whirlpools threatened to engulf us, our pilot never failed us and within half-an-hour—during which many hearts beat more quickly—we left the dangerous passage behind us and were in the calm fairway of the river.

On the left the coast rises fairly steeply about 200 feet to a height which is crowned by a dark fir-wood, at whose edge, close to the slope, there rise a lighthouse and a battery which we have already observed from the sea and recalls the great Civil War. On our right to the south the land is flat, but also covered with dense woods. Right on the water's edge, opposite the north battery, earthworks have been thrown up, and behind them a company

37

of artillery is encamped in tents and blockhouses, and as we pass by they answer our salute. We draw near the southern bank, and after rounding a wooded promontory we come in sight of *Astoria*, the port of the State of Oregon, which extends along a cove of the river.

ASTORIA, OREGON.   E.T. 1868

The settlement, consisting of small wooden houses, does not make a particularly favourable impression. The ground is hilly, and rises somewhat abruptly from the water's edge, so that some of the buildings, resting on piles, are actually in the water, whilst other scattered houses and huts seem to cling with difficulty to the side of the hill. The town, as it exists to-day, is only a few years old : the small area reclaimed from the forest is still strewn with half-charred stumps of trees which detract from the charm of the scene.

Meanwhile we had been moored to the wooden landing-stage, and were received by about a dozen stalwart sunburned men who, with their hands in their pockets, were awaiting our arrival. The start of our journey upstream had to be postponed until the evening, as we had to take in fuel and engage a river pilot, so that it was possible for me to get a closer view of Astoria.

From the landing stage we made our way past stacks of wooden boards, the chief product of the town, to the lowest street, which runs parallel with the river bank and rests on piles ; on both sides of it there are restaurants and taverns in which my fellow travellers partook of highly-peppered oyster soup, to make good the gastronomical shortcomings of the voyage, or sought by some glasses of stiff brandy to prepare themselves for the hardships still to come. At the Custom House and the Astoria Hotel, both of which are built entirely of wood, the more respectable part of the town begins, and the numerous little whitewashed houses with green blinds, each standing in a small garden, look pleasant enough when seen at close quarters. There is also a little church around which the upper class seems to reside. A few paces uphill we found ourselves on the edge of the settlement ; stumps of trees of the weirdest shapes impede the intruder with their wide-spreading roots, young fir saplings seem to be trying to get a foothold in the clearings, and it is almost as if the dark pine wood above were pressing forward to overwhelm the young settlement at its feet. For a lonely place commend me to the Astoria of to-day !

It was in 1812 that John Jacob Astor, the first and most famous fur-trader of America, established near to the site of the present town a settlement or so-called " fort," like several others which he had built along the Columbia River, for the purpose of barter with the natives. At that time no white faces were to be seen on the banks of the virgin stream ; undisturbed the Redskin hunted or fished, and rich was the booty of splendid furs which he was ready to exchange for worthless trumpery. Years have passed since then ; the white men have increased continually in numbers, steamships plough their way along the once so peaceful river, steam engines tear through the dark forests, flourishing towns full of life spring up as if by magic. Some ruins, half-rotted pillars, of J. J. Astor's fort remain, but in its place there rose a town, named Astoria in his honour, with several hundred white inhabitants.

But what, we ask, has become of the Redskins, the former inhabitants of the territory over which their white brethren now hold sway ? They have disappeared, leaving hardly any trace, decimated in useless struggles against the white men, but even more sorely ravaged by disease and every kind of vice acquired through intercourse with the whites.

To-day there are only a few remnants left—and they are mostly given to drunkenness—of those proud nations in Lower Columbia which were the terror of the first settlers and had once by their bravery gained the admiration of men like Fennimore Cooper and Washington Irving. Could those warlike figures of bygone decades have imagined descendants like those three small, dirty, miserable-looking Indians who paddled up in a canoe during our stay in Astoria and tried cringingly to sell oysters and clams to one of the American hotel keepers ?

By this time it was evening and our steamer had taken on board the requisite supplies of wood as a substitute for coal, which was not available ; but for some unknown reason the continuance of our journey was postponed till the next morning. So we had wasted another day.

Beneath a cloudless sky under the guidance of the river-pilot, a tall, thin Yankee captain who has grown grey at sea, we continue upstream, leaving the original Astor settlement on our right. The wreck, lying in midstream, of a ship laden with timber which our pilot told us had been there since 1849 and was now almost entirely overgrown with river-weeds, helped us to realise the variations in the level of the river-bed.

Some miles above Astoria the Columbia narrows considerably. Its width, which near that town is some seven miles, dwindles to about one mile, and apparently it remains of that size for a long distance. The banks, however, become relatively steeper and higher, and the further we get from the mouth the wilder becomes the scene. The dark pine and fir forests, reaching down to the water's edge, are broken from time to time by bare masses of rock, which rise in fantastic forms often perpendicularly from out the river ; and numerous gorges and gullies, cutting deep into the mountain barrier, remind the tourists of the streams and avalanches which doubtless produced them.

Very occasionally, we noticed on the bank a small clearing, in the middle of which there stood a cabin made of rough logs, generally inhabited by fishermen, white men who had taken to themselves Indian squaws, and showed themselves quite unconcernedly by the side of their brown companions and frequently surrounded by a number of dusky-hued children. As the Columbia is very rich in all kinds of fish, and particularly in excellent salmon which when preserved forms an important export from Oregon and is shipped even to China and Australia, the fishing industry is very remunerative and the fishermen on the Columbia have an assured market.

It was not till the afternoon that we passed the first little town, Monticello, and towards 8 o'clock in the evening, when off the settlement of St. Helen, we fired a signal gun in order that a telegraphic warning of our approaching arrival might be sent to Portland, which was still about 30 miles away. Meanwhile the scenery along the river had become decidedly less interesting, and the banks were less steep and high, so that we did not miss much when it grew dark, but resumed tranquilly our walks on the deck, which wiled away some of the evening hours, or leaning on the bulwark watched the sparks that poured from the funnel like a fiery shower against the dark evening sky. Reaching a bend of the river we turned sharply to the right and entered the Williamette, a tributary of the Columbia, on whose high bank about 15 miles from its junction with the main stream lies Portland, the most important town of Oregon. It was midnight when the steamer arrived there—too late for us to land and consequently, despite our curiosity, we had to postpone till the next day our first view of San Francisco's northern rival.

OREGON.

Portland, the largest and most important town in Oregon, contains at the present time (1868) about 1,300 houses and some 7,000 inhabitants, of whom 400 are Chinese and about 80 are " coloured." Situated in the fertile valley of the Williamette, and in direct and regular communication with the Pacific, it is the centre of a considerable trade.

Early on Sunday morning I went on land in order to spend a day on solid ground after eight days at sea. In

ARIGONI'S HOTEL, PORTLAND, OREGON.   E.T. 1868

Arigoni's Hotel, kept by an Italian, I found good entertainment, a clean room, and satisfactory food which was very acceptable after the monotony of ship's fare. The weather was cool and rainy, so that I made use of the

COURTHOUSE, PORTLAND, OREGON.   E.T. 1868

opportunity to look round the town itself. Sunday is observed in Portland much more strictly than in California, and so the church which I visited was quite full of decently dressed people. It was Easter Sunday, and as I was about to begin a long and wearisome journey I thought of my dear ones at home, from whom I was separated by so many thousands of miles. Our own steamer, the not very active *Actice* had postponed the continuance of her voyage till Tuesday, so resolving to make use of the time I went early next morning on board the steamer *Cascade*, which was going up the Columbia River. It was 5 o'clock

ACADEMY, PORTLAND, OREGON.   E.T. 1868

in the morning and the day had scarcely dawned when we left Portland.

The first 15 miles from the junction of the Williamette and the Columbia were quickly traversed and offered only a view of thickly wooded banks, with strips of arable and

LOGHOUSE, WILLIAMETTE RIVER.   E.T. 1868

pasture land interspersed with a few farmhouses and numerous herds of cattle ; there was no wide prospect. Rounding a wooded promontory we suddenly beheld the mighty Columbia lying before our astonished gaze with its waters broadening out like a lake. Continuing the journey we passed on the right bank Van Couver, which was formerly a station of the Hudson Bay Company, but after the occupation of the territory by the United States was made an important military post. Most of the generals who became famous in the recent war spent part of their period

FORT VAN COUVER—COL. R.   E.T. 1868

of service here. The present President of the United States, General Grant, was stationed here for a long time and it was here that he retired from the service ; only at the outbreak of the Civil War did he take up the sword again in defence of his country.

A further 25 miles brings us to the foot of the Cascade Range, which runs parallel with the coast and is a prolongation of the range forming the Sierra Nevada, which with a breadth of 40-60 miles rises to a height of 14,000-17,000 feet, with its summits covered with everlasting snows.

OPPOSITE CASCADE LANDING—COL. R.   E.T. 1868

44

It was indeed a mighty stream that broke its way through such a mountain range, and its waters rush fiercely through the narrow rocky gorge. Progress is difficult—the last five miles take almost an hour. On both sides are perpendicular walls of basalt many hundred feet high, and masses of rock of colossal size, detached from the banks, stand erect in the raging waters and remind us of the battle of the elements. At a bend of the river a pyramidal rock, named Cape Horn, rises some 600 feet out of the water, on whose rugged outline some suggestion of a human countenance may be traced. With its setting it forms one of the most satisfying features of the river. The stream becomes still more narrow, the water ever wilder ; deep breaks appear in the grey walls of the gorge, made by miniature waterfalls which look like silver veins ; the air grows cold and damp and the traveller feels as if he were in a cellar.

The end of the voyage is reached ; the ship is moored by a floating stage and we are at the Cascade landing. Beyond this the river forms a series of rapids and waterfalls which

CASCADE LANDING, COLUMBIA RIVER.   E.T. 1868

make navigation impossible for a distance of about 10 miles. Consequently passengers and goods are landed and conveyed by a five-mile railway belonging to the steamship company to a point where the Columbia again becomes navigable for a distance of 45 miles and a steamer is waiting to convey them to the eastern mining districts.

45

The majority of our passengers left the boat, which immediately began its return journey; only a few people took the miniature railway. The journey downstream was much more tranquil since we were rid of the noisiest of the passengers and the only distraction was the occasional landing of a traveller or the delivery of letters, which took place sometimes at a lonely log cabin or small farming settlement. In the first case the passenger had to point out to the steersman the precise point at which he wished to land. The steamer was brought as close as possible to the bank and a long plank, kept ready for the purpose, was thrown out to the shore—an undertaking which only succeeded after repeated attempts—and the passenger had to reach the land as best he could without getting wet. The delivery of the mail is an even more simple affair. As we approached a mail station—usually an isolated log cabin— a signal was given, a man appeared on the bank and without more ado the leather bag containing the mails was thrown to him.

When we got back to Portland towards evening, I learned to my great disappointment that the steamer *Active* had again postponed the continuance of her voyage for two days and it was only on the evening of the next day but one that she would be ready for sea.

As I feared that these repeated delays would end in my missing the steamer from Victoria to Alaska, I joined with my fellow passengers in making the most urgent representations to the captain to expedite the sailing of his ship. He informed us, however, that he must wait for coal and consequently, as no other means of transport were available, we were compelled to spend the next two days in Portland in rainy weather and to wile away our time in very successful fishing and walks in the town.

On this occasion I made the acquaintance in a book shop of a man who professed to have been in Sitka in October of the previous year, but gave such an account of the place that credulous folk would have given up for ever the idea of going there. According to his account, Sitka was a little Russian settlement consisting of log cabins surrounded on three sides by the sea and on the fourth by a palisade beyond which no white man could go without the risk of being kidnapped by the Indians, who were constantly at feud with the Russians. The American garrison, instead of protecting the few settlers left after the withdrawal of the Russians, gave itself up to excesses of every kind and theft, robbery and arson were everyday occurrences.

FROM PORTLAND TO VANCOUVER ISLAND.

Meanwhile the eagerly awaited time for our departure had come. The few passengers travelling to Victoria were on board, the saluting gun was fired, and the captain gave the order to " Go ahead ! " ; the flag was hauled down, and soon we were out in the channel of the Williamette. It was 8 o'clock in the evening when we reached the Columbia River and proceeding down the stream at half-speed under a clear sky we arrived in Astoria at daybreak. There we stayed only for a short time since we wanted to avail ourselves of the high tide, which was at about mid-day, in order to clear the mouth of the river.

The little town, which on our previous visit had been so quiet, was now somewhat excited by the arrival of a delegation consisting of three Indian chiefs from Eastern Oregon, who were about to make the long journey to Washington in order to lay before the " Big Father " (as they call the President) complaints about the non-delivery of the supplies of blankets and foodstuffs which they had hitherto received regularly, to carry them through the winter months. They were the representatives of a number of fairly important tribes from the upper reaches of the Columbia River, who lived on peaceful terms with the white men, and therefore laid claim to this support. To judge them from their chiefs they seemed to be an intelligent people, strong and stoutly built, with copper-coloured complexions and long coal-black hair hanging straight down their backs. A large number of these Indians are successfully occupied in horse rearing—some of the tribes have thereby raised themselves to a fair level of prosperity. The ponies which they rear, though small and unattractive in appearance, are unsurpassed in their endurance and suitability for the rough and trackless mountain regions, and are sold in Oregon for 25-30 dollars each.

The good relations between the Indians and the white immigrants have not always been undisturbed, and the famous Oregon Indian war of the 'fifties furnishes proof that the fighting powers of the Red men are not to be despised.

That war, which was admittedly started by some settlers who were eager for adventures or thought that a war would give them a chance of improving their personal position, lasted for several years and it was only after heavy losses in men and property that the white men were able, with the help of regular troops to subdue the rebel Indians. In connection with the war the following anecdote is current in Oregon :—

A number of Indian chiefs were assembled at a council of war ; the question was whether the struggle should be renewed at the beginning of the warmer weather. The representatives of the various tribes declared almost unanimously for the vigorous continuance of the struggle until the last white man had disappeared from the territory of Oregon—the scalp of the last Paleface would be the signal for peace. Already the eldest of the chiefs had risen to disinter (according to the ancient custom) the hatchet buried when war had come to an end, when there stepped forward an old Indian who in his younger days had been with a consignment of furs to the Eastern States of America, and there had convinced himself of the existence beyond the snow-topped mountains of those millions of Palefaces of whom his kinsmen seemed to have no idea. Plucking some blades of the grass that covered the boundless stretches of the prairie he asked the Indians assembled there in council whether the number of blades left seemed to be diminished. Those who stood round shook their heads in answer. " The number of blades of grass that cover the prairie," he said to them, " is like the number of the white men who are spread all over the world, and just as the plucking of a few blades of grass does not reduce the unending numbers that are left, so the destruction of the Palefaces that live in Oregon will not lessen the number of the Palefaces throughout the world." The comparison drawn by this travelled Indian enlightened the assembly: a deputation to offer peace was immediately despatched to the frontier and within a few days the very tribes which had been a short time before bent on a life-and-death struggle smoked the pipe of peace with the dreaded white men.

About mid-day we passed the lighthouse of Race Rock, which stands on a dangerous group of rocks isolated from the coast, and right in the channel, and a few hours later we anchored off the harbour of Victoria, which was not conspicuous as it was separated from us by a low tongue of land. The signal for a pilot was again given and this time, fortunately, with greater success than at Columbia. Within a quarter of an hour a prosperous looking broad-shouldered figure with a round rosy face, a typical John Bull, was rowed up to us by two sturdy fellows dressed in tidy seaman's garb, presented himself to our captain as the British pilot, and took over from him the command of the ship. Steering straight for the unbroken coast-line, it was only when we got quite close to it that we became aware of a narrow opening, scarcely 50 feet wide, through which, after many windings we entered the small and well-protected natural harbour of Victoria. We were greatly surprised to see spread out before us a quite attractive town of whose very existence the traveller coming from the sea would have no idea.

PREPARATIONS FOR A SAILING EXPEDITION.

My stay in Victoria was inevitably a short one, for, as I mentioned previously, I had to move on towards the north as quickly as possible. My first step, on my arrival was, of course, to enquire about a steamer bound for Alaska, and I learned to my great annoyance that the *Oriflamme,* with a contingent of American troops and war material on board, had actually arrived in Victoria, but instead of touching at Sitka had been ordered to set up military stations at two points on the newly acquired coast, the most northerly of which was 200 miles south of Sitka. It was no use thinking of any communication between these two places because the Indians there were in a state of warfare with their northern neighbours and could not, therefore, be induced to provide any transport. In these circumstances, there was nothing left for me to do but either to wait for a suitable opportunity (which would have entailed a loss of precious time) or to undertake this long journey on a vessel provided by myself. I decided on the latter course, and was fortunate enough to meet with five other people all of whom had come with the same intention as myself and having also been disappointed with regard to the *Oriflamme*, were animated by the same wish as myself to push on at all costs. Two of them had already been in Sitka, one as a clerk at the quartermaster's office, the other was a Jewish merchant ; the remaining three proved to be an engineer, an ex-rebel cavalry officer and a lawyer, all emigrating to Alaska to try and improve their position in the much vaunted North, after the failure of many attempts at making their fortune in the South. We had several discussions and eventually decided to charter a small one-masted sailing vessel, commonly called a " sloop," of the kind which is used all along the coast for trading purposes. When I first set eyes on the pompously styled *Ocean Queen*, I almost repented of my original decision—I found a flat boat of scarcely 20 feet long by 8 feet broad, a so-called " Plunger," without any gunwale or elevation except for a cabin, half sunk in the deck and half raised above it, measuring about 12 feet in length, 6 in width and 4 in height, which was intended to shelter for a voyage of a week's duration the six passengers and two seamen as well as their luggage, which had to be reduced to a minimum.

" Needs must when the devil drives "—at any rate I ought to be thankful at finding travelling companions.

I was assured that the seamen were well acquainted with the route and that the course itself was along the coast in waters sheltered from wind and waves, and so I agreed to the arrangement. We passengers made an agreement with the owner of the boat under the terms of which he undertook to convey us safely to Sitka for a payment of 240 dollars.

We had to provide our own supplies for the journey. Two of the party who were particularly expert in these matters were entrusted with the task of making the purchases and the rest of us undertook to see about the blankets, fire-arms and the numerous small requirements for a long journey.

Each of us was provided with one or more pairs of blankets of coarse but strong material, and a revolver with the requisite ammunition, while the crew was furnished with two muskets.

I myself took also a thermometer, a pocket-compass and a sailing chart, a precaution which I had no reason to regret since the nautical instruments belonging to the crew proved later on to be in a most deplorable condition.

On the evening of the 20th April, all our preparations for the journey were complete and our departure was fixed for the following day about noon. I bade farewell to my friends in Victoria, who had given me a most friendly reception, thanks to my letters of introduction ; and after I had reduced my luggage as much as possible and provided myself with the money necessary to meet my personal and some entertainment expenses in Alaska (this money owing to the lack of any notes took the form of a considerable number of 20-dollar gold pieces) I made my way at the appointed time to the harbour, where I found my fellow travellers already assembled, wearing the strangest garb. Then we had to partake of a variety of farewell " drinks all round " and so often that most of my companions including the crew were obviously affected by the strong liquors. At last, at my earnest persuasion, we got the party on board and availing ourselves of a mild south-west breeze which sprang up, we slowly passed the harbour, not without exchanging many a jest and farewell signal shots with our friends who remained behind.

Before I proceed to describe our journey, it will not be out of place to say something about the route we were taking.

From Victoria to Sitka there are three sea routes. The first, which is taken only by large sailing vessels and steamers is the so-called " outside passage," which is first westward into the open Pacific and then northward direct to Sitka. On this route land is out of sight from the departure from Victoria till the arrival at Sitka. The second route, taken chiefly by steamers, lies through the Gulf of Georgia between the Island of Vancouver on the left and the mainland on the right up to the northern end of the island, at which point the open sea is reached and the first route then followed to Sitka. Finally, the third route, the so-called " inside passage," is taken by the quite small and unseaworthy sailing boats. This hugs the coast as close as possible, taking care to be protected from the waves of the open sea by the numerous islands large and small which are strewn all along the coast.

The advantages of the first route described above are first of all greater likelihood of the breezes needed by sailing ships, smaller risk of striking rocks or shallows and a shorter passage when the wind is favourable. The second route, of which the latter part offers the same advantages as the outside passage, is utilised by steamships for the purpose of taking supplies of coal, a fuel which is produced in substantial quantities at the mines of Nanaimo, situated 70 miles north of Victoria on the eastern coast of Vancouver Island.

Finally, the inner passage, the one which we ourselves proposed to take, has the advantage of a calm sea, but on the other hand the disadvantage of a longer passage caused by the irregularity and mildness of the breezes, and partly also by the necessity of skirting the numerous bays and

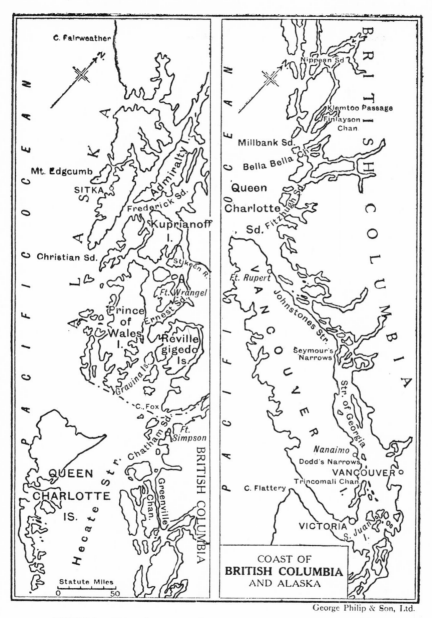

COAST OF
BRITISH COLUMBIA
AND ALASKA

George Philip & Son, Ltd.

VOYAGE OF THE "OCEAN QUEEN," VICTORIA TO SITKA, 1868.

53

promontories. To this it must be added that the coast, so far as it lies within British territory, has been surveyed and properly charted, but the northern part which formerly belonged to Russia was, on the other hand, not officially surveyed and is only roughly set down in a few sailing charts drawn by Russian captains.

One can give an impression of the nature of this coast with its channels, bays and other water-ways cutting deep into the mainland and its chain of islands by comparing it with the fiords of Norway; but it is not easy to convey any idea of the difficulties which we had to overcome in finding our way with the help of a copy of a Russian chart, when it became apparent that our captain was completely ignorant of these regions.

But none of us had then any conception of the troubles which were in store for us, and we commenced our journey in good spirits.

ON BOARD THE "OCEAN QUEEN"—I.

When we were once under way our first task was to arrange our cabin and settle the sleeping accommodation as well as possible. The hatch of the little hold was raised, the trunks and boxes of supplies were stowed in the fore part, boards laid over them and these in turn covered with blankets. Then we realised how restricted the space was; four men had to lie side by side with a two foot allowance for each, the other two men and both the sailors lying at their feet. I thought with dismay of the coming night. The small remaining space left in the cabin was occupied by a little stove which was barely adequate to meet even the most modest requirements in the way of cooking.

On deck the space was equally restricted. The stern of our flat boat, which had no gunwale, so that any water which swept over it could run off easily, held the rudder which was operated by a long spar in a strong but very primitive manner. On both sides of the hold, which rose about two feet above the level of the deck, was a space

54

of some two feet wide, barely sufficient for one to pass to the fore-deck, from which there rose our one mast, leaving only a few square feet unencumbered. At the side of the hatchway leading to the cabin stood the indispensable water barrel containing a two days' supply, and above the cabin itself a small flat-bottomed boat by which we could land in an emergency. Some large oars and poles, to be used should the wind drop suddenly, completed our equipment. The 15-foot mast carried two sails, one the four-cornered main-sail spread out horizontally from the mast, which could be swung from one side to the other of the ship according to the wind, and the other a smaller three-cornered jib-sail spread forward of the mast.

In these confined quarters eight persons as well as two large dogs belonging to one of the passengers had to live and move—a problem the solution of which remains a mystery to me to this day. It was regarded as an evil omen when one of our dogs accidentally fell overboard ; as there was only a light breeze it was easy to turn the boat and get him on board again. The impression which this incident, so unimportant in itself, made upon us was reflected in every countenance and when, soon after, the wind dropped altogether, the reaction from the extreme cheerfulness of our start was very apparent. It was already evening, and so we decided to run close to the shore and drop anchor for the night ; we were scarcely four miles from Victoria.

I shall never forget the first night aboard the *Ocean Queen*. I could not sleep a wink, my miserable couch was so hard and the air so moist and close in the hold, occupied as it was by eight men and ventilated only by the companion 3 feet high and 3 feet wide. There I lay with only my coat for a pillow and a single covering, between two snoring fellow creatures, and during this first night I had ample opportunity to reflect on my situation, which looked quite different now from what it did before I left hospitable Victoria, where I was surrounded by kindly friends.

Now for the first time I thought seriously of the great distance we had to travel and also, strangely enough, for the first time I began to wonder what security I really had that these complete strangers into whose company I had been thrown would act loyally towards me.

Although from the very beginning I had been consistently simple both in dress and manner, they must have soon realised my real standing which was in sharp contrast with theirs, if indeed they had any at all. All kinds of ideas crowded into my mind—I remembered that one of the sailors when he carried on board the small but heavy chest, containing my money and closely packed belongings, asked jestingly whether it was so heavy because it contained gold, and I thought then how easy it would be to put me out of the way somehow or other in the remote regions where we were to travel.

I was heartily glad when at last day dawned. A fresh sunny spring morning is the best cure for such fancies. After a frugal breakfast, with a favourable south-west wind we resumed our journey, in the course of which we were able to increase our food supply by the purchase of a quantity of smelts from fishermen who were returning to the town.

Towards mid-day as we threaded our way through a labyrinth of small flat but thickly-wooded islands, we passed the Island of San Juan, which at one time gave rise to a dispute that nearly brought Great Britain and the United States to war. The original cause was a lawsuit brought by the Hudson Bay Company, who in their capacity of ground landlords of several farms had come into conflict with the neighbouring American authorities over some trifling matter, and when they failed to get their rights by their own unaided efforts had invoked the protection of the British Crown. This was followed by an exchange of notes between the cabinets of St. James's and Washington, which became more and more violent. Both parties were discussing preparations for war when, on the eve of sanguinary conflict, the ingenuity of an

English statesman brought about a kind of armistice, by the terms of which the Island of San Juan was to be treated as neutral territory and both parties were to maintain a garrison there.

Owing to other and more important events these events were relegated somewhat to the background; still for many years companies of English and American troops were stationed on the island and, if report speaks true, they drank together so convivially at their secluded post that they could be distinguished only by their respective red and blue uniforms.

It was but quite recently, in the winter of 1869, that the San Juan dispute, which might have led to serious dissension, was settled by the High Court of Washington in favour of the Hudson Bay Company, whose claims were finally satisfied by a fairly large sum as compensation. Moreover, the little island of only a few square miles in extent seemed to us, who saw it from the boat, scarcely worth disputing about when a district of thousands of square miles on the mainland lies fallow and unutilised.

ON BOARD THE "OCEAN QUEEN"—II.

After San Juan came the Pender and Prevost, Admiral and Galio Islands, all bearing a striking resemblance to one another and showing no trace of cultivation save an occasional tumbledown fishing-hut nestling in the woods. Towards evening the fitful breeze died away entirely, and we sought anchorage for the night in the shelter of a small bay formed by two tiny islands, and after several casts of our sounding-lead we took up our position quite close to the shore. Even for our boat of shallow draught, it was dangerous to go too near the shore because of the great difference in depth (often amounting to 20 feet) between high and low tide and also because, being held merely by one anchor at the bow, the movement of the waves made our vessel move slowly but continuously round, as it were, its centre. The evening was cool but cloudless; a solemn silence reigned on land and sea, broken only from time to time by the rising of a fish.

In order to pass the time we tried to angle with hooks and plummet attached to a line, but soon gave up the attempt after we had pulled up one after another three so-called dog-fish, the largest of which must have weighed 15 lbs. at the very least.

The next morning we went ashore with the aid of our little boat in order to procure fuel, of which our stock was running low. While some of the party, who were entrusted with this task, hewed wood, brought the best and driest of it to the ship and kindled a large fire on the shore with what was left, we others roamed through the island seldom trodden by human feet, with its thick forest of stunted cypress trees, which seemed capable of striking only weak roots into the rocky, indurated soil.

Long after we had left the island we could see the smoke of our fire rising like a pillar in the clear transparent air. The day passed in the usual way without any particular incidents, the monotony being broken only by our modest meals, an occasional tack, or a shot at the diver-ducks floating in calm unconcern upon the waves. Sailing on at about 4 miles an hour we reached near mid-day the Gulf of Trincomatil, a stretch of water some seven miles wide and twenty long, shut in by a chain of islands which together formed a wonderful panorama. On our right there towered in the distance the snow-covered heights of the Cascade Range, lit up by the reflection of the setting sun, whilst on our left the mountain range of Vancouver Island, also covered with snow, seemed gilded by the fiery rays that fell upon it, long after the lower slopes were hidden in darkness. Gradually the glowing red faded to a dull pink tinge upon the summits; a little while and the first stars appeared in the clear sky. By this time we had reached the northern exit from the Gulf, and as it was now late in the evening had cast anchor in one of the numerous bays. We had to look forward to the passage next day of the dreaded "Dodd's Narrows," a strait which separated us from the Gulf of Georgia, and was feared because the water rushed through the narrow rocky passage in a raging torrent, and navigation was not possible except when the tide was highest just before beginning to ebb.

Our anchorage was about five miles from the beginning of this rocky pass ; the sailors reckoned that high tide would be about 3 o'clock, and so it was decided that we would resume our journey at 1 o'clock and that, if necessary, we should row the boat for this part of our course.

We had gone to sleep fairly late and should probably have missed the all important time to start had I not awakened about 1 o'clock, roused the sailors and myself taken a hand with the oars. The night was cold and still, no breath of air ruffled the dark green water—with a rattling noise the anchor chain was hauled in, and with regular strokes of the oars we moved slowly on. Either the distance to the entrance of the Narrows was greater than our sailors reckoned, or else the boat moved too slowly, but anyhow it was 3 o'clock when we reached a passage, at most 1,000 feet wide, between low thickly wooded islands with rocky shores, which formed the entrance to the three miles of the Narrows. Scarcely had our boat entered them, than a suspicious noise of waters in the distance warned us that the turn of the tide had already begun. Straining every nerve we struggled against the stream which ran perceptibly more and more against us ; no breath of air came to the aid of our drooping sails. We had managed to go about half the distance when to our dismay we saw that instead of moving forward we were being dragged back by the tide. Everything was at stake, since it was idle to hope to control the boat if it were once caught by the tide, and we remembered only too clearly the dangerous ledges of rock about the entrance to the Narrows we had come through. Those passengers who were still asleep were hastily roused, two men took each oar and with the utmost effort we succeeded in reaching the left bank. The captain and one of the seamen, carrying a towing line fastened to the prow, jumped on to the rocky but happily fairly flat shore and dragged the boat forward, whilst the rest of us armed with oars and poles kept it off the projecting rocks and also sought to help it forward.

For half-an-hour we struggled on in this way against the angry water, but to me it seemed an eternity and the recollection of that night is stamped indelibly on my mind, never to be erased. Even to-day it is a mystery to me how we managed to get through, but we did succeed after almost superhuman exertions in reaching the exit from the Narrows, just as the first faint streaks of light in the eastern sky heralded the coming day. Our comrades who had done so much to help us from the bank came on board with their clothes torn to rags and their feet wounded ; they had been obliged to force their way through thick and thin, clambering over rocks and trunks of trees in order to follow us along the shore. We others were bathed in perspiration and had to allow ourselves a short rest before we could resume our journey over the Gulf of Georgia, which lay before us like a sea. At daybreak a light breeze came to our help and, in a few hours, steering along the coast we arrived at Nanaimo, the second and last town on Vancouver Island.

NANAIMO—I.

We were pleasantly surprised to encounter at the landing-stage the familiar shape of the *Oriflamme*, which was taking in her supply of coal and from whose upper deck many a hearty welcome was shouted to us. We fastened our boat by the bank near the steamer, and went as quickly as possible on shore, where we were most cordially received by some officers of our acquaintance belonging to the American contingent on the *Oriflamme*. There was, of course, much to relate on both sides as to what had happened since leaving Victoria, and we were never weary of recapitulating our experiences on the tiring journey which, however, was only the prelude to a greater enterprise. Once more we lamented our ill-luck that we could not avail ourselves of the steamer to Sitka, and were forced

60

to spend possibly weeks in the confined space of our sailing boat. Then one of us suggested that we might be given a tow by the *Oriflamme* and taken by her, if not to our destination, at any rate as far as Fort Wrangel. In this way we should accomplish the larger part of our journey in a comparatively short time and the rest could be done without undue difficulty under our own sails. No sooner said than done. A deputation was despatched to Captain W., the commander of the *Oriflamme*, to present our request. After much discussion, and only when some of the American officers had intervened on our behalf, did the old and somewhat obstinate captain consent to take us in tow for the sum of 75 dollars paid in advance. Unfortunately it now appeared that one of the passengers and the sailors were either unwilling or unable to contribute their share of this amount, and it was not till I offered to pay a second share that the matter was settled. The *Oriflamme* was to sail the next day, but we brought our boat alongside the steamer that evening in order to be ready for departure at any time.

NANAIMO, VANCOUVER ISLAND.   E.T. 1868

A great weight was taken off our minds; the omens for our journey seemed now most auspicious. We went cheerfully on shore to take a look at Nanaimo.

61

Nanaimo, like Victoria and most of the settlements on the north-west coast, owes its foundation to the Hudson Bay Company who very early pushed their trading posts, which are also called commercial harbours, forward into the wilderness where white men had penetrated very rarely, and dealt in furs for which they paid very low prices in kind to the ignorant Indians. The officials of the company had their attention drawn by accident to the coal deposits near the fort and began a profitable business since they mined that fuel with the help of Indians who got as wages a blanket for every eight tubs of coal. With the growth of Victoria and the settlement of white men on Vancouver Island, the Hudson Bay Company suppressed its post at Nanaimo and sold its coal mine, which was but slightly developed and hardly exploited, to an English company which in the year 1850 with the help of experienced miners began the exploitation in earnest.

During our stay the little place was enlivened by the brief visit of the American soldiers ; otherwise the death-like quiet of the town seemed rarely to be disturbed. On the afternoon of our arrival, in company with two officers and one of our seamen, I paid a visit to the Indian encampment about half a mile from the town. It consisted of some twenty huts hastily constructed of old boards, trunks of trees and undergrowth, and occupied by about 300 men and some women. They were the "Flatheads," a race from the most northerly part of the island, who had come to exchange the furs collected during the past year for other commodities, as had been their custom for years past. In each hut we found ten to twenty people crouching round a wood fire that burned in the centre, and talking noisily with much gesticulation. Whilst some gnawed greedily at dried or smoked fish, others dipped long wooden spoons into a kind of fat or blubber cooking in a great pot, and others again, having no doubt satisfied their hunger, were enjoying a smoke from wooden pipes carved by themselves. Our visit appeared not to disturb them in the very least— they sat quietly while some of the older Indians who understood "Chinook," the universal language of the Redskins who come in contact with white men, immediately engaged in talk with our sailor and as a result after much discussion a number of marten, otter, beaver and bear-skins were brought out from old, blackened, roughly-carved chests and boxes or from quite skilfully plaited baskets, and these they were ready to exchange for so many blankets.

Whether because the price asked was too high or the quality of the furs too low, no purchase was effected at our first visit, but we had the opportunity of studying the character of those children of the wilds. They are generally of small build and their figures, clad simply in a blanket, are by no means attractive. Their long, coarse hair, which is in a very few cases bound up with a coloured handkerchief in turban fashion, or by a plain leather strap, their black and red painted faces, disfigured by disease, and their restless, half-closed eyes lend them a repellent aspect, which is further increased by their harsh, guttural dialect. They gave us to understand that they proposed to set out on their return journey in a few days and accordingly their boats were in a seaworthy state and already partly loaded with the goods and supplies which they had acquired. So far as we could see they had brought with them some fifteen to twenty canoes, the largest of which was 25 feet long, hollowed out of the trunks of trees and capable of holding as many as thirty men. Though the canoes varied greatly in size, they were all of the same type, and it appears as if each tribe has its own special design for the construction of its canoes. In fact anyone well acquainted with the Indians of the North-West coast can, as soon as he sees a boat, name the tribe to which its occupants belong.

These light craft can make long voyages in smooth water with the aid of short paddles or, when the wind is favourable, their small sails ; and their construction seems to be so good that they can encounter even a fairly high sea. The Indians, who sit or kneel in the canoes, keep as close to the coast as possible and lay up on the bank every evening as soon as it is dusk ; the canoes are drawn ashore, a fire is kindled round which they camp for the night, and the journey is resumed at daybreak. It sometimes happens that they are caught in a sudden storm when crossing a gulf and then they show an instinctive knowledge of wind and wave and a coolness in the handling of their light craft which generally bring them safely through. Kneeling on the bottom of their canoes they know how by tricks of balancing to prevent them being overturned or by a quick turn of the rudder to avoid a sudden breaker ; with their sharp eyes they can detect a spot on the coast protected from the waves and, though mercilessly battered by the sea and wet through from the water that they have shipped, slowly but steadily they paddle on and reach the shore in safety.

NANAIMO—II.

Our study of Indian life had occupied the whole afternoon, and when darkness set in we returned to the town, where a new spectacle awaited us. A certain Professor Martin, a ventriloquist and conjuror of some note, chanced to be in Nanaimo on his way back from an unsuccessful trip to Alaska, and had announced his high-class entertainment for that evening. On our arrival we found that the temporary theatre, set up hastily in a barn, was packed with soldiers, miners, seamen, half-castes and others, including many Indian squaws in company with the whites with whom they lived. Although the performance could only be described as moderately good, it seemed to be well received by the audience, and to be especially approved by the squaws, to judge by their delighted faces as they went away. The ventriloquism, however, nearly caused a fight, as one of the American soldiers took some of the Professor's jests seriously, and was prevented only by force from assaulting him.

The night was very dark when, in company with one of

my travelling companions, I walked along the path which led to the shore and would take us to the landing-stage ; we had gone only a few paces when I felt a touch on my shoulder.   Instinctively laying my hand on a loaded revolver I hastily turned round and was much dismayed to see immediately behind me the fantastic figure of an Indian. At first I thought it was an attempt at assault, but soon abandoned that idea as I saw him nodding and gesticulating, and my companion explained the object of his appearance. The noble Redskin was broaching a proposal to sell his wife to us, a proceeding which, originating in the immorality of the white men, has unhappily become a habit among the Indians of the West coast.   On two other occasions the same proposal was made to us before we reached our boat, and it was with a feeling of deep disgust at this horrible trade in human beings that I lay down to rest that night.

The next day we spent in making preparations for the continuance of our journey, and in improving our store of provisions by the purchase of fresh meat and new bread, of which our supply had been exhausted several days before, and even now I can recollect the relish with which we partook of both these at our mid-day dinner.   In the afternoon the sailors had set out in our little landing-boat to replenish our supply of fresh water, but had met with an accident on the way—close to the shore their boat filled with water and sank.   The two men saved their lives by swimming, but we lost our only boat, without which we had no means of landing.   A similar boat was unobtainable anywhere in Nanaimo, neither were we able to purchase from the Indians one of their small canoes ; we were therefore forced to depend entirely and exclusively on our *Ocean Queen*.

Returning to the landing-stage we found the *Ocean Queen* already fastened to the *Oriflamme* by a strong tow-rope, and both ships prepared to start.   Our vessel did not look very different, the only change being that the sails were closely furled ; but the steamer presented a remarkable appearance as she was piled high above the bulwarks with munitions and bales of forage so that the crew of 200 men had scarcely room to move about.

Had the steamer been less heavily laden, no doubt her captain would have agreed to our suggestion to carry our boat on deck instead of taking it in tow, but as things were we saw that this was quite impossible ; but to give us more room on the sailing boat, two of our companions, who had personal friends on the steamer, resolved to travel by her for the first few days and then to complete the journey with us. Our party was therefore reduced for the time being to four passengers and two sailors, so that it was possible to make the cabin, hitherto so overcrowded, rather more comfortable, though even so it was very close quarters.

As we were having our supper by the light of a small oil lamp we received a visit from an American whose acquaintance we had made in Nanaimo, where he resided as agent of the Wells Fargo Express Company. Inspired no doubt by patriotic motives, he informed us with an air of great mystery, of a plot which according to his statement, had been concocted by the English authorities against us, and doubtless would have been carried through by this time had not the accidental presence of the American war-ship impeded the measures which had been planned. The position was as follows : At this time the British possessions in North America from the Atlantic to the Pacific were in a state of great unrest owing to the numerous raids, some actually carried out, others only projected by American Fenians, who, under cover of the Fenian movement were making savage attacks on the life and property of British subjects. In Canada, where there had actually been sanguinary conflicts with the Fenians gathered from the slums of the big towns, volunteer defence corps had been formed all along the frontier and even in remote British Columbia the patriotic fervour of the population capable of bearing arms was very marked, and on all sides people were preparing against Fenian raids. Victoria with its larger population and garrison of about 1,200 sailors and marines was fairly immune from an attack, but the outlying, undefended places like Nanaimo, for example, were exposed to a sudden raid; in this particular case the important coal mines were likely to attract the attention of the Fenian organisation, and such a blow at England would be certain to receive, if not the actual, at any rate the moral support of the Americans.

To come back to our own adventure, it appeared that the arrival of a well-armed sailing-boat flying the American flag and with a crew of eight young men had aroused the suspicion of the English officials in Nanaimo—a suspicion which increased as we did not appear to be either sailors or fishermen or hunters or traders, and moreover were evidently on intimate terms with the American soldiers on the *Oriflamme*, who were open sympathisers with the Fenians. Our American friend said quite frankly that we were regarded as Fenian freebooters, and our harmless *Ocean Queen* as a disguised privateer. If we wanted proof of the truth of this story we had only to notice the detective who was walking up and down on the landing-stage. As as matter of fact we *had* noticed by the shore a person whom we took for a customs or excise officer, and had observed that he was always near our boat. At this very moment he passed along the beach and was obviously watching our movements. As we proposed to start very early in the morning in company with the steamer we had no further cause for anxiety that night. On leaving, our friend assured us that should the British officials put any difficulties in our way, we could rely at any moment on the support of fifty avowed Fenian soldiers whom he had placed at our disposal (he seemed to be one of the Fenian chiefs) and who only waited our summons for help to run down immediately from the steamer to our aid. Happily the contingency did not arise and a sound sleep quieted our excited spirits.

TOWED BY THE "ORIFLAMME."

It must have been about 6 o'clock next morning that I awoke and to my astonishment saw our seamen excitedly occupied in moving the iron blocks and heavy packages that had been put in the front of the boat as ballast back to the rear of the cabin. Half asleep and half awake I could not, for the moment, understand the meaning of their activity, but my ignorance was soon dispelled. I and the other passengers who were still asleep were summoned to get up and lend a hand with the ballast, if we did not want to be entirely dragged under. Collecting our clothes and boots in the dim light of the cabin we all jumped up as quickly as possible. In front of us, above us, on both sides we could clearly hear the rushing of the water; though our boat did not roll it trembled all over and creaked and groaned in an appalling manner as if hammered by a mighty force. We flew straight as an arrow through the turbulent water; we found out that we had already been in tow for two hours.

Hastening on deck I saw at a distance of quite a thousand feet away the dark bulk of the big steamer, which by means of the tow-rope fastened securely to our mast drew us, or rather tore us, along. Our boat was obviously too deep in the water forward, so that the waves swept over half the deck. This was clear enough and I did not delay to do my best to help in shifting the centre of gravity of the boat more to the stern. In a very short time all the ballast, the boxes of provisions, trunks and casks were piled pell-mell in the most amazing chaos at the entrance to our cabin, and thereby the sleeping arrangements which we had made with so much trouble were entirely ruined. But nobody troubled about this as it was necessary for the safety of the boat; the prow of the vessel rose quite markedly and thereby prevented the water from inundating the deck.

Matters went on in this way fairly tolerably for half an hour, and then the wind that was blowing against us suddenly increased in violence and the waves rose higher in proportion. We were somewhere in the middle of the gulf and about 25 miles from Nanaimo. A drenching rain began to fall and shut us off from anything more than an occasional glimpse of the distant shore on our right. The *Oriflamme* was hidden from us as by a veil, and only every now and then did the wind sweep aside the misty clouds and let us see her more clearly. The prow of our boat again began to sink and every few minutes a wave swept over the whole deck and to stay on it was to say the least unpleasant, though it was better to be on deck and see what was happening than to shut oneself up in the cabin. It was difficult to know how to improve the situation—we could do no more to lighten the prow than we had already done ; the wind increased and the rate at which we were cutting through the waves must have been at least ten miles an hour. At last one of our seamen had the unfortunate idea of lessening the strain on the boat by lengthening the tow-rope. It was lighter now and we could see a number of figures on the stern of the steamer ; we shouted to them as loudly as we could and tried to make them understand by despairing gestures that they must give us more rope. For some anxious moments we were uncertain if we had been heard or understood, but then to our delight we saw the rope lengthen until finally we were some 1,500 feet away from the steamer.

Unfortunately our joy was of short duration. The alteration seemed to have exactly the opposite effect from what we expected. Our poor *Ocean Queen* settled deeper than ever into the water ; whereas before although too deep we were being dragged at least in a straight line, now the longer tow-line gave our boat far too much free play. When the rope was loose the boat would rock from side to side, when taut the vessel was jerked with tremendous force through the waves. We had taken the precaution to carry below deck everything that could be moved and rope up everything else, and to close the companion as best we could. It was a good thing that we did so, for our deck was entirely swamped several times, and the only comparatively dry spot was the elevated part of the cabin, on which I, together with the other passengers had taken refuge so as to be ready for any emergency. The captain, who could scarcely keep his foothold, was at the helm ; a sailor stood at the prow armed with an axe and prepared for all contingencies. Then we suddenly noticed that the clouds of smoke rising from the funnel of the steamer were increasing in volume, which showed that the engine fires had been freshly stoked and that the vessel's speed had consequently been augmented. The result we dreaded now came to pass—a gigantic wave rushed towards us—instead of gliding over it, our ship looked as if it would be engulfed. We called out to the sailor, who was waist deep in the streaming water, to cut the towing-line. He tried to do this but without success and the force of the water was so tremendous that he sank back on the deck though he managed still to cling to the mast. Fortunately at the critical moment the rope became taut and with a powerful heave we were dragged through the wave. For the moment we were safe. In spite of our repeated signals of distress we could not make the people on the steamer hear us, and we pursued our wild course; a sudden gust of wind made the foaming waves rise still higher and, horror-stricken, we perceived another enormous breaker which threatened to overwhelm us with crushing force. In tones of despair we shouted for the rope to be cut and, heedless of danger, the sailor, swinging his axe, rushed to the prow of the ship. I myself, with the engineer (the two other passengers seemed to have disappeared) clung to the mast expecting the worst. Nearer and nearer rolled the raging water; then at the critical moment, preferring his own safety to that of the ship, our cowardly captain let go the helm and, expecting the ship to heel over every moment, leaped to the side which was bound to be uppermost. But scarcely had the engineer seen the helm abandoned than with admirable presence of mind he seized hold of it, and with a powerful twist prevented our boat being swung broadside on to the waves and capsized. Our dauntless sailor in the bows displayed equal heroism; clinging with his left hand to the mast he hacked with the strength of despair at the rope below the water. Twice his blows seemed ineffective, as they were weakened by the resistance of the waves, and the stern of our boat was already sinking beneath the rushing torrent; the angry water surrounded me and, believing my last moment had come, I wanted at any rate to face death with composure. My past life rose before me in that instant—I thought of my loved ones in my distant home and gazed passively at the unbridled fury of the sea. Suddenly I heard the sailor's reassuring shout, "We are off!" At the very last moment he had managed to sever the rope and once free of the pull our sorely tried boat rose up as if by magic, the water ran off the deck and for the time being at any rate we were afloat. The steamer, it is true, stayed her course for a few minutes in order to ascertain whether we wanted a fresh tow; but she never came nearer us, nor sent a boat to our assistance, and presently she got up steam and in a short time vanished from our sight.

So we were once more thrown upon our own resources. The deadly peril we had all escaped had at least the good result of drawing us more closely together, and henceforth we behaved like brothers. Our features quivering with emotion we congratulated one another on our safety, and our most grateful thanks were accorded to those who had played such noble parts in attaining it. On the other hand, we looked on the captain with diminished favour since he had earned our distrust by his cowardly behaviour at the time of our greatest danger—a distrust which on later occasions was renewed and led eventually to an open rupture.

Even if we were safe for the moment, we were still in a very unenviable situation; miles away from land, with close-reefed sails and at least a foot of water in the hold, we were the plaything of the angry waves. Our first care was, of course, to see whether we had sprung a leak or whether the water in the cabin had penetrated from above. Making our way with difficulty to the entrance choked with ballast, we waded through the water strewn with objects of every kind, to the pumps at which two men worked for half an hour at a time. These were anxious moments for us—not a word was uttered as the wooden pistons regularly rose and fell. After two shifts we noticed to our joy that the water was diminishing, and soon afterwards we were quite reassured that our boat was not taking in any more. A short discussion was held as to whether we should continue our journey or return to Nanaimo, and the unanimous wish was expressed that we should continue, now that we had once started. The sails were refurled as speedily as possible, the wind had become more favourable, and with good courage we continued on our way.

SEYMOUR'S NARROWS AND JOHNSTONE'S STRAITS.

It was 7.30 a.m. when we cut through the towing-line, and within half an hour we had made a fresh start; the weather became clearer and the sun even came out from behind the clouds. We opened the companion and tried in some measure to dry our cabin, which was, of course, frightfully wet, to bring the ballast forward again and tidy up our sleeping quarters; and after some hours of toil we succeeded in accomplishing all this. Fortunately our coverings were only slightly damp, but our boots and clothes had fared much worse and it took several hours in the open air to dry them. But these were all trifles in comparison with what we had undergone, and the evening found us talking cheerfully on deck and discussing the events of the day. Each of us related what he was doing at the moment of our greatest peril, and even humorous incidents were not entirely lacking.

As I have previously mentioned, I missed two of our passengers, the lawyer and the Jewish trader, when I was waiting for the boat to sink. It appeared that the former possessed several important legal documents and when he realised in what danger we were, he tried to fetch these papers from the cabin and carry them on his person in order to save this much at least. Either in his excitement he forgot which of his boxes contained the papers or in the

72

appalling confusion he failed to find it, anyhow it was too late for him to get back on the deck. A torrent of water burst into the cabin—he gave himself up for lost and resigned himself to his apparently inevitable fate. Much the same thing happened to the Jew, whose deathly pale and distorted features still bore witness to his fright. He, too, had sought to save some of his money from the cabin, but failed owing to his excitement. He lost his head and fell down in a faint there, and was found by us later half-stunned.

Had the boat capsized, both of these men would certainly have been lost beyond all hope of rescue, and so we had a striking instance of the way in which men often put their lives in peril for the sake of their worldly possessions.

Admittedly even for those of us who were on deck the chance of rescue had our boat capsized would at best have been dubious, but at any rate we should have had *some* chance of help from the steamer, whereas those in the cabin would have had no chance whatever.

The chief consolation we had in trying to forget the disappointment of the hopes we had set on the *Oriflamme*, was that probably the reckless speed of the steamer would have certainly exposed us to danger, and owing to the readily explosive ammunition which she had on board, her nearness would have been a perpetual menace to our safety. On the other hand, the thought of the money we had paid in advance to the captain of the *Oriflamme* and the loss thereby incurred was a galling one, and the faint hope then expressed that it would be refunded was doomed to disappointment.

Towards evening the south-easterly breeze which had hitherto favoured us, began to drop and about 9 o'clock completely ceased; we were still about six miles distant from Cape Mudge, a point at the northern outlet of the Gulf of Georgia. We intended to pass the cape at dawn, and as we had already sailed 85 miles during the day, we gave up the idea of continuing our journey by night and contented ourselves with lying-to, with one watchman at

73

the rudder. Quite unexpectedly a strong breeze began to blow from the coast about midnight and threatened to drive us out to sea. The sailor who had just taken over the watch from the captain awakened me at 1 o'clock in the morning, as I was regarded as the most experienced oarsman, to help him row our boat to the shore ; it took us a full hour until we could drop anchor in the shelter of the wooded bank. At daybreak the longed-for southern wind came to our aid and at 6 o'clock we passed the cape and entered a narrow strait between two mountain masses. This was not more than two miles wide, and in the course of a two hours' passage became more and more restricted until we reached Seymour's Narrows (which are also called the Ukeltah Rapids). Seymour's Narrows, like Dodd's Narrows which we passed shortly before Nanaimo, are the meeting point of the tides which move from north and south between the Island of Vancouver and the mainland ; but they are much more dangerous than Dodd's Narrows and everywhere notorious on that account. The narrow channel is strewn with a multitude of rocks, some of which are visible while others lie just below the surface. Through these the angry current runs at a pace of 7-8 miles an hour, and drags the largest sailing ships and even big steamers which entrust themselves to it unresistingly with it. Consequently there are frequent accidents, and what is very remarkable is that no fragments of any wreck caught in the whirlpool and dragged down have ever appeared above water again. As a rule small light craft are much safer than the heavily-laden steamers with deep draught.

Happily the tide was with us, and towards 8 o'clock we observed the first indications that we were caught in the current. So the sails were furled, the deck cleared and the oars and boat-hooks got ready for any emergency. We kept as close as possible to the left bank, but when we came to the narrowest part we rowed our boat with powerful strokes into mid-stream, where we were swept along with irresistible force. Steering was impossible ; I well remember that we escaped a rock by a very few feet and suddenly found ourselves caught in a foaming breaker which whirled our boat round in a circle five times, and it was only after crossing a number of great and small rapids that in a quarter of an hour we came into smoother water.

We all breathed more freely when we had left the dangerous passage behind us, and with a strong favouring south-west wind we sailed merrily onwards at a speed of some six miles an hour. The scenery after leaving the Narrows was wonderfully fine. The channel, scarcely half-a-mile wide, was shut in on both sides by steep mountain walls at whose feet the dark green cypress woods were mirrored in the clear water, whilst higher up the bare mountains covered with snow gave place to ice-fields and glaciers, some of them at a height of 5,000 feet or more. The stillness of nature was broken from time to time by the splash of small mountain streams which had their source in the snowy heights and formed numerous miniature water-falls leaping from rock to rock. The charm of this part of the journey was increased by the fact that the stream was very winding and constantly presented new vistas to our gaze. Sometimes it became no wider than a canal, sometimes like a sea it was so broad that its outlet was difficult to find.

The rocky walls on both sides were broken by numerous small channels and the mouths of larger streams which caused the whole landscape to resemble Norwegian fiords. An inexperienced captain might easily lose himself for days in this labyrinth of channels and passages, and even a boatman who knows the neighbourhood well can only find his way by observing certain familiar landmarks, consisting sometimes of curiously-shaped masses of rock and sometimes of high mountain tops which can be seen from afar off and enable him to take his bearings. On the other hand a compass or a map, especially if the latter is not absolutely accurate, is of much less use.

About mid-day we passed a small Indian settlement at the mouth of a tiny river ; it consisted of some poorly constructed huts with a few inmates, some of whom seemed

75

to be busy with the making of a new canoe, as we could see them hollowing out a long tree-trunk. Towards 4 o'clock the wind dropped altogether and as shortly before this we had noticed a small bay with gravelly bottom we decided to go ashore until a breeze sprang up again. All along the coast the banks are so steep that a boat can be brought close to the land, and though the gravelly bottom sloped very gently we were able to jump from the boat right on to the shore. Near to the bay, which was enclosed by beautiful encircling woods, we found a little stream of fresh water at which we filled our two casks. The dogs also found the remnants of a deserted Indian camp near which the game they had caught had evidently been cooked. The place had certainly been chosen with true native instinct, and was by no means to be despised as a summer abode. Stately cypresses and cedars were mingled with towering fir trees whose lichen-covered trunks seemed bound together by a tangle of rankly-growing creepers and drooping mosses. The ground was strewn with rocks and decayed tree trunks and covered with a layer of moss a foot deep, so soft and springy that it made a most comfortable couch. The district owed this luxuriance to the cool and humid atmosphere which, however, we were assured would be very unhealthy for Europeans.

An hour was spent in taking in our supply of water and firewood, and when towards evening a light south wind sprang up we started again and coasted along the western shore. The nature of the scenery was unchanged. About 6 o'clock we passed on our left a larger bay, the estuary of the Salmon River, one of the chief streams of Vancouver Island, and shortly afterwards two large canoes manned by Indians who, as soon as they saw us, disappeared swiftly into one of the side channels.

In order to make full use of the favourable wind, and as our sailors professed to know the way exactly, we decided to travel all night. The steersman was relieved every four hours and next morning found us at the entrance to Brougham's Straits, which steadily broadened out till gradually towards the north-west they formed an open arm of the sea strewn with numerous islands. We held as close as we could to the Vancouver shore, since to the east the great masses of rock and channels cutting into the mainland made the fairway unsafe. As the gulf broadened the banks became flatter and the snow mountains in the background were less frequent and at last ceased entirely on our left. Near Beaver Harbour we passed Fort Rupert, a trading station of the Hudson Bay Company, concealed from our view by a headland, and close by it an Indian village which a few years ago had a population of 1,600 but now, owing to the epidemic sickness caused by the devastating " Fire Water," can show hardly one-tenth of that number. There are coal deposits in this neighbourhood but owing to the difficulties of transport they have been worked only occasionally and to a small extent.

A VISIT TO THE NUKLETAH INDIANS IN THEIR SUMMER CAMP.

Steering northward from Fort Rupert we came to a stretch of water some fifteen miles wide whose northern part, between the Galiano Islands and the mainland, forms the entrance to Queen Charlotte Sound. It was our intention to anchor for the night at the entrance to the Sound, but unfortunately the south-easterly breeze which had filled our sails dropped about 4 o'clock, and to make matters still worse it began to rain heavily, so against our will we were compelled to seek a premature anchorage for the night ; this we were fortunate enough to find quickly in the form of a quite small island lying in the middle of the gulf. We had to row hard to reach it, but we did this willingly and soon found ourselves close to what proved to be a whole group of islands. One of our sailors told us that he had once been here before, and found an Indian village on one of the islands. Only after we had passed half-way round the group did we succeed in finding the narrow entrance, which according to our steersman would

77

bring us to an anchorage. It took us half-an-hour's journey between the low islands or islets, emerald green in their covering of cypress trees, until we came into a large bay, almost surrounded by land, at the end of which the Indian village was believed to be. A shot from our boat was answered quickly by the appearance of a canoe paddled at incredible speed by five Indians, which came towards us and was soon alongside. The occupants of the canoe, thin, half-naked, ape-like figures with dirty brown complexions and long coal-black hair, some having rings through their noses and others decked with chains of mussel shells, sought with many gestures and unintelligible guttural sounds to be

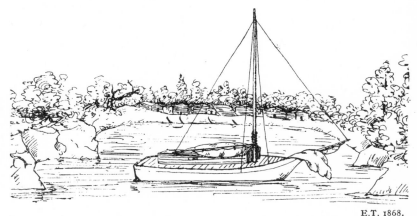

E.T. 1868.

THE "OCEAN QUEEN," FISHING GROUNDS OF NUKLETAH INDIANS,
QUEEN CHARLOTTE SOUND.

allowed to come on board. This, of course, we did not permit, but made signs to them to conduct us to their village. Passing round a small promontory we found ourselves in a short time opposite the Indian village, whose picturesque situation tempted me to make a small sketch of it.

Before us there was outspread a little crescent-shaped bay whose two ends, formed of rocky wooded land, protected the already calm water in the bay from any breath of wind and kept the blue surface smooth as a mirror. Inside the bay the gently sloping beach was covered with pure

white sand strewn with shells like a girdle.   At the edge of
the sand where the dark green cypress wood, distant only
a few paces from the shore, formed the background of the
picture, stood the few native huts built of tree-trunks,
thatch and matting.   The smoke from them rose straight
up in the clear air and stood out in sharp contrast to the
roseate hues of the evening sky.   I could not gaze enough
at the idyllic beauty of the landscape before me, and it was
with the greatest regret that I heard the confused cries of
the excited Indians and the wolfish howls of the Indian
dogs which rose from the camp and brought me back to the
commonplaces of life.

By this time the canoe which had guided us had reached
the land, in order to give information as to what we were like
and what we wanted to do—information which a crowd
of forty to fifty natives received with great interest, as we
gathered from their gestures.   Our appearance seemed to
win their confidence as, after a short consultation, a number
of the canoes drawn up on the beach were put afloat, each
with a crew of four or five Indians, and paddled towards us.
Soon a number of these boats were gathered round us
and an old Indian, who seemed to be a kind of chief, invited
us by signs and a few words in " Chinook " to visit his
camp.   We gladly accepted the invitation, since we already
had in mind the possibility of renewing our store of water
and fire-wood.   The sails were closely furled and the anchor
dropped and leaving two of our party as a watch on board
the remaining four of us, prudently armed with loaded
revolvers, made our way to the shore in canoes paddled by
the Indians.   This was my first opportunity of appre-
ciating the insecurity of these fragile boats ; crouching in
Eastern fashion at the bottom of the canoe I thought every
moment to be overturned, since even the slightest movement had the inevitable result of bringing the side of the
boat dangerously close to the surface of the water, and had
it not been that the Indian steersman, evidently conscious
of my insecurity, balanced my every movement by a
counter-movement of his own, I should not have been able

to reach the shore without a ducking. Thanks to his skill, however, all went well and our whole party came safely to land. The discomfort which I experienced during my first trip in a canoe disappeared in the course of time, and later on I was able to handle a canoe by myself. A natural poise I found to be the chief requisite in keeping one's balance, and the experienced canoeist knows instinctively how to counterbalance by certain movements of the body the shock caused by the waves or anything else. The short paddles used by the seated canoeist and dipped alternately from one side to the other also help to keep the boat balanced.

When we reached the shore we were surrounded by the whole company consisting almost entirely of women, children and old men, to whom our arrival caused no small excitement as we judged from their inquisitive looks and lively talk.

The old chief signed to us with great respect to follow him into his house, the best of the six huts, and invited us, when we had entered, to sit down by the fire. The interior of the hut, which served only as a temporary dwelling-place for the summer, was remarkably simple. The floor was covered with dry leaves and in the middle, as I have related previously, there was a big fire the smoke from which filled the whole room and then found its way out, as best it could, through some opening in the roof. We sat round the fire on stumps of trees or chests covered with mats amidst the dusky figures of some old Indians, whilst in the centre sat the chief smoking a wooden pipe which he himself had carved. Round the sides stood a number of wooden chests, mats and baskets which no doubt contained the property of the inhabitants of the hut, a few old flint-locks and some fishing tackle leaned against a corner and, finally, a number of nets were suspended from the ceiling containing dried fish in the process of being smoked, which filled the air with a smell of train-oil.

After exchanging the customary " Kld how ya " (How are you ?), the chief, who spoke more and more fluently in Chinook, entered into a long conversation with us, from which we gathered that we were with a tribe of the

Nukletah Indians which was on a fishing expedition and had made a temporary camp here, whilst its actual " Smoke " (derived from a Mexican term and meaning " settlement ") that is, its permanent winter home, was several days' journey away on one of the fiords that cut into the main-land. All their men and youths were at the moment further out at sea engaged in fishing and only sent their catch to this place from time to time in order that the fish might be prepared, that is, dried and smoked, by the women who remained behind. It was for this reason that we found the population of the camp to consist almost exclusively of women and children. Our host would not have been a true Indian had he not attempted to do some trade or barter with us. The wonderfully made chests and boxes were opened and skin after skin was carefully laid before us in the expectation that we should make an offer for them. But as none of us except the seamen were prepared for a deal, we expressed our thanks for the opportunity given to us and for our part presented the old " Tyhee " (chief) with a clay pipe and some tobacco as a gift. But then we were so beset on all sides with similar requests for tobacco and pipes, that we withdrew through the narrow doorway to get into the open air again. On the shore we found a number of squaws busy unloading a cargo of fish, which had apparently just arrived in a canoe in charge of two youths. It seemed below their dignity to take any part in the preparation of the fish, since they both sat there motionless with folded arms, looking at us in a way which was by no means friendly. As we found later, the men consider themselves a privileged race and jealously guard their rights, which consist in occupying themselves exclu-sively with fighting, hunting and fishing, whilst all the really indispensable work is without exception put upon the weaker sex. In general, that is so far as we were able to judge, the Nukletah Indians were of medium height and not remarkably robust ; the squaws on the other hand, were small and well-built with unusually small hands and feet, which were adorned with numerous silver rings and bangles ;

their clothing consisted as a rule of a single blanket reaching from head to foot. I was much struck by the scars which were visible on the upper part of their bodies and on their shoulders, the cause of which was by no means apparent, but I was assured that they were simply the marks of bites inflicted on them as signs of affection in the madness of winter time orgies and dances. At dusk we embarked on the canoes again and returned to our ship, where we found the two sailors busily employed in taking on board the two casks of water and a good supply of wood from the hands of a number of Indians who had volunteered to do this work for a small gift of tobacco, and carried it out to our complete satisfaction. After some time we managed to get rid of the importunate crowd and, leaving a watch on deck, the rest of us settled down in the cabin for the night.

QUEEN CHARLOTTE SOUND.

At dawn next day we weighed anchor, bade farewell to our Indian friends, who despite the early hour had come out to us, and sailed before a light south-east breeze to the exit from the archipelago. It was only by the exercise of the greatest care that we reached the open channel unscathed, since the low tide revealed a number of dangerous reefs which we had not noticed when we entered. Some of these were indeed not yet visible above the water, but were already so near to the surface that the lurking danger was indicated by a line of foam. Towards 8 o'clock in the morning we passed on our left the low-lying Galiano Island, encircled with rocks, and we were about to pass between that island and the mainland into Queen Charlotte Sound when the faint south-east breeze gradually died away and suddenly a strong north-westerly wind sprang up which precluded any idea of steering northward. To avoid being driven on the reef-strewn coast of the mainland we had to seek an anchorage on the coast of Galiano Island, where we should be protected against the wind ; but in order to find this we had to tack in a south-westerly

E.T. 1868

FIGURES ON HOUSES OF NERVITTY INDIANS, NEAR CAPE SCOTT, NORTH END
OF VANCOUVER ISLAND.

direction for five hours against a fairly high wind and in a rough sea (as the wind blew straight from the ocean) and it was not till 3 o'clock in the afternoon that we managed to reach the natural harbour known as Nervitty.

At the upper end of the deep bay we found the settlement of the Nervitty Indians. This was quite an important village of about twenty huts built regularly and solidly of planks, each of which would hold about twenty persons. The front or gable side of each hut, which was provided with a small and very low door, faced towards the water and in most cases was painted with designs and figures quite remarkably executed. The figures represented grotesque bird-like or human forms and were rather repulsive. Besides this the better class of dwellings had high flag-staffs and a few of the huts had on both sides of the entrance curious figures carved of wood, which were no doubt idols. The rather large number of canoes drawn up on the shore seemed to indicate that the population was a considerable one, and as a matter of fact we counted no less than eighty Indians assembled on the beach. It was not long before we were surrounded by a crowd of curious natives, who overwhelmed us with offers of every kind and tried to barter with us a number of quite worthless skins. When they discovered that we were not traders they were somewhat puzzled, and possibly the crew of our little vessel seemed too numerous; anyhow they all fell back, with the exception of one old man who seemed to be a sort of interpreter and whom they left with us to find out what he could as to our purpose there. The old man, who had tied his boat alongside, came on to our vessel and asked us a string of questions in fluent Chinook. Finding we were not so responsive as he expected he sat down with unruffled calm and, smoking hard, blinked cunningly at us with his crafty eyes. We had anchored a few hundred yards from the shore and as I was much interested in the architecture of the houses I gave the interpreter to understand that I should be very glad to land. A call from him immediately brought out a canoe into which I stepped together with one of my companions. The reception which we had was much colder than any I had hitherto experienced from the Indians and, although the sailors assured me that there was no danger in broad daylight and within hail of our ship, nevertheless I felt somewhat apprehensive when I began to draw and noticed that I was surrounded by a number of Indians pointing at me with an air of mystery. It was evident that my occupation intrigued them, and involuntarily I placed my hand on my revolver to make sure that it was there. However, my visit was concluded without any mishap, and having made various little sketches and thoroughly inspected the settlement, I returned to the ship and nothing happened to me except an onslaught by a pack of Indian dogs ; these half-tamed, hungry animals, not unlike small prairie wolves but mostly spotted, are found in hundreds in the Indian villages and make their presence known from a distance by their hoarse yelping.

Back on board again I found our intrusive visitor still sitting there quite oblivious of our requests for him to depart at once ; it was only when we threatened to cut his boat loose that he sulkily prepared to obey our orders. As we were rather dubious about the behaviour of the Indians altogether and had also heard various rumours that were current about them, we thought it advisable to keep a watch on deck all night. It was quite uncanny in that dark starless night on the deck, rendered slippery by the dew. The ebb and flow of the water swung the ship slowly in a circle round the anchor, so that she seemed to be moving continually in the dark water towards the ghostly outlines of the shore hard by.

Now and then the bark of a dog was heard from the village wrapped in slumber, and at the entrance to the Sound the waves beat against the granite rocks with a dull thud. The four long hours which form a watch, namely, the ones from midnight onward, seemed unending and we hailed the dawn with delight. There were also signs of stirring in the Indian camp and a small flotilla of canoes paddled towards us as soon as our preparations for starting

85

were noticed. Our departure seemed to be welcomed by the Indians, who were rather suspicious of us and, as if trying to make up in some measure for their reticence of the previous day, they now offered to sell us fish and game. In exchange for a few clay pipes and some tobacco we obtained four magnificent codfish, each weighing 10 lbs., an enormous so-called halibut of at least 30 lbs. which was rather similar to a pike, and a fine wild goose.

The old Indian who acted as interpreter in this bartering accompanied us to the mouth of the harbour where he took leave of us with the ominous words, " Skokum pask, heyu chuck, helo illihe," which means " Strong wind, heavy weather, little land." We attached no importance to his warning as the cloudless sky seemed to presage a pleasant day. Once we were well away from land the moderate but steady south wind carried us along at about four miles an hour, and so we calculated that we should cover the fifty miles which separated us from our next anchorage by the beginning of dusk. In the best of spirits we prepared with the help of the supplies we had bought a dinner which for people in our situation was quite magnificent, consisting of fish-soup and boiled goose. We thoroughly enjoyed it, and had already begun to congratulate each other on having crossed the quite open and dangerous stretch of Queen Charlotte Sound under such favourable conditions, when about 1 o'clock—we had gone halfway and were quite twenty-five miles from the nearest land— the southerly breeze suddenly changed into a south-westerly wind blowing from the open sea and increasing in violence every quarter of an hour. Our speed increased quickly to six miles an hour, and the waves rolling in from the ocean rose so high that we found ourselves compelled to shorten sail so as to lessen the pressure of the wind. In an amazingly short time the " white horses " rose up— the foaming masses thrown up by the waves—and the overcast sky lent to the whole scene a strangely desolate and gloomy aspect. Only the sailors' shouts as to the handling of the sails and rudder broke the silence of our speechless company. By 3 o'clock the land behind us was no longer visible, and straight before us there appeared in the misty distance the steep outlines of the rock-strewn coast, on which every now and then we could perceive the white foam of the breaking waves. How our steersman kept his course, how he managed not to miss the entrance, a quite narrow passage, into the Fitzhugh Sound was a marvel to us all. But he must have recognised some landmarks along the coast, since about 5 o'clock we came without the help of compass or chart to the entrance of the passage. Here the sea was raging furiously, yet we saw in the distance a canoe with one tiny sail steering towards the land. Sometimes it seemed actually to fly through the air, and sometimes to shoot down a wave as though it were being engulfed in the sea; how so light a craft managed to live in such a sea, or how it succeeded in getting through undamaged was a mystery to us. We quickly lost sight of it and were glad enough when we reached a channel where the water was quieter because it was sheltered on each side. Shortly after 5 o'clock we passed Safety Cove, a natural harbour which we had originally chosen as our anchorage for the night, but as some hours of daylight still remained and the wind continued in our favour we decided to go on and to travel through the night—a decision which nearly cost us dear. At first all went well; the scenery, though as a whole unchanged, had features somewhat different from those we had hitherto observed. On our left we had Calvert Island, on our right the jagged, irregular coast of the mainland. The height of the mountains, covered from base to summit with needle-pines, ranged from 1,000 to 3,000 feet and bore the signs of great convulsions of nature. Whole mountain-sides, particularly the spurs that sloped to the sea on the western side, seemed to have been swept by tempests. Vast masses of uprooted and shattered trees were interspersed with huge grotesquely shaped masses of rock, whilst the existence at intervals of numerous broad tracks leading down to the water's edge seemed to be due to earthquakes or avalanches. Probably the rocky ledges with which the coast was strewn owed their origin to these same convulsions.

OUR LAST NIGHT JOURNEY.

Meanwhile there had unfortunately been no improvement in the weather. The wind blew in violent, irregular gusts behind us and a damp mist hastened the fall of darkness, so that, as early as 8 o'clock, we were forced to depend on our compass. Already we were regretting that we had not dropped anchor at the entrance to the sound. The nautical knowledge of our sailors we well knew to be extremely small, and we could not rely on them for anything that was not within their actual experience hitherto. Besides this, our chart, a copy of an ancient Russian map, was extremely defective as we had already discovered on many occasions, and the old ship's compass in its wooden box was so out of order that occasionally the needle would not move at all, and we could only get our bearings by using my pocket compass, which was very small but quite accurate. It was on this occasion that we noticed for the first time that the sailors were no longer quite sure of the route, and as a matter of fact, it appeared later that only one of them had ever been so far.

At 8 o'clock, when it was already quite dark, I was standing by the steersman on deck and clad in my waterproof, was looking at the compass by the dim light of a lantern, when suddenly there was a crash forward and our square sail, struck by a sudden gust of wind, collapsed and was swept overboard. Our shouts brought our companions promptly to our aid, and after great efforts we succeeded in hauling the sail on deck; it was still held by the ropes and so water-logged that, until we regained it, it threatened to overturn the boat. As if this accident had been a signal the violence of the elements was renewed. The wind had risen to a veritable hurricane, which seemed to stir the sea to its very depths. Lashed by the storm the rain fell in torrents on the deck and the darkness of the night added a touch of horror. Soon we had to take in our foresail because of the violence of the wind that blew from our right. Up to now we had managed to keep in the middle of the channel which was not very wide, but now we had to take care lest we should be driven by the storm, that beat on our side, against the left bank. Our only safety lay in tacking against the wind with as little sail as possible and in reaching, if we could, the shelter of the right bank. Though we flew swift as an arrow, we saw only too plainly that we were being driven more and more to our left, and about 9 o'clock we had come so near the coast that we could plainly hear the breaking of the surf and could see the foam of the onrushing waves. According to the reckoning of our steersman we must be quite near the Bella Bella Rocks, a conspicuous landmark showing the entrance to the Bella Bella Sound that stretched to the west. If we could reach this before we were driven on to the coast we should be safe.

The storm increased in violence. The steersman could hardly see a ship's length in front of him and besides this the sail was between him and the land. The other sailor had stationed himself in the prow and looked out in vain for the rocks we sought. Fortunately, as he possessed only an old and useless telescope, I had lent him my small but very good binoculars. We had shortened sail as much as possible, and contented ourselves with a small triangular jib, which was fastened on a boom that stretched hori-zontally far over the ship's side and threatened every minute to capsize us. At last there came from the prow the cry, " Rocks ahead ! " We dashed forward and through the glass we could see clearly the white foam breaking over a rock that lay immediately ahead. Right by this should be the entrance to the Sound. Now our seaman could see the rock; for a moment he seemed uncertain and to doubt if it was the right place, then suddenly with a powerful twist of the rudder he swept the boat away from the land. The ship trembled under the mighty blows of the storm, and with a mad rush, we passed, scarcely fifty paces on our left, the foam-covered ridge that we had mistakenly thought to be the entrance to the passage—a mistake which had very nearly cost us our lives.

Now the wild struggle began again, but this time with the courage of despair. We had no time to think about taking our bearings—we could only think of saving our lives. Phantom-like the coast flashed by us as a perpendicular wall, its base battered by the waves. Far as we strained our eyes there was no bay that broke the coast line, no channel came in view—whenever we thought we saw one we were doomed to disappointment. Silence reigned among us, broken only from time to time by a shout from the seaman posted in the prow to warn us of a dangerous-looking spot in the channel, or summoning us to a special effort to keep the boat off the coast. Now the ever increasing waves began to break over our deck, so that it was only possible to remain there by holding on to the mast. A heavy sea of this kind washed one of our dogs overboard, and it was only with great difficulty that we rescued him half-suffocated. The poor beast owed his safety to the strong iron chain by which he was fastened to the deck. I shall never forget the faithful creature's look of gratitude as we snatched him from a watery grave. After another quarter of an hour we gave up all hope of being able to hold out any longer against the storm that was driving us shorewards, and we unanimously resolved to run the boat on to the first place where a landing seemed possible and to try at least to save our lives, even though we had to lose the ship and all our baggage. The choice of the place we had of course, to leave to the steersman, and soon his practised eye observed a little spit of land, behind which he was resolved to run ashore at any cost.

On his advice we had equipped ourselves with the barest necessities and carried on our persons some food and our weapons. Now we waited apprehensively for the decisive moment. Each of us, of course, asked himself whether he could make the leap. For a few minutes it seemed as if we were steering straight for the rocky coast, but just as we were

90

about to strike it the steersman turned the boat to the right, tacked for a short time against the wind and then, once we had passed behind the reef, turned the helm to the left towards the coast.

FROM FITZHUGH TO MILBANK SOUND.

Who can describe our astonishment when we saw in front of us, instead of the inexorable and cruel rocks which we expected, a narrow channel cutting like a gap into the steep shore, which not only afforded us protection from the raging breakers but even offered the hope of an anchorage for the remainder of the night. We did not even ask ourselves where we could be, but directly we entered the calmer water took soundings and dropped anchor in about a ten fathom depth of water on a somewhat rocky, uneven bottom.

It was 10 o'clock at night when we had accomplished this ; we made sure that we had sufficient space on both sides, so as not to be driven by the rapid current against the shore which was only a very short distance away, and exhausted by our violent exertions of the day lay down to rest with a feeling of deepest gratitude towards Providence which had preserved us in such a marvellous manner from this second deadly peril.

We passed a restless night. Whether the cause was the storm, accompanied by gusts of rain, which howled over the hills all through the night, or the rocking of the ship which, though sheltered from the violence of the storm, was buffetted by the waves rolling in from the Sound, or possibly the effects of our tremendously severe exertions —at any rate, all of us without exception were unable to sleep and rushed on deck several times under the impression that our anchor had broken loose and we were being driven on shore. I need not try to describe how welcome was the dawn after such a night.

Our first task was, of course, to make a thorough examination of the boat in case it had suffered any damage the preceding day. There was a fearful mess in the cabin ; all the contents of the boxes and trunks were thrown together pell-mell and were soaked with the sea-water which had penetrated into the cabin from the sides and through the deck, whilst clothing, shoes, toilet articles and kitchen utensils of all kinds were strewn about and filled all the space amidships. A half-hour shift at the two pumps convinced us that, although we had taken in much water, it was not rising and so we need have no apprehension as to a leak.

After we had roughly taken our bearings with the help of our chart and compass and come to the conclusion that we were about twenty miles from the entrance to the Bella Bella Sound, we prepared to continue our journey. Some essential repairs had to be made to the sail which was torn in several places ; but, owing to lack of time, we did not replace the square sail which had collapsed the day before. Many repairs were necessary on deck, the small lead chimney of the cabin was badly twisted and partly broken, so that we were much troubled by the smoke from the fire, and lastly, one of our oars, a boat-hook and many small things, though we thought them securely fastened, had been washed overboard and lost during the night.

Soon after 6 o'clock in the morning we were ready to weigh anchor, and with a last thankful glance at the rocky cleft that had given us shelter we steered for the open channel. The day was warm and rainy, the sea was some-what less rough although a strong south-west wind blew in irregular gusts, and proceeding northward we made quite rapid progress. The rocky coast on either side stood out steep and straight without any foothold, so that we realised even more vividly the danger which had threatened us in the night.

About 9 o'clock, that is to say after three hours' sail, we came in sight of the Bella Bella Rocks, which showed that on the previous day we had covered not less than a hundred miles, a record we never surpassed on any day during the whole of our journey. Whilst from this point onward a number of arms of the sea formed by numerous islands stretched deep into the mainland to the east and north, our course, going northward past the rocks, lay through a narrow passage to the west between moderately low-lying wooded islands. The wind was almost dead against us so that we were compelled to tack, a manœuvre for which our boat was not at all well designed, since it was of shallow draught and flat-bottomed and instead of a rigid keel was provided only with a centre-board, which had to be pushed up and let down whenever we changed our direction. Besides this the weather was not calculated to raise our spirits ; rain and hail alternated the whole morning and forced us to remain in the narrow, evil-smelling, smoke blackened cabin. The channel was at times so narrow that we could almost touch the bushes on either side, but the scenery was not worth looking at.

At 2 o'clock we passed a settlement of the Bella Bella Indians on a small island ; so far as we could see it consisted only of a few huts. Through the trees we thought we caught a glimpse of masts which must be those of a large ship. Welcome as the society of civilised people would have been we did not think ourselves justified in losing on that account the chance of a favourable breeze which had sprung up, and we passed the settlement without being observed. As we learned later, the ship anchored near the settlement was the schooner *Thornton*, of Victoria, engaged in the coasting trade.

Two hours later we reached the Kokai Settlement, also inhabited by Bella Bella Indians with whose chief named Charley Hamsched (probably an assumed name) our steersman was acquainted. We anchored about fifty paces from the shore and made our way to land with the help as usual of canoes paddled out to us by the Indians. The settlement consisted of six roomy huts built of timber, with a population of rather less than two hundred, many of whom were suffering from small-pox or scarlet fever— diseases which cause terrible mortality among the poor ignorant natives since when the fever is highest they try to get cool by plunging into the ice-cold sea, which only too often causes death. The incantations of their medicine men are harmless but quite useless ; in every illness they see the work of an evil spirit and seek to drive it out by all kinds of fantastic contortions.

The Indians themselves, who seemed to consist mainly of women (part of the " Bucks " were no doubt away hunting or on the war-path), were generally of a darker hue than any we had previously seen and had thick, coal-black hair which hung down in long straight strands ; their clothing consisted of the usual blanket, mostly blue in colour. The chief, Charley Hamsched, who received us with great dignity, wore as a symbol of rank a cap with a silver band of which he was evidently very proud. He invited us into his hut. Entering, we shook hands with all the inmates amid innumerable repetitions of " Glachoja " (" Good day, how are you ? "), and sitting round the fire were regaled with a kind of wild rhubarb, a plant which the Indians consume with great relish in the summer months. The Kokai and Bella Bella Indians are much superior in intelligence to those we had previously visited further to the south—the Nukletahs and the Nervittys. Not only could Hamsched stammer out a few English words, but many of the inmates of his house could speak Chinook fluently, so that we were able to talk with them as much as they liked. Hamsched, who seemed to be very loquacious, told us in the course of conversation about the loss of the English schooner *Growler*, of Victoria, which during a voyage to Sitka had been wrecked near the boundary between British and Russian America (we could not obtain more definite information) and had gone down with all hands. The schooner *Thornton* had some fragments of the wreckage on board which left no doubt that the ill-fated vessel was a total loss. During the narrative a knowing smile played over the faces of many of the Indians who were listening, and we could not help thinking that our hosts knew a good deal more about the shipwreck than they thought fit to tell us.

Greatly pestered by the importunities of the squaws, we returned before dusk to our ship, which was still for some time surrounded by a swarm of inquisitive canoes. A few small gifts secured for us in the evening a supply of firewood and fresh water, and after arranging for a night watch on the deck we retired to rest.

THE FINLAYSON CHANNEL.

At dawn next day before there was any movement in the settlement we were ready to resume our journey, and with a good south-west breeze we made our way between small islands to the Seaforth Channel by means of which at about 8 a.m., we reached the entrance to Milbank Sound, a stretch of water about fifteen miles wide, exposed to the open sea. A strong south-west wind caught us at the entrance to the Sound and carried us in two hours through a fairly high sea to the opposite coast where we expected to find the Klemtor Passage leading northward ; but to our surprise when we were near the entrance indicated by the neighbouring lofty and conical mountain called Mount Diavolo, which could be seen from a long way off, our steersman turned to the west in order, as he explained, in reply to our urgent enquiries, to look for Crow Creek, a so-called " canoe " passage which could be traversed by only very small vessels and at high tide, but which, he thought, would be a shorter route. Though we were by no means averse to the steersman shortening the journey, the captain as owner of the boat was not at all willing to risk his property or we passengers either to risk our property or to imperil our lives in the dangerous passage. Completely outvoted the steersman had to yield to our wishes, though it went much against the grain, and after he had got within a few hundred yards of the entrance to the Canoe Passage he had to turn back and steer against the wind towards Mount Diavolo. Whether it was that he wanted to pay us out a little for our objection to his course, or whether it was the inevitable consequence of tacking in a fairly high sea and in a strong wind, anyhow our poor boat was ruthlessly tossed about and heeled over so much as we tacked, that we feared to be overturned despite the centre-board. Fortunately this uncomfortable journey, which lasted fully two hours, was completed without mischance and about 12 o'clock we reached once more the entrance to the Klemtor Passage. The coast, which sloped down westward towards the open sea, rose on the east to a considerable height. The two banks of the narrow passage which cut at right angles through the coast must be some thousand feet high and above them towered a huge landmark of a mountain like Mount Diavolo. After leaving the Klemtor Passage we made rapid progress to the Finlayson Channel, its entrance guarded by the sugar-loaf mountain of Monte Christi. The scenery reminded us vividly of that we had enjoyed in Johnstone Straits, and was an effective contrast to the bare and later flat districts of the Fitzhugh and Bella Bella Channels. Nevertheless, despite the channels which cut their way like deep gorges into the mountains; despite the crystal clearness of the water; despite the almost perpendicular mountain walls clad in dark green cypresses and their summits covered with snow; despite the silver threads of the mountain streams that leapt down over the rocks, our eyes soon grew weary of the monotony of the scenery and we yearned for some signs of human life, if only the smoke of a settlement or a canoe gliding by the shore. The stillness, the loneliness of the whole district, had a somewhat oppressive effect from which the newcomer could not easily escape. The weather, hitherto favourable, changed towards noon and the wind blew irregularly and in gusts which kept us continually on the alert. Here we had our first experience of the disadvantage of the inner passage as compared with the outer one, which was always exposed to the wind. Shut in as they are on both sides by very high banks, the channels of the inner passage are characterised generally by a complete absence of wind; if however, a breeze gets into the narrow cuttings it does not blow steadily, but comes now from this direction and now from that, according as mountain hollows or valley-like clefts give it scope. Sometimes, but very rarely, a hurricane sweeps in and then to be caught in the narrow arm of the sea shut in with rocks and stirred to its lowest depths is an extremely dangerous experience for ships of any kind.

Towards evening when we were thinking about our anchorage for the night we had a great surprise. We noticed a sail a good way behind us and at first took it for that of a canoe ; but it gained on us rapidly, and as it came up we saw that the vessel was the *Red Rover* sloop of Victoria ; on its deck four people appeared in blue soldiers' cloaks and asked the name of our ship and its destination. The *Red Rover* and its captain, one Mr. King, were well-known to our sailors and passengers, and in order that we might have an opportunity of exchanging experiences it was decided that at least we would spend the evening together, and therefore drop anchor by a bank of shingle, formed by the mouth of a mountain stream, in a fairly sheltered position. Amid torrents of rain we anchored side by side, and Mr. King and his steersman, George, came on board and formed with our party of six a quite pleasant gathering which would have been thoroughly enjoyable if we had had rather more room. But despite this we did as well as we could, and with the aid of a glass of rum and the recounting of marvellous adventures the evening seemed extraordinarily short.

From the conversation it appeared that the owner of the *Red Rover* was one of those restless characters that one so often encounters in America and particularly on the West Coast, where California is so strong an attraction. Coming to California by the overland route early in life at the time of the discovery of gold, he was at first one of the most enterprising miners and in that capacity faced dangers of every kind—adventures with hostile Indians, fights with wild beasts and with still more dangerous savage white men through the gold areas, from the shores of Colorado and the Mexican boundary right up to the inhospitable regions of the Cariboo district in the far North. At one time rich, at another poor, he would not exchange his adventurous life in the wilderness for safer residence in civilised places, and so at this time he was again on a hunting expedition towards the boundary of Russian-America, and for this purpose he had procured the boat and had engaged these men who were skilled in fishing and hunting ; a Nukletah Indian who acted as pilot and a fine big New-foundland dog completed his party. The dog, after whom he had named his ship *Red Rover*, seemed to be greatly treasured by him and accompanied him on all his adventur-ous expeditions, and had given proof of remarkable intelli-gence. According to his owner if the dog were allowed to go on shore at night he would be certain to see him return next morning with some game in his jaws. The appearance of this animal showed quite clearly that he was ready to fight with any kind of wild beast whatsoever, and presented a striking contrast to the utter uselessness of our own dogs. During the night we were awakened several times by the hoarse baying of wolves who no doubt had come down to the shore in search of prey and joined with our dogs in a regular concert, which repeated by the echo resounded far and wide through the clefts of rock.

When we awoke next morning, the 3rd May, we found the deck and all the rigging covered with snow and the two banks were clothed in white to the water's edge ; there must have been a very heavy fall during the night, and at 4 a.m. my thermometer registered 44° F. = about 5° Reaumur. There was no sign of a breeze, but on the other hand the tide running fairly swiftly in the narrow channel favoured us and furthered our progress to some extent. I myself took the opportunity of obtaining some exercise (which was almost impossible to get in the confined space of our vessel) by helping with the long heavy oars and at least keeping the boat on a straight course. About 10 o'clock the tide changed and as there was still a complete absence of wind, we were compelled to drop anchor for a while to avoid being carried back, and we made use of the time to take in supplies of fresh water and wood and to stretch our legs again on dry land. A mountain stream, which here leapt down over the rocks, filled the already moist air with a fine spray and gave an unwonted freshness to the almost tropical beauty of the various mosses, those ornaments of the northern clime, which covered the ground and the trees, sometimes forming a soft springy cushion, sometimes hanging down from the branches in fantastic forms. Though the coloured glory of flowers was lacking, there was compensation in the varied shades of green, from the almost yellow tint of the hanging mosses to the dark shades of the cypresses. No sound disturbed the heavenly peace of nature's unchallenged reign, and it was not without a start that the intruder heard the noise of a stone rolling beneath his feet or the cracking of a dry twig ; he seemed to realise that he had no right to set his foot on the virgin soil.

Before we returned on board one of the party thought he discovered traces of silver-bearing quartz. On closer investigation by an experienced miner it appeared that the silver content, if it existed at all, must be quite insignificant, nevertheless we took careful note of the place and carried away some specimens of the stone with us for more exact analysis. But who of us will ever visit the spot again !

About noon the watchful eye of our steersman detected the first signs of a rising breeze, which gave warning of its approach by a slight ruffling of the surface of the water and eventually filled our drooping sail and made it possible for us to go on. We had of course hoisted every rag of canvas that we had, and as our boat was more speedy we should soon have left the *Red Rover* far behind us, had not its crew, who had already spread out their blankets as additional sails, helped to quicken her pace by hard work at the oars. The only notable event in the afternoon was the appearance of a black wolf, who stood for some minutes on a rock some hundreds of feet above us and seemed to be watching us closely. It was only when our dogs gave tongue that he deigned to retreat. To judge by his size he must have been a dangerous beast, as the wolves of the north-west coast generally far surpass the comparatively small bears in ferocity and strength.

The banks became steeper and higher the further we went along the Finlayson Channel ; towards evening they were over 3,000 feet high and the mountain streams on both sides became much more numerous. The left bank, formed by the Princess Royal Island, was an almost straight unbroken line, but the coast of the mainland on our right was indented by many bays and channels, some of which were like narrow passes, others broad as inland seas and altogether formed an enchanting scene.

Unfortunately every breath of wind ceased towards evening, and at the same time the apparently inevitable rain warned us to seek quarters for the night. After two hours' hard rowing against the current we reached at 6 o'clock, a little bay near Work Island, not far from the exit of the channel. Here amidst heavy rain we anchored side by side with the *Red Rover*, whose captain had already invited us on board.

The cabin of the *Red Rover* (which was of the same tonnage as our sloop) was no larger than our own, but it was divided into sleeping and living rooms and was altogether cleaner and better fitted than ours. The equipment was characteristic of the owner and included a regular arsenal of weapons and a complete supply of fishing and hunting gear, traps, etc. Antlers of deer, every kind of skin and hunting trophies of all sorts decked the cabin and there was evidence of the geological interests of our host in a collection of ore-bearing specimens. We were much less impressed by the nautical knowledge of this strange hunting party, as in spite of a quite good chart and the presence of the Indian pilot, they seemed to be very uncertain about their course up to now and had to get their first information as to their precise position from us.

THROUGH THE GRENVILLE CHANNEL TO FORT SIMPSON.

By daybreak next morning we were already under sail again, this time with the help of a favouring south-west wind, thanks to which at 11 o'clock we reached the Nipean Sound, a stretch of sea about 10 miles wide and 20 long almost shut in by islands. At its north-east shore the big Salmon River empties itself into the sea through two branches each several miles wide, known to seamen as the First and Second Kittimat Arms, and gives to the otherwise clear dark green water of its estuaries a muddy whitish hue. Our course lay north-west towards the entrance of the Grenville Channel, which lies between Pitt Island and the mainland and forms the connecting link between the Nipean Sound and Chatham Sound, the latter lying further to the north.

We had traversed about two-thirds of the Sound and were off the mouth of the Second Kittimat Arm, our pace must have been quite six miles an hour, and the whole party with the exception of the steersman had gone below for our simple meal of salt meat and potatoes, when suddenly we felt a severe shock which made the boat tremble in all its timbers and gave us a terrible fright. We ran on deck in breathless excitement, but were met by the steersman with the assurance that there was no danger. Our vessel had struck with great violence against a huge drifting log which he had not noticed, and had received a very severe shock but was undamaged, as the pumps quickly proved.

Our meal was quite spoiled and all the afternoon we stayed on deck in our anxiety to avoid another collision with the numerous trunks and logs which were floating in our course ; they had no doubt been swept down into the Sound by the Salmon River, and called for great care on the part of the steersman.

At 1 o'clock without further mischance we reached the entrance to the Grenville Channel, through which we sailed steadily in torrential rain, but with a strong south-east wind, and about 4 o'clock we passed on our right the Kittcattle Arm, with a settlement of the Kittcattle Indians. Two hours more brought us to a very sheltered anchorage on the left bank, formed here by Pitt Island, near the northern end of the channel, where we had arranged to wait for the *Red Rover*, of which we had lost sight during the day.

Despite the rain which poured down as if the clouds had broken and even penetrated into our cabin, I could not but admire the wonderful and impressive beauty of the neighbourhood. With the crystal, glacier-like stream, the steep banks and boldly hewn sturdy cliffs now covered with dark woods, the fantastic masses of rock rising amid the trees, and finally the mountain peaks that sometimes were lost in the clouds and sometimes were covered with eternal snow or gleamed with the blue of glaciers—it presented a picture which could bear comparison with the scenery of the Grisons or the Tyrol. Noteworthy also was a range of mountain gorges stretching from east to west, in which at high altitudes there appeared cup-shaped hollows suggesting the presence of mountain lakes.

Although the left bank of the channels and arms of the sea which we had traversed was formed exclusively of islands, whilst the right or eastern coast was generally that of the mainland, the scenery on both sides was so much alike, that one was forced to believe that the chain of islands which lies along the coast from Victoria to Sitka had originally formed part of the continent and had been separated from it by some great upheaval. Further evidence in support of this view is afforded by the fact that the fauna and flora of almost all the islands, some of which are quite small and lie miles away from the coast, are identical with those of the mainland.

Darkness had fallen by the time the *Red Rover* had at last come in sight and taken her place alongside. It was our last night together, for we proposed to proceed next day direct to Fort Simpson whilst the other vessel intended to go eastwards and first visit Methlakatla, a native settlement and mission on the Skinner River.

Next morning the weather had not improved, and when we resumed our journey at 4 a.m., the rain fell in torrents despite the fairly strong south-west wind. Before we came to the outlet of the Grenville Channel we had the rare opportunity of seeing a specimen of the mountain sheep, which are regarded by hunters as the most elusive and therefore most highly prized wild animals on the North-West coast The creature seemed to be twice the size of an ordinary sheep and was covered, legs and all, with a dirty brown fleece. It was standing on a rather high ridge of rock at the entrance to a deep inlet, but vanished inland with a great leap before we could get near.

Shortly after 6 o'clock we reached the mouth of the channel in Chatham Sound, and here we parted from the *Red Rover*, whose crew responded to our farewells with three cheers.

From this point our course was north-westerly over the Sound, which is about 40 miles long and 10 wide. Its southern portion is hemmed in by islands, but the northern part is fairly open. Its numerous shallows and dangerous ridges of rock make it one of the most dreaded parts of the coast. As a matter of fact the Sound deserved its reputation, for it needed every conceivable precaution on the part of our steersman to find a safe channel in that jumble of islands and reefs, and also the dogged patience of an experienced seaman to keep in a good temper amid the heavy rain, tempestuous sea and a strong wind that came in gusts.

We passengers kept ourselves to the cabin as we could do nothing to help on deck and the captain, to whose guidance in such stormy weather we were not inclined to trust ourselves, was summoned on deck from time to time at a word of command from the steersman to help him. Frequently it was necessary to counter the gusts of wind that blew so strongly against us by a slight turn of the wheel or the lowering of the sails, and great skill was needed to do this at the right moment. Thus in the course of time the captain of the *Ocean Queen* was reduced to the rank of a sailor, whilst the sailor by virtue of his seamanship took command—a reversal of positions which gave rise to some apprehension on our part.

The further we got from the channel, the more uninteresting became our surroundings. The islands we passed seemed to be more and more flat and were covered with low copses, whilst the rain-soaked haze shut off any wider view. Had not the danger from the reefs on the right and left of our course and the occasional pulling up or lowering of the centre-board as we tacked kept us in activity, we must have regarded our journey across the Chatham Sound as one of the most monotonous parts of our voyage.

Nevertheless we made good progress and at noon we passed the entrance of the Skinner River and the Methlakatla Settlement, and after another four hours' passage in a high sea we dropped anchor at last on the evening of the 5th May in sight of Fort Simpson.

FORT SIMPSON—I.

Fort Simpson, established by the Hudson Bay Company in 1834, is one of the most northerly points of the British North-West coast, and lies about 600 miles (by our reckoning 619 miles) from Victoria and approximately 300 miles from Sitka. So for fourteen days (one of which had been wasted at Nanaimo) we had voyaged at least 45 miles a day, and so could not complain of the speed at which we had travelled. True, a third of the entire distance to Sitka remained to be traversed, but at this rate we should take at most a week—a hope which proved to be unfounded.

Situated as it is on a quite safe bay of a flat peninsula, Fort Simpson is an important place of call for the small trading vessels which ply along the coast, and as such is widely known. One of our sailors had spent some time there recently, and had roused our curiosity by his descriptions of its importance. But nevertheless we were greatly surprised when on entering the bay we saw a great fort formed of palisades and comprising towers and large buildings and surrounded by a veritable town of Indian houses decked in many cases with flag-staffs and carvings. Lying stretched along the shore this Indian town made a complete semi-circle, formed of several hundred wooden houses ; and the smoke which rose from every house led one to suppose that they were all inhabited.

Immediately we dropped anchor we were beset, as usual, by a crowd of canoes manned by Indians, and with their help three of us went on shore. When we reached the approach to the stately fort, over which there floated the

FORT SIMPSON FROM THE BEACH.   E.T. 1868

British flag with the arms of the Hudson Bay Company, we were met by two white men, well dressed in English fashion and of very respectable appearance, who introduced themselves to us as the Factors, gave us a hearty British welcome and invited us to the fort.

Although we were total strangers to them, we accepted this invitation with pleasure, told them our names and business, and made our way, through a number of loitering natives, up the short road to the fort, the gate of which was opened as we approached.

We were now able to examine the fort close at hand. It seemed to be of great extent and was surrounded by a double palisade. The outer ring consisted of strong pointed stakes about ten feet high. The second ring, which was some forty feet inside the first, was about twenty feet high and flanked at the sides by massive towers constructed of logs laid diagonally and provided with gun embrasures ; it was so high that only the roofs of the

E.T. 1868

ENTRANCE FORT SIMPSON.

buildings inside rose above it. Passing through the outer palisade we reached the heavy entrance door, with its iron clamps and loopholes ; this was kept shut, but a small postern door gave us admittance to the interior of the fort. But even this gateway, above which rose a tower with a bell, was equipped with gun embrasures on both sides within the door, so that to get into the fort against the will of the garrison would be no easy task. Under the guidance of our hosts we entered a spacious courtyard, surrounded by five blockhouses built of wood, and went across it to the entrance to the main building or dwelling house. There we were conducted into a large room, extending almost the whole depth of the building, in the centre of which was a long table—this with a row of chairs along the walls constituted almost the only furniture. The room was made more habitable by a glowing fire which crackled on an immense hearth ; an Indian of quite civilised appearance stood ready to replenish it with huge logs.

106

Realising the very neglected state of our toilet we were delighted to find in a small room to which we were conducted, washing materials which enabled us after fourteen days' deprivation to enjoy once more to our hearts' content essentials of civilisation. Anybody who for a fortnight has been able to wash only with salt water and the very coarse so-called salt-water soap, and to dry himself with ships' towels stiff with salt, will be able to appreciate the feeling of comfort with which after thorough ablutions we met our host.

In the living-room or parlour the table had been laid in the meantime and we were invited to partake of a lunch which with the conversation that accompanied it, forms one of the really pleasant memories of our tour. The participants were only our two hosts and we three visitors ; we were waited on by the young and intelligent Indian, who acted on the slightest hint from his master. The meal was excellent and consisted of tender mutton with sauce and vegetables, good English beer, bread and cheese, served in real English style and perfectly cooked, and to our palates which were not spoiled by a great variety of food it was a veritable feast, for which we could not be sufficiently grateful to our hosts.

INTERIOR OF FORT SIMPSON. E.T. 1868

Mr. Cunningham, the elder of the two gentlemen, who with his jolly round face, strikingly white skin and very light curly hair, was a typical Englishman, was not really the Factor but was temporarily in charge in place of a

Mr. Manson (or Mansell ?) who had gone to establish a new trading post on the Stikeen (Stikine ?) River, closer to the American boundary. His companion, Mr. Hawkins, was a much younger man who had come to Victoria in the service of the company a few years before and was now assistant to the Factor.

After lunch we were invited to inspect the interior of the fort. Proceeding from the dwelling house towards the entrance, we went first into the warehouse where not only were there European goods of all kinds carefully packed in cases and bales, but a great variety of the skins traded by the Indians were also stored.

Amongst the goods of the first class the chief place was taken by blankets ; there were whole rows of bales full of these commodities which are in such demand among the Indians, and there were also other articles of clothing. A second very important group consisted of iron goods, axes, knives and smaller wares and fancy goods (strings of beads, mirrors, etc.) ; then there was Colonial produce such as sugar, syrup, coffee, tea, and in addition flour, tobacco, pipes, tinder, and finally, fire-arms, powder and lead, small shot, flints, and in the cellar there were alcoholic drinks, namely, brandy, rum, beer, etc.

The collection of skins was fairly comprehensive, and also very large as the steamship *Otter*, which belongs to the Company and takes the pelts twice a year to Victoria, was expected to arrive shortly. The skins of each kind were sorted out into numerous grades and most carefully arranged. The most abundant were the small otter skins, which are used to some extent as currency on the North-West coast. The classes were :—

Sea otter value	$20–100	Marten	value	$2–7
Fur seal ,,	3–5	Small otter	,,	1
Hair seal ,,	$\frac{1}{2}$	Silver fox	,,	20–60
Bear ,,	6–10	Cross fox	,,	5–7
Wolf ,,	3–5	Red fox	,,	2
Lynx ,,	2	Wolverine	,,	5
Small lynx ,,	1–1$\frac{1}{2}$			

These skins were all exchanged for European goods imported from England *via* Victoria, and almost exclusively by Indians of the coast districts. The stations further inland send the skins collected in the winter down to the coast station in the spring and thence the whole consignment is brought by the steamer mentioned above to the chief depot in Victoria. That town is the great centre not only for all the skins collected on the North-West coast, but also for the European goods which are distributed to the smaller trading stations. Consequently every station, even the most remote, is in communication with the chief depot to which it sends its skins and whence the whole supply is despatched twice a year to London to be sold at public auction. Thus the Hudson Bay Company has established a chain of stations over the whole northern part of North America except the extreme North-West coast (Alaska) and until recently it could claim a monopoly of the trade, but now the Company has given up this monopoly on payment of compensation by the Canadian Government and the trade in furs is now open to all. But nevertheless the collections of skins made by the Company are by far the most important, since the Indians know the Company's representatives well and are, as a rule, much more fairly treated by them than by the grasping and unscrupulous smaller traders.

The skins thus dealt in are paid for entirely by goods, and as the Company is entitled to import all its goods free of duty the profits made in this bartering are always high.

Money is never seen amongst the Indians, but it sometimes happens that dealers add to their stocks of bartered goods by purchases at the Hudson Bay Station and pay for them with gold ; but they also frequently pay partly in skins.

From the store we made our way to the "shop." At the entrance there was hung up a list of prices for the various commodities and the number of skins taken as equivalent to the price in each case. Here the actual deals were carried out, the skins bartered and goods delivered in exchange. It presented a curious jumble of all kinds of articles ; there were even Indian weapons, knives, muskets, hunting and fishing gear which served, Mr. Cunningham explained, as pledges in respect of deals not yet completed.

Passing the entrance we came to the quarters of the staff (assistant factors, clerks, etc.) and then to those of the workmen and so back to the main building.

FORT SIMPSON—II.

In order to get a wider view of the surroundings of the fort and also of its defences we mounted the gallery which runs round the whole fort inside the inner palisade, whence we could get an extensive view through the numerous gun openings. Behind the fort, but within the line of the inner palisade, was a fairly large kitchen garden, watered by a small stream flowing through it, where with difficulty a few potato and cabbage plants were being grown. On one side of it lay the modest burial ground, marked by a few crosses. Lonely graves of white men so far from the place of their birth! With sympathy for the lot of our hosts, probably destined one day to die in this remote spot, we continued our tour. I was particularly interested in the watch-towers at each corner of the fort, whose height and massive construction seemed such as to baffle any attack by the Indians, and besides in each there was a cannon, which alone would suffice to put an army of Indian braves to flight.

As a matter of fact there was no danger from the Indians. Their disposition was friendly and it was so much in their interest to keep on good terms with the occupants of the fort that there was not the slightest reason to apprehend their hostility. Formerly the fort had a garrison of fifty men, and had to withstand many an attack, but at this time there were only four white men in the population— the others were Indian servants who at a wage of half-a-dollar a day were good workers.

An additional fact was Mr. Cunningham's marriage to a squaw, which greatly strengthened his position in regard to the Indians around him ; it is the practice of the Company's officials to marry Indian women. It is reported that they make very good wives, and are very devoted to their husbands and children. The differences between the offspring of such mixed marriages are very striking. In one and the same family some of the children of an Indian mother have all the characteristic features of the full-blooded Indian, whilst others, offspring of the same marriage, are scarcely distinguishable from the children of white parents. Generally these half-castes are of poor physique and have bad health, so that they seldom reach any considerable age, but are frequently victims of consumption. The marriage of the Governor of British Columbia to a squaw attracted much attention at the time ; it was, however, a happy marriage and there were a number of children.

Whether or not because our host at Fort Simpson did not regard his wife as a social equal and presentable, at any rate he did not introduce her, and had we not accidentally seen two healthy and lively children in the courtyard we should have remained for that day quite ignorant of his domestic circumstances.

On our return from inspecting the fort we encountered in the parlour a very intelligent looking Indian fully dressed in European fashion, who was introduced to us by our host as P. Legaic, chief of the neighbouring Methlakatla Indians. Legaic, who conversed with Mr. Cunningham in the Tshimpsean dialect, had also a fair mastery of English, and his manners were far superior to those of many of the white men in these regions. Not only had he a high reputation amongst his own people on account of his acute intelligence, but his wealth had made him well-known in a wider circle, and he had great influence over other tribes, including the Indians of Fort Simpson. Legaic had a house of his own near the fort, and occupied it during his frequent visits.

According to our host the number of Indians settled round the fort was about 2,000, divided into eight tribes each under its own chief. At this time the majority of the "Bucks" (or men) were away on a fishing expedition to the River Nass, which enters the sea north of the fort and affords an extraordinarily rich fishery which is particularly famous on account of the great quantities of small fish (a species of herring) which are caught there. At the fishing season in the spring a host of Indians of various tribes gather there to lay in a stock of this popular fish, which is generally salted and on account of its oiliness is greatly esteemed. Such a heterogeneous gathering of Indians unfortunately seldom passes off without disturbance and thus there were recently open hostilities between the Fort Simpson and the Nass Indians, in the course of which, besides a number of lesser braves, two chiefs of the former tribe were killed. This act of violence the friends of the slain chieftains managed to avenge in native fashion by killing the next five Nass Indians that they encountered.

The dead chiefs had been brought to the fort only on the preceding day and were lying there still unburied, or rather still unburned—burning is the customary method by which the coast Indians dispose of their dead—in houses of their followers, so that naturally the whole settlement was in mourning. Whilst we were in the fort the squaw of one of the victims came to beg for some candles, as she intended to watch by the dead man throughout the night. Mr. Cunningham gave them readily and tried to comfort her, but her dark countenance showed no signs of cheering up ; by the dim light of a lantern her close-cut hair and face painted black as signs of mourning gave her a most repellent appearance.

By this time it was late and our captain, who had come on shore with us, had gone back to the boat some time before without taking leave ; we, too, now bade a hearty farewell for the night to our hosts and were conveyed to the *Ocean Queen*, where we found the companions we had left behind still engaged in a lively discussion with the Indian men and women.

I shall always remember how the stillness of the night was disturbed by the animal-like howling which reached us from the Indians, who were mourning their dead, and seemed to stop only at dawn.

Before we went on shore next morning we had a consultation as to whether it would not be advisable to obtain an Indian pilot from Fort Simpson, as it had now become quite clear that neither our captain nor the steersmen had ever been further than this point and could know nothing of the remainder of the route. Our seaman professed to know an Indian pilot at Fort Tongass which was near by, but we thought that the Factor's authority was sufficient assurance that we should be able to engage through him an Indian for this purpose, and we decided that at any rate we would try this first.

Quite unexpectedly on visiting the fort we found Mr. Cunningham about to sit down to breakfast in company with his wife and children; on our entrance the latter disappeared at a sign from Mr. Cunningham, despite our attempts to avoid this disturbance of their meal.

With his usual kindness our host immediately sent a messenger to find some pilots from whom we could choose, and we occupied the time of waiting in purchasing some provisions for our journey. These consisted of three small barrels of the famous salted herrings, for which we paid 2½ dollars per barrel, and some bottles of good brandy or cognac for special occasions, the price being 1½ dollars per bottle.

Mr. Cunningham, who seemed to be well acquainted with everything that went on in the settlement, complained to us about the behaviour of the white men who visited it, and said that in the short period of their stay amongst the Indians they heedlessly counteracted all his efforts to improve their condition, and seemed to take a delight in introducing the ignorant and credulous Indians to their characteristic vices.

The drunkenness and infectious maladies from which the Indians suffered so much were the outcome of their contact

113

with the unscrupulous whites and consequently—this was our friend's conclusion—it was with great regret that he saw any intercourse between strangers and his Indians. As appeared later, our captain, who had spent a night on shore amongst the Indians, had behaved disgracefully, and it was probably his conduct which had given rise to Mr. Cunningham's remarks. There was complaint also against one of our sailors, who had wisely not put in an appearance at the fort. A short time previously he had been at Fort Simpson in company with a French trader in a small merchant vessel, and during his stay had sought to form a liaison with the squaw of the captain of his boat ; and when the jealous husband threatened to shoot him he was compelled suddenly to leave the ship (in which he had a share) and take refuge on land. Being entirely without resources he was looked after in the fort and promised a passage to Victoria on the next steamer of the Company. Instead of showing himself grateful for this kindness he left the fort without saying good-bye, spent several days in the company of some dissolute Indians and finally joined an Indian trail to the south, whereby he got to Victoria.

Thus we got an even poorer opinion of our two sailors than we had had before and our confidence in them was entirely destroyed. Yet we were probably bound to these wretches for some weeks to come.

FORT SIMPSON—III.

Meanwhile the messenger came back to the fort and brought with him only one old Indian who was ready to go with us as pilot. From our conversation with this man, in which the Factor acted as interpreter, it appeared that many of the " Bucks " in the settlement knew the way but none of them were disposed to make the journey with us because of the Stikeen Indians who dwelt midway along the route to Sitka and with whom they were in open feud. The old man who *was* ready to go proved, on cross-examination, not to have been at Sitka himself, and

114

only once, as he explained in rather an original manner, had he seen from a distance the mountains behind which he was told Sitka was situated. We could, of course, not conceal the fact that we were reluctant to trust ourselves to such a guide and as Mr. Cunningham, who clearly knew the character of his Indians, held out no prospect of overcoming their timidity, there was nothing for us to do except try our luck with the next Indian tribe, the Tongass. Possibly some of the soldiers landed at Tongass by the *Oriflamme* which had passed Fort Simpson, some eight days before, could help us to find a pilot.

E.T. 1868

INDIAN CARVING, FORT SIMPSON.

Accompanied by the Factor and despite the rainy weather (which seems to be the general rule here) we went to the Indian town to buy a canoe to replace the small boat which we had lost at Nanaimo and missed greatly whenever we wanted to land. The canoe, together with paddles and a bailer, we obtained for six dollars. The vendor was credited at the fort with the amount which we paid to the Factor.

I could not lose the opportunity of making some sketches of the fort and its surroundings. Particularly interesting

115

and novel were the wooden carvings that stood above the entrance of almost every house ; the grotesque designs showed much ability. These carvings seem to take the place of coats of arms, since no two of them are alike. The quaint images placed in a curious manner one above another and carved on a single tree-stem were sometimes 20 feet high and more, and rose considerably above the huts, whose apparently quite small entrances were between the carvings.

Over the houses of the Methlakatla chief was a copper plaque with an eagle on it, and beneath the name of the owner the motto : " My crest is the eagle, the king of the birds "—truly a proud device ! The houses are all very large and can shelter 20-25 persons comfortably. Those which stand by the water's edge are built on piles, and when at high tide the water sweeps under them they can only be reached by means of ladders.

We did not go into the houses, as our guide advised us not to do so on account of smallpox and scarlet fever, which was rampant at the time. But we were everywhere received with a friendliness that bordered on respect, and my sketches seemed very greatly to interest the Indians who stood round me. It was quite amusing to see how, looking over my shoulder, they were delighted when they thought they saw that the drawing resembled the original and they called my attention to any instance in which they thought I had overlooked any detail of the carvings.

The people whom we did manage to see were very sturdy and well-grown, many of them being quite six feet high without their shoes ; and as a whole they seemed quite superior to the Indians whom we had met hitherto. All the men and women wore as their sole garment a blanket sometimes decked with beads. The squaws generally had silver bangles and rings on their arms and feet and in a few cases through the ears and nose. The children, even the bigger ones, went about quite naked. The boys exercised themselves with bows and arrows, whilst the girls plaited and sewed. Amongst the older people many of the

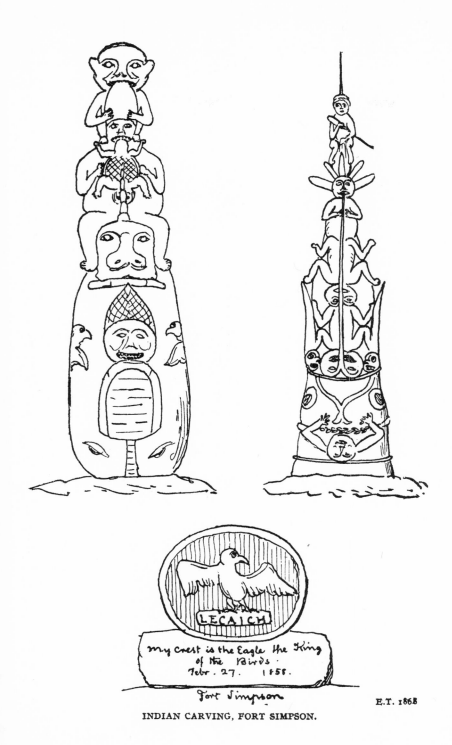

my crest is the Eagle the King
of the Birds:
Febr. 27. 1858.

Fort Simpson

E.T. 1868

INDIAN CARVING, FORT SIMPSON.

women were painted black and had their hair cut off as a sign of mourning.

When we arrived at the beach we witnessed the departure of Chief Legaic of the Methlakathla Indians. A large canoe fully 20 feet long packed full of goods of every kind (obtained mostly from the Hudson Bay Fort) had been launched on the water by six sturdy fellows. Legaic was still on the beach, quite elegantly dressed in a kind of travelling costume and distinguished by a large pair of opera glasses slung over his shoulder, of which he seemed to be very proud. After a long conversation with the Factor he finally took leave, sprang with great agility into the canoe, waved us a ceremonious farewell and then lying back comfortably gave the order to start. The six short paddles struck the water with machine-like precision, and it was not without a feeling of respect for this Indian dictator that we gazed after the rapidly disappearing canoe. P. Legaic certainly displayed a higher degree of civilisation than any Indian we had hitherto encountered, but Mr. Cunningham assured us that the case was by no means an isolated one in this particular tribe and that amongst the Methlakathla Indians, thanks to the unceasing efforts during many years of an English missionary named Duncan, a certain level of civilisation had been reached. At the time more than 300 Indians, including 80 children, belonged to the Mission, which was carried on by Mr. Duncan in quite a patriarchal manner. He watched over the worldly interests as well as the spiritual well-being of his flock, and acted not only as a pastor but as a judge. He had established a kind of police, and small coasting vessels manned by Mission Indians carried to market the skins which they wished to barter and brought back other commodities in exchange. In short, his self-sacrificing activity had at any rate met with a measure of success, in that at least a superficial culture had been reached by his Indians, although their general condition still left much to be desired.

A second Mission recently founded on the Nass River, directly north of Fort Simpson, by a missionary named

Tomlinson was only in an early stage of development, but it was likely to be ultimately of far-reaching influence, since every year there was a gathering at that place of many Indian tribes.

One immediate result of the Mission activities in the Tshimpsean peninsula is that the domestic conditions of the Indians inhabiting that part, their language, customs and habits and their religion has been studied more carefully and thoroughly than is the case with the other tribes of the North-West coast. It is the Tshimpsean language in particular which has aroused very great interest as it was found that it is not only an entirely independent language, quite unrelated to the dialects of the neighbouring tribes, but that it has also a grammatical form with conjugations and declensions, which could hardly be expected in the case of coast Indians, who dwell in such remote districts. Moreover, the importance of this language seems to be recognised by many other tribes who dwell in the interior since they regard Tshimpsean as a kind of superior language of which every intelligent Indian should at least understand the rudiments.

Through the instrumentality of the missionaries, books in Tshimpsean have been printed at Victoria, and I have before me now a dictionary and phrase book from which the following words will give an idea of the language, which is unaccented but rather too guttural. I should add that in contrast with Chinook it is a genuinely Indian language.

Numbers : 1 Kooll 4 Tum-alp 7 Tup-old
2 Koopel 5 Shtones 8 Yugh-talt
3 Kwula 6 Ha-gold 9 Kist-more
10 Keap
20 Koo-pel-wul-keap
100 Kwe-stin-sole
½ De sto

Pronouns : I Nu-yu you Nu-a-sum
thou Nu-un they Tup-ne-ed
he Ne-ed we Nu-und

119

Adjectives :

Black	Dotsk	Blue	Kus-kwash
White	Moxk	Green	Meet-leth
Red	Musk		

Cardinal Points :

North	Ke-seas	World	Ke-am-a got
East	Hy-wass	Sun	Seo
South	Ugh-pala	Star	Be-a-list
West	Gu-il-Ka	Snow	Ma-tum
		Rain	Wass

Natural Phenomena : (see above, merged)

Days and Seasons :

Sunrise	Tse yoost	Mid-day	Suego-llh
Sunset	Koo pell	Morning	Kum Klay pa
Evening	Mla wo rumel	Night	Kl hoop
Spring	Koy un	Summer	Soond
Autumn	Kwus-oot	Winter	Kome-sam

Conjugations :

I thank	Nu-ya-chrodote	I see	Neet sote
thou thankest	Lil-chroda	thou seest	Neet sin e
he thanks	Lip-chrod-ca	he sees	Neet set
we thank	Lip-caro-dum	we see	Neet sund
you thank	Lip-carod-sam	you see	Neet se sund
they thank	Lip-carod-ca	they see	Neet set ca

UNITED STATES.

FORT TONGASS— I.

Such time as we had to spare had been spent in inspecting the settlement and purchasing all we required, and so, shortly after mid-day on the 6th May, we bade farewell to our kind hosts and set sail once more. The weather, which had been rainy during the whole of our stay at the fort, now cleared up, the sun shone bright and warm, the wind was favourable and, towing the canoe we had purchased, we soon left the flat coast of the Tshimpsean peninsula far behind us and about two o'clock, favoured by a moderate south-east wind, we passed the mouth of the Nass River, near which the land again rises to a considerable height.

From this point our course was almost due west, obliquely across the northern part of Chatham Sound towards Tongass Island, which was about 30 English miles distant.

This journey which was a somewhat slow one as the wind dropped from time to time, was about four o'clock interrupted by an accident which nearly cost the lives of some Indians who were coming to meet us. We had already noticed for some time a canoe under sail approaching from the opposite direction and apparently making straight towards us. As we had no wish to meet the Indians and were just being carried by a favouring breeze we kept on our course ; the canoe, however, had got its paddles out and was already within hailing distance of our ship. Whether it happened that the Indians were trying to cut across us at the last moment or that our steersman deliberately turned the helm round towards them, at any rate we struck the canoe broadside with such force that we all believed we had cut it in two. However, despite the violence of the collision, which hurled the canoe some distance backwards, the five Indians in it escaped with nothing worse than a fright. Their canoe, constructed of tough cedar wood, was of such light build and consequently offered so little resistance that we did not sink it. Without paying any heed to the gestures and loudly expressed protests of the Indians against the brutal treatment they had experienced, we continued on our way and soon lost sight of them. According to our calculations they must have come from Clement City and were making for Fort Simpson, where they probably gave vent to their grievances against us.

It was eight o'clock and already dusk as we drew near the flat, thickly-wooded Tongass Island, surrounded by numerous reefs, when a canoe manned by ten armed Indians suddenly blocked our entrance to the bay. We were at first somewhat alarmed at the forbidding aspect of the savages who, holding their muskets between their knees, bombarded us with unintelligible questions. A few words from our steersman, who knew and pronounced the name of the Indian pilot, had the effect of pacifying them, and when shortly after this the pilot himself came on board our ship, we were permitted to enter the bay; but as it was quite strange to our steersman and was rendered dangerous by strong currents and sunken rocks, he gave over the helm to the pilot with whom we were quite easily able to make ourselves understood in Chinook. It was not our intention to drop anchor by the Indian settlement, which we recognised by its lights in the distance, but in the vicinity of the military station, which was about a mile distant; and as the wind had died down we had to make our way along the shore with the help of our oars. It was not till 9.30, with a very dark night, that we anchored opposite the watch-fire of the troops encamped on the shore. After we had answered a few questions by the sentry we decided to dismiss for the night the pilot, who was allowed to make use of our canoe with instructions to return to the ship at daybreak.

When we awoke next morning we found ourselves in a narrow channel—it could not be called a bay—with flat, thickly-wooded banks on both sides. In front of us there was a space cleared of trees on which were erected some twenty tents amidst the undergrowth which still remained; their whiteness against the green background made a picturesque sight. Some officers who were already on the shore despite the early hour invited us to land, and fortunately Charley, as we called our pilot, had already come alongside in the canoe accompanied by his wife, so we could make use of it to go on shore. Charley had already had an accident with our boat, as he and his " Klootschman," as he called his squaw, had been upset. But he seemed to regard this as nothing unusual and if we had not seen him bailing out water he would probably have said nothing about it. This made us cautious and though subsequently the canoe justified its claim to be regarded as seaworthy, we never allowed more than two people to be in it at once.

In the camp we were most cordially greeted by the officers with whom we were acquainted; most of them were already about, but others we sought out in their tents and there were some amusing episodes. There were 50 men and 10 officers of the 2nd United States Artillery Regiment; they had been landed eight days previously from the *Oriflamme* and had found it necessary in the first place to form a tent encampment. Now they were busy clearing a large area of trees before commencing the building of the block-houses. Consequently it was not

E.T. 1868

U.S. MILITARY CAMP—TONGASS ISLAND.

surprising to find the camp in a state of confusion; the path up to the tents, which were very irregularly placed, passed through many felled tree-trunks, stumps and roots which had been left, so that communications were greatly hindered. It was laughable when the garrison drew up on the parade ground and it was manifestly impossible for the men to form a straight line and the commanding officer could only supervise a part of his forces.

By this time a table had been laid in front of one of the officers' tents and we were invited to breakfast, which was a very pleasant meal. The most interesting person present was certainly Dr. Chismore, attached to the force as surgeon, whose wide acquaintance with the country and people of the whole North-West coast seemed to give him special qualifications for his present appointment. His knowledge of the Indians of this neighbourhood dated from the time of the American-Siberian Telegraph Expedition which he had accompanied for several years and on which he had had some remarkable experiences. Dr. Chismore was consequently in the best position to form an opinion as to the condition of the troops in the camp, their relations with the neighbouring Tongass Indians, and particularly the importance of a military station here, and I am indebted to him for the following information.

The troops sent here from Fort Vancouver in Lower Columbia were made up, like practically the whole of the standing army in time of peace, of men who hailed from the older countries, the Irish element being predominant. As they came mostly from the rough and reckless element of the big towns (the " rowdies ") and had enlisted as a last resource, there was need for the strictest discipline, which could not, however, always be maintained whatever efforts were made. Spirits were entirely prohibited in the camp ; the troops could not go out of bounds without special permission ; and the neighbouring Indians were forbidden to enter the camp on pain of death. Nevertheless a number of soldiers had already managed to slip out to the Indian settlement, so strong was the attraction of the Indian squaws.

The commissariat of the troops consisted of provisions which they had brought with them, and game and fish sold by the Indians, of which there seemed great abundance. Outings for the garrison, hunting and fishing expeditions for the officers and communications with Fort Simpson and the American Fort Wrangel lying still further to the north were made feasible by two very long, narrow, open rowing boats, so-called " whalers," which could carry the greater part of the troops. A flat raft, also lying at anchor, was used for the transport of munitions. The state of health of the troops was at the moment fairly good, but though they had been landed only eight days the wet weather and the damp mist rising from the woodland in which they were encamped were already having a bad effect and rheumatic complaints were on the increase. The novelty of their surroundings made the officers for a time, forget their somewhat unenviable position, but already most of them were looking longingly back at the garrison towns of California and Oregon which were less cut off from the world, but which they had been compelled to exchange for their lonely station on Tongass Island.

FORT TONGASS—II.

The relations of the military officials with the Indians were very good, thanks to the mediation of the doctor, who enjoyed in the settlement a respect which was not common amongst the Indians in consequence of some successful operations and cures which he had performed, and his reputation had already spread beyond the boundaries of Tongass. Strange Indians now came from great distances to be treated by the white Medicine Man, and his services among the natives were the more acceptable because they were given gratuitously. Medicine was also supplied without charge to the natives whom he befriended. The diseases most prevalent amongst them were scarlet fever, smallpox, skin complaints and rheumatic affections. The Indians never reached an advanced age—fifty years seemed to be about the limit. Those who were not carried off by disease lost their lives in war or hunting. At this time the Tongass natives had a feud with the Stikeen Indians who dwelt in the north ; the Tongass had recently inflicted a defeat on their enemies and were now expecting an attack in their own territory. The state of war explained the action of the canoe which we had seen guarding the harbour and, as we were told, kept watch day and night for the dreaded Stikeens. The Tongass had, however, not much reason for alarm since the American troops would not have allowed a conflict between the two tribes so near their camp, and would certainly have taken the side of the Tongass Indians.

What advantage the American Government expected to derive from the existence of Fort Tongass is not very apparent, unless its purpose was to check the quarrels amongst the Indians ; the weak and isolated garrison could not have resisted a serious attack from a foreign enemy. No more unfavourable site could have been chosen, but Tongass was the most southerly point of the newly-acquired territory which had formerly been Russian and possibly had some importance as a frontier post in the eyes of the military authorities. But in these undeveloped areas only sparsely inhabited by natives a strict surveillance of the frontier was of little importance, and the station itself was so situated amidst a labyrinth of islands and channels and the mobility of the troops on the only lines of communication available to them was so hampered, that the establishment of the post, which had involved considerable expenditure, seemed quite superfluous.

The English in the neighbouring British Columbia make use of a much simpler and less costly method of guarding their customs frontier and of taking action against insubordinate Indian tribes. This takes the form of some gun-boats of shallow draught, built for coastal service, which are constantly cruis ng up and down the shores and have not only suppressed smuggling almost entirely, but by firing a few well-directed shots into the settlements of some tribes which had become notorious for their deeds of violence had imbued the Indians with a wholesome respect.

After two years' experience the American Government appears to have seen the error of its ways. It is stated that all the military posts established on the coast of Alaska, that is to say, Tongass, Wrangel and Kadiac (in the Aleutian Islands) are to be abandoned and Sitka alone retained as a military base, whilst the coastal service, following England's example, will be maintained solely by light cruisers.

At the time of our visit, however, no one imagined that the newly-erected fort would last so short a time, and when after breakfast Dr. Chismore produced a bottle of his medicinal brandy (which should really only be given to the sick) we all drank to the health and long life of the first American fort in Alaska.

In return we invited the officers on board our vessel, where, thanks to the purchase of spirits which we had made at Fort Simpson, we spent a very pleasant hour despite the rather limited accommodation of the cabin. Naturally there was much talk of our adventures and perils, and it was a puzzle to our guests how the *Ocean Queen*, with its small dimensions, had held together so valiantly. At the time of the accident with the tow-rope, the *Oriflamme* had given us up for lost, so perilous was our position as seen from the steamer. We learned that we owed to our friends the fact that the rope which was dragging us to destruction was cut on the steamer at the same time as we cut it, and that she was forced to heave-to at least for a time. Our two fellow travellers had gone on by the *Oriflamme* right to Fort

Kainook Cutlayam Skutleyikáh - Koaigh - Kayaghs. Eldest son of Hovats, the chief of the Tongass tribe of Indians, our Pilote

E.T 1868

CHARLEY.

Wrangel, where they had to find the best way they could of getting to Sitka. The steamer herself had passed Tongass on the previous day on her return journey and reported that troops and passengers had been landed safely at Wrangel. When we parted from our friends the commandant of the post handed us an official letter which he asked us to take to Fort Wrangel, which we were in any case bound to visit.

Meantime the negotiations between our captain and Charley, the pilot, as to the latter's engagement, had been completed, and Kainook - Skutleyikah - Koaigh - Kayaghs-Cut-layam-Klaytohts, elder son of Hovats, chief of the Tongass Indians, *alias* Charley, was taken on as pilot

127

and interpreter for the journey to Sitka, on condition that he was guaranteed a free passage back to his native village. This Charley, as we called him for short, presented a remarkable appearance; about 30 years old, of medium height and rather squat, with black hair cut short, a stupid-looking face covered with a beard, cunning eyes which were always half-closed, well-shaped features and wearing European clothes he would hardly have looked like an Indian had not the silver ring hanging through his nose betrayed his descent.

From his youth onward Charley had been engaged as pilot and interpreter on the small ships carrying on barter with the Indians, and besides this he had made a trip on a steamer to Victoria and seemed to be very proud of it, although on that journey he had had the misfortune to lose his left hand when splitting wood. To compensate him for this loss the captain of the steamer gave him the outfit in which he appeared before us. Besides knowing some English words our new pilot possessed a qualification of great importance to us; he spoke Chinook quite fluently and so could carry on detailed conversations with us. As, in addition, the Tongass dialect, his mother tongue, was closely allied to those of the six other tribes along the coast between this point and Sitka (the Stikeen, Kaigh, Hennega, Tacon, Chilcaht and Kolosch or Sitka Indians), we found him an extremely useful interpreter on our journey.

He assured us that he was well acquainted with the route to Sitka and when we asked him if he were not afraid to go through the territory of the Stikeen Indians, who were hostile to his tribe, he asserted that they would not recognise him in his European costume, and he would take care that his dialect did not betray him as a Tongass. Charley's luggage was very simple; it was brought on board to him by his " Klootschman," and consisted of a tanned deerskin for him to sleep on and a small pouch quite prettily embroidered with beads containing a small wooden pipe, flint and steel and some ammunition. He did not appear to carry any weapons, or at any rate he did not show them to us.

FROM FORT TONGASS TO FORT WRANGEL.

At 9 o'clock in the morning, with a strong south-east wind blowing, we left our anchorage after exchanging final greetings with the friends whom we were leaving, and quickly lost sight of the camp. As we passed from the channel into the open Chatham Sound the sky, which had been overcast all the morning, dissolved into torrential rain and the wind increased in violence and came in gusts. We had been spoilt by the two fair preceding days and now at the very beginning of our journey had to encounter the rage of the elements. Our course was westerly; to the right was the flat bare coast-line of the mainland thickly strewn with rocks, and on the left at a greater distance the island of Old Tongass and smaller rocky ledges marked only by the white foam of the breakers and, though lying between us and the open sea, not big enough to serve as a barrier against the ocean waves.

At noon we passed Cape Fox, and then took a north-westerly course in order to reach Ernest Sound which lies between Prince of Wales Island and Revillagigedo. But before we could reach the Sound we had to traverse a stretch of more than twenty miles which on the western side was completely exposed to the full force of the ocean beating through Dixon's Passage, and so we were likely to have a stormy voyage. At the south-western extremity of Prince of Wales Island, that is to say, only some 50 miles from where we were, lay Cape Chacoum near which, as we had heard at Tongass, the *Growler* had been wrecked, and as we had not been able to glean any further information as to the mysterious disappearance of that ship our nearness to the scene of the catastrophe increased our perturbation.

We had shaken out all three sails and with a wind that filled them blowing strongly right behind us we were making six miles an hour at the very least, a very remarkable achievement considering the kind of boat we had. The sea became rougher—the water which at first beat against us in short irregular waves had gradually risen into mountainous billows that followed each other with great regularity and threatened to engulf our cockleshell boat. As one stood at the stern of the deck, which was only a few feet above the water and was quite flat and without a bulwark, it was a strange sensation to be lifted as it were by a magic hand suddenly to the summit of a gigantic wave and after a wonderful but terrifying glimpse slipping down almost unconsciously into the depths on the other side of it, and seeing the dark green breaker rearing itself up like a threatening monster behind us again.

So long as we could carry enough sail not to lose ground in the race with the waves that threatened to overtake us, and so long as they did not begin to break over us, we were fairly safe. In fact the movement of the boat was less violent than we would have expected in such a high sea, thanks to our pace and the regular intervals between the breakers. Our boat was so light that it offered little resistance to the waves and rose and fell with them.

But when about 4 o'clock a gust of wind tore down our square sail and the sailors nevertheless proposed to go on, we passengers resolved to seek shelter on the first coast that came in sight. After some grumbling the sailors gave way and asked the pilot which was the nearest anchorage. As soon as we had come in sight of Chatham Sound in the morning, Charley had pointed to the lowering clouds, ominously shaking his head, and advised that we should not venture into the open Sound. When his warning remained unheeded he had sat down on deck, despite the rain, in silence and with his legs crossed gazed at the increasing violence of the sea as if he had no longer any interest in the matter ; if he *had* any fears as to our safety there was no trace of them in his impassive face which never moved a muscle. But when we turned to him and asked about landing, he became animated at once, and springing up quickly, stood for a few minutes gazing out over the foaming waves. He did not strain his eagle eyes in vain, but must have recognised a familiar spot, for he indicated with his one arm a point lying not far from our course where we would find a safe anchorage. Hard as we tried we were unable even with the aid of a telescope to distinguish anything except the white foam of the raging waves, which could just as well have been caused by the breaking of huge masses of water as by the surges upon the coast. But the atmosphere was so cloudy and the movement of the boat so violent that our observations were likely to be of no great value and so we trusted ourselves blindly to the keener sight (or perhaps instinct) of the Indian and steered our course in a more westerly direction. Fortunately we could then go with the wind and though our speed was somewhat diminished by the loss of a sail, we were able to dodge the waves which were already beginning to break over us and within half-an-hour to reach a low island which lay to our left, the existence of which we should never have suspected were it not for the guidance of the pilot, so completely was it hidden from us by the towering waves.

A small sandy bay into which Charley steered us offered a fairly safe anchorage and we were all glad when our sorely-tried boat lay once more quietly at anchor with furled sails. Despite the rain, which had streamed down all day without a break, we went on shore in the canoe to replenish our stock of firewood and fresh water.

The small island seemed quite uninhabited and was covered with dwarf cypresses and undergrowth. Nevertheless we found a small brook with clear fresh water, as in the case of almost every island along the coast, and near it what were probably the remnants of an Indian camp fire. It appeared that we were on one of the small islets off the south-west end of Gravina Island and therefore, though we had only been seven hours on the way, we had covered about fifty miles, which meant a pace of more than seven miles an hour.

We spent an uncomfortable night; the rain beat on the deck, the storm which continued all night whistled and howled over the flat islet and through our rigging and, as the tide was higher, the waves swept up to us through the opening of the bay. Scarcely was it dawn when at 5 o'clock in the morning we were again under sail; the sea was somewhat moderated by the heavy rain, and a strong south-east wind presaged a quick passage. Our course lay between Gravina Island and Revillagigedo Island to Ernest Sound, which we reached about 8 o'clock. On our left, that is to say to the west, there now lay Prince of Wales Island with the Indian Settlements of Georgina and Kasan, and on our right Revillagigedo Island with the small trading-post, Fort Stewart, with coal deposits in the neighbourhood. The breadth of the Sound, whose northern part is known as the Clarence Straits, is from ten to twenty miles; both shores, so far as we could judge from a distance, seemed to be steep and rocky with deep gaps in them like gorges. Soon after, we noticed to our left but at a considerable distance, a two-masted vessel steering towards Georgina, which was recognised by our seaman as the *Nanaimo Packet* schooner.

About mid-day the wind which was carrying us forward became stronger but more irregular and there was rain with it, so that we were compelled to take a reef in our mainsail which had become waterlogged, but kept our two other sails still fully spread. At 2 o'clock we had to take in the square sail, which we had set up again during the morning, so that our spread of canvas was reduced to a minimum. An hour later we passed on our right the canoe passage which leads between Etoline Island and the mainland to the Stikeen River. About 4 o'clock the storm increased so much that we began to look about again for a place of refuge, which we found after another half-an-hour's sail in the form of a quite safe bay almost shut in by rocks on the west coast of Etoline Island.

This was now the second day since our departure from Fort Simpson that we found ourselves compelled by the violence of the weather to drop anchor before darkness had set in, and although on this day we had done 75 miles we began to be apprehensive about the duration of our journey. We were still some 200 miles from our destination and the further north we went the more dangerous our journey seemed to become. We were suffering particularly from the unfavourable weather (frequently at 6 o'clock in the morning the thermometer stood at 42° Fahrenheit = 5° Réaumur), and some of us began to suffer from rheumatic pains. If the journey were prolonged we could not escape serious illness in the form of scurvy owing to the absence of fresh meat and vegetables from our dietary; and we hardly dared think what might happen if we and our vessel met with any accident or perhaps were wrecked.

FORT WRANGEL.

After a night of rain and storm we started again at 5.30 a.m. and reaching in two hours the north-west point of Etoline Island, keeping its shore to our right we steered in a north-easterly direction with a good favouring breeze. At 10.30 we passed to our right the so-called " Canoe Passage," between Etoline and Wrangel Islands (the southern entrance to which I have previously mentioned) and an hour later, steering towards the estuary of the Stikeen River, we came in sight of Fort Wrangel, whose white tents we could distinguish clearly against the dark background.

Wrangel Island is the eastern limit of a group of water-ways of considerable extent formed by a series of small and large islands, and into which the Stikeen River flows at its north-east corner. Low-lying and thickly wooded, the island is dominated by the lofty and snow-clad mountains of the neighbouring mainland, through which the great river has forced its way in gorges strewn with glaciers. The scenery in the estuary of the Stikeen is rightly ranked with the finest along the coast, and the glaciers and ice-fields which give it a special interest are among the largest in the whole territory.

At 12 noon we were opposite the Fort, at about four miles distance, and had already decided to spend the night there, when to our surprise we observed that the steersman apparently intended to leave the Fort on our right and to keep our course to the north. The captain and steersman now declared that they proposed not to call at the Fort, but to take advantage of the favourable wind in order to reach Kuprianoff Island by the evening ; this lay to the north in Hennega Strait. This proposal conflicted so directly with our original intention that we passengers protested strongly. Whilst the matter was being discussed suddenly a gun was fired from the Fort, no doubt as a signal to us to heave-to. Our steersman nevertheless kept on his course, but when after a short time a second gun was fired and the shot passed over our boat, our seamen were compelled to drop sails and wait to see what would happen. Meanwhile we had gone a considerable way past the camp, and could only have returned to it by tacking against the wind. The garrison appeared to realise this, as we soon perceived a sail coming from the camp and overtaking us rapidly, and in half an hour a canoe commanded by an American officer and with a crew of five Indians came alongside. Lieutenant King, who was discharging at the time the duties of a customs officer, as was shown by the customs' flag flying at the stern of the canoe, came on board to search for dutiable goods and particularly for spirits which it was forbidden to import. He was greatly surprised at seeing us as we had made his acquaintance at Nanaimo, and without troubling further about our cargo or papers he accepted an invitation to take a glass of cognac with us in the cabin.

It appeared that the fact that we were carrying three sails—one of which, the square-sail, we had set up only after leaving Nanaimo—had misled the garrison and prevented them from recognising our boat ; they took us, especially when we seemed unwilling to stop for search by them, to be one of the many trading ships which came up from British territory to engage in smuggling along the Alaska coast. The lieutenant assured us that a third shot would have given us clear evidence of their prowess as gunners, had we not stopped in the nick of time.

Our sailors, who as appeared later, carried many kegs of rum and must have had uneasy consciences, excused their discourtesy by saying that the wind had prevented them from making for the fort, and as on our account the lieutenant did not trouble himself about the incident, the conversation soon turned to other matters.

The garrison had been landed only a week previously by the *Oriflamme*, and was already complaining bitterly about the hardships suffered since then, which were due chiefly to the extraordinarily damp climate. As at Tongass Island, so here, the soldiers had to clear the site proposed for the fort from the dense cedar woods, hitherto untouched by the axe, before they could think about erecting the block-houses which were to shelter them, and for which they had to bring the materials with them. But this took a good deal of time, and meanwhile they had to camp on the damp woodland under canvas and the sickness returns already began to be a cause for anxiety. Moreover, since the landing they had had a good deal of trouble with the neighbouring Stikeen Indians, and were able to induce the latter to bring supplies to the camp only by paying high prices; the Indians showed themselves generally much more unfriendly and sullen than was expected.

The position of the Fort seemed on the other hand to be much better than that of Fort Tongass, since Fort Wrangel was also a customs office, and all the coasting vessels which made use of the Inner Passage (many of which were trading to the Stikeen River) had to pass within sight of the fort, and so it was able to exercise a real check upon the lucrative smuggling trade, especially in spirits, although despite this many gallons of rum and whisky were disposed of to the ignorant Indians.

We were much disturbed by information which had recently come to light and was given to us by the lieutenant as to the loss of the *Growler* at the southern point of Prince of Wales Island. It was reported by Indians on Tongass Island that the natives in the Georgiana and Kasan settlements, near to the scene of the wreck, had recently been in possession of a great quantity of modern firearms, articles of clothing and ship's provisions, which they professed to have obtained by barter from Indians living at Cape Chacoum, but which certainly formed part of the rich cargo of that ill-fated vessel, as the Chacoum Indians maintained that they had picked them up on the shore. It was a remarkable fact that of the crew of the schooner, ten in number and all experienced men, not a single one was saved, though the greater part of the cargo was picked up ; and in Fort Wrangel the belief was openly expressed that the crew had been murdered by the natives whilst attempting to get to the shore by means of their boat. A report of the facts, so far as known up to the present, had already been sent to the chief command at Sitka, by a coasting vessel that was going there, so that further investigations might be made immediately on the spot.

As regards our two former companions we learned that they had resumed their journey to Sitka five days previously, on board the schooner *Sweepstakes*, which had chanced to touch at Fort Wrangel ; and so they had got several days start of us. The *Sweepstakes* was the ship in which our steersman formerly had a share, and it was by its captain, a Frenchman known on the coast as " Frank," that during a stay at Fort Simpson he had been put on shore in so discreditable a fashion.

So there was now a prospect that the culprit would meet his enemy on his arrival at Sitka, and would perhaps overtake him even before that ; and he had a strong motive for pushing on with our journey as rapidly as possible. He had kept his weapon, a long five-barrelled so-called cavalry revolver, loaded for a long time with a view to a possible meeting with his foe, and his boast that when they met he would put a bullet through the Frenchman's brain was distinctly disquieting to the peaceably-disposed passengers who were expected to be witnesses of the proposed murder.

Whilst we were talking in the cabin the Stikeen Indians in the canoe that lay alongside tried in vain to enter into

CURIOSITIES, STIKEEN INDIANS.

E.T. 1868

137

conversation with our pilot Charley, whose nationality they probably guessed. The noble son of the Tongass chief Hovat sat like a mummy near the entrance to the cabin, his legs crossed and his arms folded in oriental fashion, and with stoical indifference answered the innumerable questions addressed to him in Stikeen by a long drawn out "Waak Kumtux " (" Don't understand ") and by using only a few words of the universal language, Chinook, was able slyly to conceal his nationality. He must have been very glad when the lieutenant again took his place at the stern of the canoe and gave the Indians the signal to start.

It was a curious spectacle, that vessel steered by an American officer in full uniform and manned by a crew of savage-looking Indians which now, tacking against the wind, made its way back to the Fort ; and the builder of the canoe certainly never imagined that one day the Stars and Stripes would be seen floating over his craft.

WRANGEL CANOE PASSAGE.

Our sails were quickly hoisted again, and with a strong breeze we steered towards the Hennega Strait, as we proposed to pass the night on its coast ; but before we were out of sight of Fort Wrangel we unfortunately ran on the sands in a channel near the estuary of the Stikeen. Happily just as we had made up our minds that we should have to go ashore in our canoe, the tide rose and floated us again. Nevertheless we lost a good deal of time in finding by sounding the deeper channel of the muddy and yellowish sea, and it was only at nightfall that we reached on the northern coast of the island an anchorage formed by a shallow and only partially sheltered bay.

Here by the dim light of a lantern the charts were spread out and we had a consultation as to the course which we should take. To arrive at Frederick Sound, which lay to the north but with a group of islands intervening, there were three distinct routes. First, a western or outer passage through Christian Sound was very exposed to the open sea ; secondly, an eastern course by a channel passing the estuary of the Stikeen River and skirting the mainland was well sheltered, but in addition to the fact that the stretch by the estuary was full of shallows and quicksands, this had the disadvantage of being much longer. Finally, a third course directly opposite us ran from south to north cutting across the Sound at right angles and was only indicated on the chart but not properly marked, which meant that it must be regarded as navigable only by canoes.

In choosing between these three routes the experience of our Indian pilot should have been helpful to us, and our annoyance was great when it eventually became apparent that he knew absolutely nothing of the two inside channels and that his information was confined to the outside channel which led through Christian Sound—a channel which we were not disposed to attempt in view of the limited sea-going qualities of our boat, although the steersman was in favour of taking it. Thus, though we had a pilot, we were entirely dependent on our charts and as these had more than once proved defective, we must be prepared for deviations from the right course. We could certainly return to Fort Wrangel and engage a new pilot there, but after long discussion we decided at any rate to make one attempt on the middle " canoe passage " which was marked on our chart as the Wrangel Channel.

From now on Charley, the one-armed pilot, had a very bad time on the *Ocean Queen*, since the sailors, finding themselves misled as to his utility and that he was now rather a burden than a help to them, would give him neither food nor drink and never ceased reproaching him for his duplicity, whereas it was largely their fault that they had not made certain as to the extent of his knowledge.

I believe that had we not taken pity on him and intervened, " Klaytohts," *alias* Charley, would have remorselessly been put on shore by these rough seamen and left to his fate, so embittered were they against the hapless Indian. The rascals forgot that whilst our deception by the Indian might be due to ignorance and insufficient knowledge of the language, they themselves had deceived us far more when before our departure they professed to know the whole route to Sitka. Unfortunately it was we passengers who were the victims of these repeated frauds, in that they prolonged our journey indefinitely.

We had a disturbed night; the movement of our vessel, which was only partially protected against the waves that rolled in from the sea, was so violent that during the night we had many times to look to our anchor cable, and it was only with great trouble that we avoided being driven against the reef-strewn shore of the shallow bay. On the following morning at low tide there were visible many rocks which we had not noticed as we entered the bay, so that great care was needed to enable our boat to reach the open sea again undamaged.

At 6 o'clock in the morning we made our way, steering by chart and compass, to the entrance of the Wrangel Channel, and after a number of vain attempts we found it at 7 o'clock, amid torrential rain. The entrance to the channel, which is only a few hundred yards wide, is hidden by an island lying before it in such a way that no one would expect to find an opening there, and we should have probably passed it unwittingly had not our Indian pilot, though he had never been in the place, instinctively realised that the entrance to the channel was close at hand.

As soon as we were in the narrow channel, which was often so blocked with small islands and rocks as scarcely to give us room to pass, the south-east wind which had hitherto been blowing strongly began to fail us and consequently we made only slow progress; about 9 o'clock the wind dropped altogether and as the current was against us we dropped anchor in the middle of the channel which was as unruffled as a mirror. Both banks were low, rocky and covered with dwarf pines and similar trees, but to our right, looking across the flat island, we could see in the distance the snow-covered mountains of the Stikeen territory towering to the sky, and despite the showery weather we could pick out with the naked eye their fields of ice.

At 10 o'clock the tide turned and ran northward so, resuming our journey, we were carried slowly forward by it. Numerous flocks of wild ducks and smaller water-birds covered the low banks of the small bays which extended on either side, and they often let us come quite close before they flew away uttering harsh cries. One of the sailors shot a very fine specimen of a wild duck which was brought on board by one of our dogs. It was the first time that this animal, which we had taken with us  primarily for hunting purposes, had brought us anything at all though we had taken a lot of trouble with him; and as if he wished to maintain his bad reputation, he devoured next day our last ham, which rather carelessly was being got ready for cooking on deck.

Directly afterwards we heard some little way behind us many shots which at first we took to be the echo of those we had fired, until we were undeceived by the appearance of a canoe in the distance. As the firing by the Indians made us somewhat apprehensive and we did not wish to be overtaken by them in the narrow channel, we paid no attention to the shots which signalled to us to stop, but attempted to get out of range of them. But the wind was so light that the canoe paddled by five Indians soon overtook us and was alongside almost before we realised it. They were Stikeen Indians, who were evidently on a hunting expedition and wanted to sell skins to us. As we desired to keep on friendly terms with them we made a deal, and for a sack of flour and some powder and shot the sailors got five mink and one sable skin, which was certainly worth double what they gave for them. There was one curious thing—in the canoe we saw a small girl about ten years old with beautiful black hair and eyes and a remarkably fair complexion, who particularly attracted our attention.

She was very pleased when we gave her a few ship's biscuits and some apples (a delicacy greatly prized by the natives who have very little fruit). We had the impression that the little creature was of white parentage, and as slavery is customary in all the tribes along the coast, it was not impossible that the child had been kidnapped. Unfortunately it was not in our power to investigate the matter, since the neighbourhood of the Stikeen Indians was by no means agreeable to us, and we were only able to get rid of our visitors by promising them through Charley's intervention to wait at that place for their fellow tribesmen who could not be far away. But their canoe had hardly passed behind the next spit of land than we had spread every scrap of canvas in order to get out of their reach as quickly as possible.

In great anxiety we approached the exit from the channel as the fairway was so shallow that the plummet showed a depth of scarcely ten feet. We were particularly afraid that our craft might not be able to cross the mouth of the channel into the Sound as it might be entirely silted up, and that we should consequently be compelled to retrace the whole of the route which we had covered that day and run the gauntlet of the Stikeen Indians who were certainly trying to overtake us.

Shortly before 3 o'clock, looking ahead over the bank which was covered with low bushes we saw the broad, dark-green surface of Frederick Sound, whose white foaming waves we could clearly see on the opposite shore and were a sign of a strong wind. But even yet the exit from the channel might be barred. We looked expectantly at the captain whose plummet showed that the water was getting shallower every minute. Finally it marked only one fathom, and a few minutes later we should have had to give up in sight of the open sound. Fortunately we had passed the shallowest part of the channel and we joyfully greeted the sight of Frederick Sound, that stretched out before us like a vast sea between two low tongues of land, rising only a few feet above the surface of the deep.

FREDERICK SOUND.

Frederick Sound is a stretch of water extending from south-west to north-east; it is bounded on the west by Baranoff Island (on which Sitka is situated) on the east by the mainland and on the south and north by the two large islands known as Admiralty and Kuprianoff Islands, the former of which rises to a considerable height. The Sound is connected with the open sea on the south-west, whilst at its north-easterly and north-westerly corners, which are formed in the one case by Cape Fanshaw and in the other by Cape Fairweather, the Stephen Channel and Christian Sound form its two northern outlets; and at its extreme end the Tacon and Chilcaht Rivers flow into it.

GLACIER ON FREDERICK SOUND, OPPOSITE WRANGEL CHANNEL.   F.T. 1868

In order to reach Sitka which is situated in the most northerly part of Christian Sound (called the Chatham Straits) we were bound to take a south-westerly course and get off Cape Fairweather before we could continue to the north.   We decided to sail along the coast of Kuprianoff Island, so as to be sheltered from the south-east wind, which was blowing with great violence across the Sound, and to escape being driven by it against the unusually steep and rocky northern shores of the sound formed by Admiralty Island, which like a gigantic granite wall rose almost perpendicularly from the sea.   There was a wonderful view of a field of ice set between colossal masses of rock not far from Cape Fanshaw; it was no doubt a frozen river whose many windings could be clearly followed up into the mountains.   The summits of the mountains and all the gorges were glittering with eternal snow, whilst the bare rocks of which the lower slopes were mostly formed were tinged with blue. And as the reflection of the setting sun gave to the whole range a crimson hue, even our rough sailors were filled with admiration. Long after the shades of night had covered the lower stretches and only the very summits were coloured a faint violet, I stood on deck to watch the wondrous spectacle.

We did not make much progress that evening. It may have been that the nearness of the shore robbed us of the wind, but towards 7 o'clock every breath of air ceased and we began to look for an anchorage. An island close to the shore seemed likely to afford this, but in order to reach it we had to row for three long hours—so difficult was it to make our way in a sea which was rough, though the wind had dropped, and against the tide. Though we needed two men for the oars, one of the sailors was asleep in the cabin owing to the effect of too much rum during the day; so I offered my help, and I remember well how anxiously we watched the rocks on the neighbouring shore to see if we made any progress at all, and if so how much. They were three very trying hours that we spent at the heavy oars, and only the thought of being overtaken by night whilst still out in the open sound and of being driven on shore in the darkness gave us the strength which we needed to reach the shelter of the bay. When we got there it was very dark, and we lay down to sleep feeling most resentful against the captain whose drunken state had left the passengers to take charge of the vessel.

Favoured with a strong south-west breeze we left Island Point, as we called the anchorage, early next morning, and in order to get away from the area in which the coast shut off the wind from us we sailed some six miles further out from it. About 9 o'clock the wind began to rise and in the course of the next hour became so boisterous that we were forced to take a reef in the main-sail. In a remarkably short time the sea rose dangerously high and its billows striking us broadside on often swept over the deck and even penetrated into the hold. With dull thud wave after wave beat against the side of the ship and splashed in streams over our helpless vessel. The situation began to make us very apprehensive as we did not know how long the deck, which was not a very strong one, could withstand the violent onslaught of the sea, and we made every effort, even putting out the oars, heavy as they were to handle in the rough water, in order to reach once more the shelter of the coast from which we had now been driven a good long way.

Though tossed about unmercifully we had towards 11 o'clock the satisfaction of seeing that we were getting nearer to the coast, though our progress was very slow, and that the sea was becoming less rough; though further out in the Sound the surface of the water was a mass of white foam, which was conclusive evidence of the increasing violence of the storm.

Shortly after this, when we must have been some three miles distant from the shore, our pilot, who was looking anxiously for a bay, saw rising above the trees on the shore a column of smoke which must come from an Indian settlement, and soon we noticed a canoe making towards us from the shore. There must have been some very strong reason for the Indians to put out in such a sea; the small craft which carried a single sail sometimes disappeared entirely behind a towering wave and the next moment reappeared suddenly on its crest. But it kept its course despite wind and waves and came rapidly towards us. The canoe was manned by four Kaigh Indians; at their request we threw them a

Kaigh Indian on Frederic Sound

R.T. 1868

rope so that they could keep near us. The purpose of their visit seemed to be to induce us to anchor near their settlement; but when we explained to them that it was not possible for us to get to the shore at this point, and asked about a bay lying further to the west,

145

they seemed to become unfriendly and flatly refused to give us the information which we desired. After a short consultation they cast off the rope and turned back towards their settlement. A little later we observed to our surprise that another small canoe steering along the shore seemed to have us under observation, and when, at last, after many fruitless attempts to gain the shore, we reached about noon a fairly well-sheltered bay, this canoe which had followed our movements closely was already quite near to us.

Whilst the two sailors made use of the half-day off to which they were entitled to put the ship in order after the battering she had received during the morning, and especially to mend the sail which was badly torn and almost in rags, we passengers went on shore with our pilot, making use of the canoe which despite the storm had so far proved to be completely seaworthy, in order to get water and firewood. Then we encountered two Indians carrying guns who, interpreted by Charley, told us that if we would supply them with powder and shot they would procure us a supply of game.

As we were very glad to have some change from our everlasting salt meat, we gave them what they asked and in a moment both of them had disappeared behind the nearest trees.

Four long hours passed without our seeing or hearing anything of them, and we began to think that the natives had regarded the ammunition we had supplied as a gift and had left us for ever—possibly they had returned to their tribe. We sat on the shore, where no sound disturbed the silence of Nature. Behind us a dense wood of cedars enclosed the sandy crescent-shaped bay into whose centre a clear mountain stream flowed over the clean shingle. Directly in front of us, some hundred paces distant, but inside the shelter of two tongues of land which stretched far out, our vessel rose and fell on the clear water and further out still, where our view was bounded by the open sound, there rolled unceasingly the dark foam-crested

146

waves. It was a wonderful but solemn sight, and involuntarily we also grew serious as we thought on the dangers through which we had passed and those which were still to come.

At odds with our sailors, on whose reliability we depended for our very lives, we were here in the lonely wilderness without a guide and entirely at the mercy of these ignoble wretches. What guarantee had we that they would not at any moment abandon us to our fate and, from fear lest they should be made to answer for their fraud, desert and make off in the ship with our arms and supplies and indeed with everything we possessed. Without any provisions, on a lonely coast very seldom visited by white men, and exposed to the rapacity of the Indians our position would not have been at all enviable, and although I myself had always with me my revolver and some money the latter would have been of very little use to us among the Indians.

As if he had guessed our thoughts the interpreter, who kept more with us than with the seamen since they treated him so badly, began to talk about the dangerous and treacherous character of the Kaigh Indians, who had a bad reputation all along the coast. Only in the previous year they had wrecked a steamer after a quarrel with its crew, killed everyone on board and burnt the ship, after plundering it completely, so that there was nothing left to reveal the crime they had committed. Unfortunately the Indians kept the matter secret and it had not been punished as yet, since at the time it took place the ownership of the territory was being changed and the American officials were only just beginning to take possession of it. Whilst we were sitting on the bank, oppressed by these disquieting thoughts, suddenly two shots rang out in succession in the wood near by and before long the two Indians who we so unjustly thought had played us false, came towards us and with delight at their achievement showed us their booty, two fine hazel-hens.

The greed of the Indians and the meanness which they display in their dealings with the white men was once

147

more brought to our notice on this occasion. We had given the two Kaigh Indians at their request a considerable supply of powder and shot for their hunting and we expected that the game which they obtained would be handed over to us without further payment. The Indians thought quite differently. As is usual with all the Redskins they had been extremely sparing with their ammunition and had fired only when quite sure of their prey, and so they had kept the greater part of what we had given them intact and yet now demanded also full payment for the two birds. Though this consisted only of pipes and tobacco it was a comparatively high price.

At nightfall the two Kaighs went away, assuring us that they would return the next morning and bring their fellow tribesmen with them. As the proximity of these Indians caused us some anxiety we decided not only to keep a good watch but to resume our journey next morning if possible at dawn, without waiting for them to appear. Charley, who did not seem in good spirits, now explained that he associated the somewhat repellent appearance of the elder of the two Indians with a plundering raid towards the south which had recently taken place. It was difficult to tell whether he was giving play to his imagination, but certainly that Indian with his strongly-marked features, close cut hair which stood up like a bush, and his deep sunk, shifty eyes seemed capable of any sort of crime.

A STORMY JOURNEY.

We must have made a very early start the next day, as when I woke up at 7 o'clock, being very tired from my night watch, I already heard the heavy thud of the waves as they beat against our craft. The movement was so violent that it was only with great difficulty that I could extricate my outer garments (we never removed our under-garments during the journey) from the chaos in the cabin. Going on deck I was met by a violent south-east wind that blew in great gusts. Clouds torn to ribands swept across the horizon, showers of rain and hail were interspersed with brief periods of sunshine. The sea was violently agitated, some threatening whitecaps already appeared on the crests of the high waves, sure signs of an approaching storm. We had left Kuprianoff and our anchorage far behind us; Cape Fairweather, which marks the entrance to the northern part of Christian Sound, was already in sight and to our left the ridges of the high ranges of Baranoff Island showed themselves on the horizon.

With a steadily-increasing wind we passed at 9 o'clock the cape, recognisable by some rocks, detached from the coast and rising perpendicularly out of the sea, and found ourselves in the Sound, which was only some 6-8 miles wide and stretched straight away to the north; its two rocky banks rising like steep mountains enclosed it, as it were, within natural walls. We had to follow this as far as the "Peril Straits," which branched off in a northerly direction at a distance of about 40 miles, and could hope to cover this stretch long before nightfall.

We had indeed hoped that inside the comparatively-narrow channel the water would be smoother than in the much broader Frederick Sound which we had previously crossed, but were sadly disappointed. The strong south-east wind that came from the open sea must have been blowing here violently for several days, for the form and size of the waves that rolled in the Sound clearly indicated that they had swept in direct from the ocean in unbroken succession between the Kuprianoff and Baranoff Islands. But whilst the violence of the wind was driving the waves into the Sound, they met at the entrance with the seaward current of the falling tide and the cross-currents were so strong that we would gladly have abandoned the attempt to go on had it been possible to turn back. But the wind now rising to a storm swept us forward so that only one direction was practicable for us; happily it coincided with our proper course, for tacking was out of the question. Our sailors themselves seemed to think we were in grave danger, for a thunderstorm rising and sweeping after us with great rapidity foretold a more violent tempest. All our sails were furled as quickly as possible except a small three-cornered section of the mainsail; it was only by exerting all his strength that the steersman managed to keep the vessel to her course. The captain, who seemed completely unnerved, was stationed at the bow holding on to the mast and with an axe in his hand, often enveloped by the sweeping waves but ready, should the mast or yard-arm snap, to cut it loose so as to free the ship from the wreckage, but ready also, should the worst come to the worst, to look after his own safety first, as he had done on the previous occasion. I was the only passenger to keep near the steersman, by holding on to the hatchway of the cabin, and was often in danger of being swept away by the torrents that dashed over the ship. Wave after wave towered up, the same threatening monsters that we remembered only too well encountering near Cape Fox. The canoe which we had in tow was violently tossed about and sometimes disappeared entirely from our sight; half-full of water it seemed likely to sink and only the idea that it might conceivably prove a means of safety in case of shipwreck kept us from cutting the tow-rope which caused it to act as a drag on us.

I had gone down to the cabin to see my comrades in danger, who were in great trepidation, when suddenly the companion-way to the deck was closed from outside and a number of heavy blows on it made it clear that we had been put under lock and key by the sailors.

In vain did we beg and pray and threaten the relentless fellows to let us out; in vain we hurled ourselves with all our strength against the hatch to force an exit. The oak planks were too strong; they withstood even the attack of desperate men. It was no use, and we had to submit to the inevitable. Then all at once the tempest broke over the boat; whipped by the storm, mingled rain and hail rattled furiously on the deck and even in our prison we could hear the shrill whistling of the wind through the rigging. Our craft heeled over now to one side now to the other;

sometimes it seemed to sweep straight down into the depths, sometimes to rise as sharply from them. Under the pressure of the rudder the weather-beaten timber of the ship strained and groaned against the raging sea, and it seemed as if at last, weary of the unequal contest, they would go to pieces. And every time the mountainous waves swept over our poor craft and made it tremble in every joint we thought our last hour had surely come.

This unequal struggle with the violence of the elements lasted a full hour. In the darkness of the cabin I could hardly distinguish the faces of my companions; they were all deadly pale, sometimes resigned, sometimes indifferent, sometimes following every movement of the ship with straining eyes and faces distorted by fear. The worst case seemed to be that of the Jewish trader; every day since our departure from Victoria he had shown an increasing nervous irritability, which whenever the slightest danger threatened changed to a state bordering on madness. During the previous days, when the weather was growing worse, his behaviour had been most unpleasant for the rest of us, but we had at least been able to avoid him as he kept in the cabin; but now we were shut up with the madman in a confined space and compelled to listen to his despairing outbreaks. His features were no longer those of a human being; his eyes rolled wildly and seemed to be starting from their sockets; a white foam gathered on his lips; he dug his nails deep into the woodwork of the deck to which he clung in terror. It was useless for us to talk to him, every movement of the ship served to excite him more and more; he had become a wild beast, and finally sank unconscious on the floor of the cabin.

The Indian was altogether different; he sat as usual, only looking from time to time with a pitying smile at the Jew, and had it not been for an occasional remark of " Hayuh Pask " (" Much wind "), we should hardly have been aware of his presence. The rest of us seized a chance when the ship, which had been heeling well over on her side, righted herself a little, to open a small porthole, which was closed by a wooden shutter, and to take a swift survey of our position. At the moment we were running quite near the shore, which lay to our left but was so steep and rocky as to preclude all hope of a landing there. Shortly before noon during one of these observations, often interrupted by a sudden dash of water against the porthole, we saw at a distance in front of us a spit of land stretching well out to sea. The surf was beating against it so violently that it was only visible every now and then between the white spray. Our sailors evidently meant to seek shelter behind it if they could. If they succeeded we should be safe, but if we were driven by the violence of the storm against the projecting rocks we should inevitably perish.

The waves, whose violence was increased by the reefs on which they broke, raged with terrific fury; great masses of water thundered over the deck. On one occasion our vessel was so buried in the water that suddenly every movement ceased, every noise from outside was silenced, and it seemed as though sinking deeper and deeper in the merciless sea we should find an unmarked and watery grave far from our native land.

These were moments which could never be forgotten by those who had lived through them—it is true they *were* but moments, but they seemed to last for an eternity. Suddenly there was a jerk, a quiver of the oaken planks, and swept forward mightily by a fresh wave our gallant vessel righted itself again. How reassuring it was to feel once again the movement of the boat and the pressure of the rudder; even the crashing of the waves and the howling of the wind were greeted with delight, for they told us that we were still alive, that we had escaped the death-like silence of the deep even if we were not yet safe. And now our ordeal was at an end. After a few minutes we must have rounded the promontory, for all at once the sea became calmer, we heard the hatchway that confined us being opened from outside and with cries of delight we rushed out into the open air. Words fail me to describe the rapture we felt at finding ourselves safe within a bay sheltered against wind and weather ; suffice it to say that weeping with joy we fell on each others' necks, and congratulated ourselves on our marvellous escape.

LOST.

When the excitement over our experiences of the morning had abated to some extent there arose a violent dispute between ourselves and our two seamen, whom we reproached for their inconsiderate behaviour in confining us to the cabin. Their excuse that our safety was due to their action and that we should have been in their way on deck was naturally not good enough for us, and although the steersman in particular (who had fastened himself to the rudder with a rope) had shown great courage and resource during the storm, we knew only too well that he would not have done anything for us had not his own safety depended on his handling of the ship. So the relations between passengers and crew became still more strained.

A mid-day meal which had meanwhile been prepared and was particularly tempting because it included the two hazel-hens helped to calm us down, and as we had had nothing to eat since the previous evening it was thoroughly enjoyed. The next problem was, of course, to find out exactly where we were. So far as we could see from the boat we were at the entrance to a bay which stretched far inland and was cut off from the sound by a number of islands, but it was quite possible that it was really a channel running to the open sea.

Our sailors thought that we were at the entrance to Peril Straits, which led to Sitka, and their opinion appeared to be confirmed by our map, as the entrance to the Straits, as shown on it agreed fairly well with our surroundings. The general position, the width of the estuary, the small islands, all seemed to justify this assumption. Certainly we did find a small bay marked on the chart about twelve miles south of the passage, but its shape and depth did not seem to tally in the least with our position, and it was so difficult to estimate the distance we had traversed in our wild rush during the morning that it did not seem impossible for us to have sailed eight to nine miles an hour during the storm—a speed that would have enabled us to reach the passage, which was about 60 miles from Kuprianoff Island.

As soon as the draggled state of our sails permitted we started on our course at 2 o'clock, steering westward towards the land and keeping close to the northern bank. With the help of a gentle breeze we sailed along the clear and almost motionless water, but the further we went the narrower became the channel and after half-an-hour we found ourselves opposite the sandy estuary of a little river where there was no sign of a passage. One of the sailors went in the canoe with the Indian to reconnoitre, but soon came back to report that there was no passage of any kind. The hills which rose to a thousand feet on three sides of us seemed also to bar our progress. We must have missed the passage, and we remembered that during our course we had noticed on our left hand two channels that branched off more to the south—these must lead into the main channel. So we had to make our way back against wind and stream to our first starting point, which we reached after a toilsome three hours' cruise at 6 o'clock in the evening. Within the shelter of a quite small natural harbour which offered just room for our craft we dropped anchor for the night, giving up all idea of going further. But a reconnaissance made by the Indian resulted in finding again the two channels which branched off at a short distance from the bay.

Very early next morning we were again under sail, testing the various channels one by one, always hopeful that we had discovered the passage we were seeking, only after wearisome tacking and rowing to find ourselves once again shut in by the land. From the main bay there branched off a number of arms of the sea which, sometimes broad and sometimes narrow, were enclosed by high mountain ranges of bare rocks covered on the western

154

side with snow, and into which there flowed streams fed from the field of snow. In vain did the scenery offer much of interest, in vain from time to time we heard avalanches rolling down the gorge-like rifts in the mountains and re-echoed from the neighbouring heights until at last they sounded fainter and fainter like shots in the lowest depths of the valleys. Even the sight of a bear within range at the edge of a snow field failed to arouse us from the depression caused by our disappointment. Slowly the beast crawled away, standing out like a black ball on the white surface, and disappeared behind some stunted bushes that clung to the mountain side.

Utterly discouraged we returned at 8 o'clock in the evening after many hours of futile cruising to our starting point at the entrance to the bay. After a three weeks' journey, after all the dangers we had succeeded in overcoming, after great privations and despite pilot, compass and chart we had completely lost the way. If we were really off Baranoff Island, Sitka could be hardly 20 miles away from us in a straight line, but how were we to get there if we could not find the passage? How could we cross the mountains which separated us from our destination? The more we thought about our position the more hopeless it seemed and we began to wonder whether the passage we sought existed any longer or had been closed by some convulsion of Nature since our chart was made. But the mountain ranges that enclosed us seemed so primæval and weathered, as if they had seen the storms oᶜ centuries beat on their stubborn rocky slopes, and the Peril Straits were so clearly marked on the chart as a channel between Baranoff and Chicagos Islands, that finally we came to the conclusion that we had overlooked the entrance during the storm of the preceding day and had passed by it.

In the course of the day we had repeatedly fired shots in order to attract any Indians who might be in the neighbourhood, since in our helpless condition any information even from the Indians would have been welcome. The reports, though repeated far and wide by the echo, died away each time without bringing any response and we were forced to conclude that no human beings were anywhere near the bay. So we were all the more pleased when almost before our boat came to anchor in the shelter of the little island a canoe came in sight, apparently steering towards us. The wild-looking Indians on it, who were unusually big and strongly built, came alongside, and with Charley acting as interpreter we entered into a parley with them from which we learned that they were Chuznus and had been attracted by our shots. Sitka, about which we naturally asked most eagerly, lay to the west (indicated by the setting sun): only the passage thither was not at this point but some ten miles further to the north. If the wind were favourable we could get there in two days; to indicate the length of the journey they pointed twice to the course of the sun. When it disappeared for the second time behind the mountains Sitka would not be far away.

Naturally we tried to engage one of them immediately as pilot, but they rejected the proposal, excusing themselves by saying that they must communicate with their fellow tribesmen who were camping some distance away on the sound. Persuasion was useless, but a substantial present induced them to promise to bring us an answer on the following morning. Soon the canoe and its crew disappeared behind the nearest spit of land.

During the day we had given vent to our grievances by frequent complaints against our sailors, to whose false statements about their knowledge of the whole route we owed our present plight. Whether because of these repeated complaints or because of their own annoyance at the length of the journey, anyhow the mutual recriminations became more and more violent and on that night ended in an open quarrel. We passengers, who had no desire to cruise around for weeks in uncertainty in this wilderness, announced our intention not to move from our present position without engaging one of the Chuznus as a pilot. The sailors protested against this on the ground that they had already engaged one pilot (the Tongass Indian) and were unwilling to pay for a second. Even when we announced that we were prepared to pay the pilot ourselves they asserted that they would not allow a second Indian to come on board, and finally they declared their intention of sailing away the next morning without awaiting the arrival of the Chuznus. We could not tolerate their behaviour any longer. We were absolutely determined to prevent by force the resumption of the journey, and if necessary even to compel the two seamen to leave the boat and to take charge of her ourselves with the help of the Indians. If it came to a fight we were the stronger party, since there were four passengers—all of us armed—and the Indian pilot would certainly have joined us against the men who had treated him so badly.

This was the position of affairs when about 10 o'clock we sought our rough couch. We quickly took off our outer garments and wrapped our blankets around us as well as we could, and used as we were to our humble quarters soon fell asleep one after another.

A NIGHT ATTACK.

I alone sought sleep in vain ; no doubt the excitement caused by the quarrel and the prospect of further unpleasantness next day kept me awake. I lay with half-closed eyes, looking in the dim light of the lantern across my sleeping companions towards the hatchway. The fire in our small stove was almost out, but from time to time an unburned fragment of wood flared up suddenly and for a moment faintly illuminated the interior of our humble cabin. Overhead there was heard occasionally the footsteps of the watch and the whining of the dogs. The weather must have been terrible, for the watch came in dripping with rain and half-melted snow to get a light for his pipe, with the help of which he was trying to pass the weary hours. I asked him the time. It was 10 o'clock. He could scarcely have got back on deck when suddenly the dogs

157

began to bark loudly. Before I could ask myself what was happening the watch rushed down breathless, shouting, " Get up, canoes in sight ! " We started up in a flash ; the appearance of Indians at such an hour must be with hostile intent—an attack was undoubtedly intended !

Throwing on our clothes and snatching up our weapons, which fortunately were ready loaded, we tried to get on deck, meaning to sell our lives as dearly as possible. There were six of us, all armed with revolvers, the two sailors had their guns also and in presence of a common danger all internal quarrels were forgotten.

But the Indians had forestalled us ; they must have crept close up to the boat before the alarm was given, as before we could get on deck the steersman, who was trying to bar the entrance to the cabin against them, was driven back into it and with him a crowd of Indians broke into the narrow hold. We had just time to fall back behind our principal luggage, which was piled up in the centre of the cabin like a barricade, so that if there was a fight we might keep together. The end of the cabin near the companion was quickly crowded with Indians ; ten were inside it and how many more there were on deck we could not tell, but it seemed to be thronged up to the hatchway and we reckoned the total number of natives to be at least eighteen, as a third canoe must have followed close on the heels of the first two.

Between us and the Indians who stared at us with glittering eyes sat our pilot as if on thorns. He seemed disinclined to side with either party and to want to keep neutral, at any rate to begin with. From time to time he looked longingly at the entrance, but it was useless to think of escape. An ominous silence prevailed in the little cabin, broken only now and then by subdued whispers. The dim lantern cast a meagre light on our surroundings and made the dark faces of our uninvited guests still darker than they usually were. Some of them had even blacked their faces, covered their foreheads and cheeks with red lines, and given themselves a diabolical appearance. Apart from one old Indian who seemed to be their chief, they were mostly young men in their prime. They carried no weapons, or if they had any they were concealed under the broad folds of their blankets. In the foremost row we noticed one of the two Indians who had visited us during the evening, but he behaved now as if he did not want to know us and seemed to be telling the chief, who was distinguished by the way his hair was coiled, about our first encounter, as he kept pointing at us.

The position became more and more intolerable. We would gladly have commenced to parley but could not induce the interpreter to open a conversation with the Chuznus. Our steersman, who had the most experience in dealing with the Indians, bade us above everything to give no sign of our uneasiness with regard to the natives : " Be ready to use your weapons at a moment's notice, but don't show the Indians that you distrust them. If they once make up their minds to attack us that will only have the effect of putting them on their guard without abandoning their intention. The Indians are remarkably quick in reading from their enemies' faces courage or fear." Then he stepped forward, bowed to the chief and said to him a few phrases in Chinook, which, of course, were not understood, and then handed to him a small clay pipe and some tobacco as a token of friendliness. The little gift, combined with the bold demeanour of the donor, had the desired effect. The eyes of the old man brightened at once ; the pipe was passed from hand to hand and its contents tried by each. The faces of the old chief's followers quickly became more friendly. Then they appeared to hold a consultation the result of which the chief told our Indian interpreter. The latter, who had behaved at first as if he did not understand the Chuznu language at all, now translated a long speech quite fluently. The substance of it was that the chief thanked us for the present of the pipe and asked for gifts for the other Indians who were all " Closh tum tum " (" friendly disposed ") towards us.

We were so delighted at the pacific outcome of our adventure that we were quite ready to bestow further gifts, and the next half-hour was taken up with the distribution of pipes, tobacco, matches, syrup, ship's biscuits, apples, etc., on a scale which, in our circumstances, was quite extravagant. The Indians changed places until all had taken their turn. Amongst the last comers was a young and quite good-looking squaw, carrying on her back a papoose who from his primitive cradle gazed out wonderingly on a world which was still so new to him, and for whom his proud mother demanded tribute. Only the flat, expressionless face of the little creature could be seen; his body was hidden in a cradle consisting of a cushion on a board about three feet long and rounded at the top, with a deerskin bound over it by leather straps. It was amusing to

Squaw of the Cheyenne Indians

E.T. 1868

see how the Jewish dealer, who had been greatly agitated by the sudden appearance of the Indians, now sought to curry favour with them. With hands still trembling with fright he prepared some coffee and distributed it among them with a lavish helping of sugar (of which the Indians are very fond); he surpassed himself in friendly speeches to the natives, which were quite unintelligible to them, and even tried by small attentions to the baby to get into the good graces of the mother.

So far all was well; we were on the best possible terms with our guests, who voluntarily promised us a pilot to Sitka; and now we wished for nothing better than to bid them farewell, for it was getting late and the Indians gave no sign of departure though they could have nothing against us on the score of generosity.

However much we urged our interpreter to convey to them our wish to be left alone and even to promise more gifts next morning, however much we tried to make them understand by signs that we were very tired and needed rest, the Indians were importunate as usual and would not move. Either Charley had not the courage to tell them to go away or believed that he would offend them if he did so, or the Indians found themselves far too comfortable by the glowing stove; in any event our desire had no effect. We were beginning again to be uncomfortable as to what was their real purpose, although the sailor declared that the presence of the squaw and the child was a sure indication that they were friendly disposed. It was past 11 o'clock before the old chief, who must have seen that his people were not likely to get anything more out of us, gave the signal for departure, and to our great relief the whole party got up. Following them on deck we saw them go in three large canoes to a little island only a few yards distant from us, and land there directly opposite our boat. Soon a great fire was crackling on the shore; the Indians began to lie down around it and soon they all seemed to have fallen fast asleep. A log or a bundle of brushwood

Tahi of the Chugun Indians
E.T. 1868

thrown from time to time on the fire showed us, however, that we were not going to be let out of sight and warned us of the need for a good look-out, which was maintained all night despite the appallingly cold and wet weather. The nearness of the Indians was disquieting to us all, and as not one of us got much sleep that night the first glimmer of dawn was hailed with delight by all. During the night it snowed heavily, and at 5 o'clock in the morning our deck was covered with snow a foot deep and the shores around us were hidden by a white mantle, and though it was the middle of May they looked as if it were mid-winter.

Our Indian friends did not keep us waiting long. We had scarcely appeared on deck when their canoes left the bank and came across to us. Consequently the sailors had no opportunity to carry out their threat of the previous day, and with Charley as interpreter we began at once to negotiate for a pilot. After endless discussions and many difficulties the old chief, Takuschki by name, said that he was prepared to give us as a pilot his son, a very intelligent but extremely ugly youth of 16 or 17, for a payment of ten dollars to be made at Sitka. At the request of Takuschki who seemed, unlike most other Indians, to know something about monetary affairs and who repeatedly asked us for a "paper," we gave him a kind of agreement which he took with a satisfied smile, wrapped in a piece of deerskin and hid under his dirty robe. In this way the business, which to us was the most important of all, was satisfactorily settled, and we could now give our undivided attention to our visitors.

In bright daylight they appeared by no means so formidable as we had thought when they surprised us on the previous night. Certainly so far as physical strength went they would have been foes not to be despised, but their conduct generally convinced us now that they were quite friendly and there was absolutely no reason to be afraid of them. A quite lively barter took place between them and the sailors who made many cheap purchases from the Indians' large stock of bear, otter, sable, mink, bear and seal skins.

Whilst they were bargaining with the grasping natives, who were very acute in trade matters, about the price of a skin, I occupied myself in sketching the chief personages amongst our visitors and particularly the old and very astute chief and his squaw. I had nearly finished when all at once one of the Indians noticed what I was doing. The friendly looks of the chief grew hostile and there was general excitement amongst the others; in a fright our interpreter begged me to stop the "picture-making," as the Chuznus were annoyed by it. I found out later from our new pilot that the Indians whom I had sketched were greatly exercised and thought that if I took their portraits I should have some power over them in the future. Fortunately it occurred to me that by tearing up some pieces of paper I could make them believe that I had destroyed their pictures;

this little trick was so successful that the " entente cordiale " between us was completely restored.

About 9 o'clock we were prepared to start, although there was a thick mist over the bay and complete absence of wind. Keste, as our new pilot was named, bade farewell to his kinsmen, was provided by his  father with a bright shirt made out of the coloured ends of blankets which the old man touchingly exchanged for his son's torn cotton shirt, and joined us on our vessel. A tanned deerskin for a couch and a piece of smoked fish by way of provisions constituted the whole equipment of this untutored child of nature. The sails were unfurled and the oars put out ; a rope was thrown to the three canoes and at a signal from us the Indians, old and young, seized their paddles and amidst loud cries, partly by towing and partly by rowing, the strange flotilla moved forward towards the open Sound.

KESTE. E.T. 1868

As there was still a complete absence of wind we made slow progress, despite the noisy help of the Chuznus, and it was 11 o'clock before we reached the mouth of the bay. At that time the mist which had hitherto enveloped us dissolved, the sun shone out brightly and a fresh breeze coming from the sound swept the mist more and more inland and soon filled our swelling sails. The Chuznus left us at this point, with loud cries and many gestures of farewell, and turned their course towards the settlement, whose position on the southern shore of the bay we could distinguish by the pillars of smoke rising straight up in the air.

Thus the supposed attack ended harmlessly. Whether the Indians when they saw the strength of our party changed their minds, or whether they were friendly disposed from the first remained uncertain, but their sudden visit so late at night was bound to make us suspicious, since owing to

163

the position of their settlement they must have seen us from the moment we entered the bay, and possibly had followed us unnoticed for some time.

FROM THE PERIL STRAITS TO SITKA.

In gorgeous sunshine we sailed cheerfully along the Sound, keeping Baranoff about four miles to our left. The fine clear weather seemed to have brought the Indian fishermen out from their settlements, since we met a number of small canoes, mostly with only two Indians in each, gliding over the gently-rippling water and dragging their fishing-lines — made of gut—behind them. Some came quite close and asked for tobacco ; they were engaged in halibut fishing, as was shown by the wooden hooks 8-10 inches long which they carried in the canoes. How different it was on the Sound now than on the day of our arrival ; then the angry elements were in conflict with almost despairing men, now all nature was peaceful and calm.

The nearer we approached the northern end of Baranoff Island the lower were its banks which, however, were thickly wooded to the water's edge. On the opposite side the coast of Admiralty Island rose to a considerable height, and, despite the distance, we could see its snowy peaks and projecting masses of rock rising out of the blue mist and glittering like silver in the sunshine.

After a three hours' journey Keste pointed out the entrance to Peril Strait, which certainly resembled closely the bay we had left twelve miles behind us. Though the two banks were somewhat lower, and the width of the entrance perhaps rather greater, nevertheless the outline of the coast, the small islands lying in front and the general direction were in the two cases almost identical. An Indian village was evidently close by, for a number of poles set up on one of the islands, decked with wisps of straw, and the canoes hung between the trees (each marking the last resting-place of its owner) denoted a burial place, as the coast Indians prefer to have their cemeteries on uninhabited, isolated and rocky islands.

A short time only elapsed and the inevitable canoe appeared. Its steersman waved a fragment of white cloth, and with the help of a torn sail came up to us. He was an old, grey-haired man very ragged and dirty, but with great dignity he handed to us a number of yellow and almost illegible documents which he produced wrapped in a piece of leather from under his grimy blanket. From what he said to our pilot it appeared that these papers were evidence of his qualifications to pilot us through the passage, but we found that they contained little in the way of praise of their holder—even if they related to him at all. They consisted mainly of reports, short notices and extracts from the logs of ships bound for the north, some of remote dates in which the reader was asked to give news and greetings from people who had perhaps long been dead to their friends in the south. Others contained information about dangerous reefs and shallows, warnings about the Chuznu Indians in the neighbourhood, and even an amusing verse about the pilot himself, which ran as follows :—

" This Indian is a rascal
    Who committed many sins,
  But although you may mistrust him
    You will find him to have good skins."

As we already had two pilots we declined his services in spite of all his " papers," but gave him some biscuits which pleased him very much and with which he went off in his worm-eaten, half waterlogged canoe. More interesting than anything else was his report that a two-masted ship en route for Sitka had passed through the Straits seven days before, and had taken a Chuznu as pilot. From his description it must have been Frank's schooner, *The Sweepstakes*, on which our former companions had taken a passage from Fort Wrangel. During the afternoon we passed a fleet of Chuznu canoes all engaged in halibut fishing. Some of their occupants wore very unusual garb —costumes of deerskin trimmed with fringes and beads were not unusual in place of blankets; many had cloaks of fox and marten skins and one old chief appeared in a costume made of sable skins, for which we vainly offered him a very high price.

Unfortunately there was very little wind in the narrow passage after leaving the Sound and as it died away altogether at 7 o'clock we were forced to anchor only about 12 miles from the entrance. For a supply of fresh water and firewood we were indebted to young Keste, who also showed us a deserted Indian camp. The seamen, who were already treating the young man as a kind of slave, set him to work to wash their things, a menial task which the chief's son carried out unwillingly but skilfully.

Towards evening the rain began again and lasted all night. The next morning we looked in vain for any sign of a breeze—the persistent and heavy rain seemed as if it would prevent one from rising. Sometimes rowing and sometimes making use of the tide we got by noon to the neighbourhood of the " Peril Strait Narrows," but through the turn of the tide were driven back about half the distance we had come. The shores on both sides were quite flat, the low ranges of hillocks densely wooded ; the channel, frequently impeded by small islands and sandbanks, was shallow and would not have permitted the passage of a large vessel of deep draught. Great flocks of water-fowl, particularly wild ducks, let us come quite close and seemed to be rarely disturbed in their haunts. For a change, here and there appeared out of the water the flat head of a seal, who looked at us for a moment with his bright eyes and disappeared before we could make use of our weapons. We were especially interested in the yellow water-snakes, about two feet long, which swam a few feet beneath the surface, but our efforts to catch a specimen were unsuccessful. Before dusk we decided, as all hope of a breeze must be abandoned, to take to the oars and try at least to regain the ground which we had lost since mid-day. After two hours of this work, which was made doubly unpleasant by the persistent rain, we managed to drop anchor at the entrance to the Narrows. The whole distance travelled during the day amounted only to 15 miles, which afforded little satisfaction to people in such a state of impatience as ourselves.

Early next morning we passed at high tide without mishap through the Narrows, which are dangerous in some places, with a very slight breeze and soon met a large canoe painted black and manned by twelve Indians who had evidently left Sitka early that morning, so that now we could not be far from our destination. The noisy and rather overbearing behaviour of these Sitka Indians, who were evidently bound on a fishing expedition, did not inspire us with great confidence, and we were glad when the turbulent party continued on its way. At 11 o'clock a strong northwest wind suddenly sprang up and at first we tried to tack, but owing to the narrowness of the channel we made no progress in that way. So in order to avoid being driven back we decided to drop anchor in the shelter of a small island. Opposite us there was a poorly-built hut, and an overturned canoe lay near it on the sandy beach. A thin column of smoke rose from this lonely dwelling and after a while a single Indian appeared in the entrance. Our presence did not disturb him in his occupation of getting fish and drying them at the fire, and in contrast to our previous experiences he did not even come over to us and soon disappeared from our sight. After a four-hour halt, made thoroughly uncomfortable by the incessant and heavy rain, we tried our luck once more. The light breeze had died away completely and when the tide turned in our favour we again took to the oars and made some progress, though it was very slow—scarcely three miles an hour. There was no lack of volunteers for the oars that evening, as we were all equally anxious to press on, and even the two Indians took the short paddles of the canoe and, sitting one on each side of the boat, helped us as well as they could. For a time we put them in the canoe in front of the boat, but their powers of endurance at the paddles were not great. Despite their shouts and gestures at the commencement, their energy soon flagged and only persistent efforts on our part prevented them from sitting quite idle.

Pushing on slowly between the narrow banks, which bore only occasional traces of snow, we came about 7 o'clock in sight of Mount Edgcumbe, a lonely mountain visible from a great distance which stands at the entrance to Sitka Bay and serves as a landmark for all the ships approaching from the sea. Looking across to the low-lying banks we saw quite clearly the cone-shaped cliffs of the mountain that sloped downward at the further end and bore only too plainly the traces of volcanic action in the past; even at the present time the smoke that rises occasionally shows that within the mountain that activity has not entirely ceased.

It will be readily understood that we hailed this welcome landmark with rapture but we could not hope, whatever effort we made, to reach our goal that evening and so we decided to spend another night—we hoped it would be the last—on board the *Ocean Queen*. Living in that little boat had become for all of us in the course of time almost unendurable. In wet weather we were compelled to stay in the cabin, even during the day; it was impossible to have any ventilation when the rain was heavy—on the contrary even the porthole had to be kept closed to prevent the water from driving in. The chimney was defective and quite useless when the wind was against us, and the pipes, or rather the tobacco, of my fellow travellers was not the most odorous. The mixture of blubber and fat with which the two Indians were accustomed to rub themselves all over gave them a very unpleasant smell, and so the whole atmosphere at night, when of the eight men at least seven were shut up inside the cabin, was such that I was often compelled to go on deck for a while to get a breath of air, since sleep was hopeless—so close and oppressive was it in there.

For other reasons it was high time that our journey came to an end. Rheumatic complaints, warning us of scurvy, were being felt more and more. Lack of exercise and bad air destroyed the only thing which hitherto had not failed us—namely, our appetites—and during the last days especially the general apathy had become so great that no proper cooking was done and we contented ourselves with what was absolutely necessary; and we often had nothing all day except biscuits and cheese and perhaps potatoes, although there was no lack of other provisions, such as salt meat and fish, if anyone had been there to get them ready for us. Our relations with the sailors were so strained that often we did not exchange a word with them all day.

We were again under sail next morning before it was light, and tacking against the gusty wind that was mingled with rain—a toilsome task for which our flat-bottomed boat was ill-adapted. To cover the first ten miles took us eight hours, and it was 11 o'clock before we turned a tongue of land and saw at the far end of a deep bay the town of Sitka. We greeted it with loud cheers; our long-sought goal was before us. With what impatience we endured the zig-zag course of our boat, the handling of which would in any case have been difficult enough in the rough sea, and what discomfort we felt as our craft heeled right over on her side again and again beneath the violence of the wind. To meet with an accident in sight of the harbour that offered us shelter and security after all the perils we had passed through, and to have our good fortune suddenly fail us—that would have been too appalling! About 2 o'clock we were so near the town that we could plainly see the Government building on a small elevation and the cupolas and pinnacles of the Russian church, and soon an open sailing-boat came out to us with two customs officers on board to take the mail bag, which we had brought with us with as many newspapers as possible from the post office at Victoria. At first they would not believe that we had really made the long journey in our insignificant little craft. The high sea made it impossible for the two vessels to keep alongside each other, and so we parted after a few brief questions and each boat made for the shore as quick as she could. At this point we dismissed the two Indians,

ENTRANCE TO SITKA, 1868.

giving them permission to go in our canoe to the Indian settlement which lay close to the town, on condition that it was returned to us in due course.

Soon we passed a buoy which marked the entrance to the harbour, and then a number of steamers and warships lying at anchor, one of which—a sailing-vessel—sent a boat whose crew rowing with uniform stroke came up and asked us for letters. Then passing on our left some smaller schooners and sloops and a number of Indian canoes we came, at 4 o'clock in the afternoon, opposite the wharf and dropped anchor. The examination of the ship's papers and our baggage by the customs officers was quickly over. In a rowing boat we made our way to the steps of the landing stage and there our two former shipmates rushed forward to give us a hearty welcome and congratulate us on our safe arrival. They themselves had reached Sitka a week before us in the schooner *Sweepstakes*.

I breathed freely when I once more felt the solid earth beneath my feet, and with the deepest gratitude I gave thanks to Providence which had so wonderfully preserved us, and vowed to heaven that I would not tempt it a second time in that way. I would sooner wait for months in Sitka than risk my life again on the *Ocean Queen* with her untrustworthy crew. So our wearisome sailing-trip came to an end. We had left Victoria on Tuesday, the 21st April and arrived at Sitka on Sunday, the 17th May, after a journey lasting 26 days, during which, according to our reckoning, we had covered 987 English miles.

PART III.

SITKA—I.

The town itself lies on a sheltered bay, and to those approaching from the sea it presents quite a foreign aspect, with its churches built in the Grecian style with pinnacles and cupolas, its palatial Government building, and houses mostly painted white; and this impression is intensified by the adjoining Indian settlement and the numerous shipping basins which are used as warehouses.

VIEW OF NEW ARCHANGEL, SITKA.   E.T. 1868

Sitka is built along the shore of a peninsula which stretches out into the bay, and on the landward side is surrounded by a palisade with bastions at intervals. At the extreme point the Governor's residence stands on a rock some 50 feet high, and so in the event of an attack would be the key of the position. By it, near the landing-stage, are ranged the warehouses and offices of the old Russian-American company; on slightly rising ground close by the palisades are the so-called Indian church and burial ground. Below there are some roughly-built block-houses and adjoining them, standing by itself, the cathedral, if one can bestow that name on a building made entirely of wood, which, however, is regarded as a model of a Greek church.

172

Close by, facing the sea, is the casino or club of the officers and officials, constructed of wood and painted yellow like all the other buildings in Sitka, and rows of one-storied barrack-like houses of the Russian work-people. And finally, separated by a narrow brook and surrounded by a number of small block-houses, there are the hospital and the episcopal palace which, however, is not distinguished in any way from the other houses except by its size.

Close to the town, and only separated from it by the palisade, the Indian village stretches along the western shore of the peninsula for about one English mile, and the whole terrain that slopes down to the bay is enclosed at its rear by a range of wooded hills that rise steeply to a height of some 500-600 feet, whilst further back still the mountain heights, covered with eternal snow, give the

GOVERNOR'S HOUSE, SITKA.   F.T. 1868

whole district an Alpine character. On the south the bay is hemmed in by a multitude of small islands and islets, some of which are only visible at low tide, and right to the west where a quite narrow passage leads to the open sea there rises in the blue distance on Krooze Island that extinct volcano, Mount Edgcumbe, from whose depths even to-day sulphurous smoke rises from time to time and which, as already observed, serves as a landmark for this, the most northerly harbour of the west coast. The low swampy ground, covering only a few square miles, which lies between the town and the chain of hills, is overgrown with heather and low bushes which at the foot of the hills merge into the dense primæval forest.

173

The population of Sitka consisted at the time of our visit of about 800 persons of whom 250 were American soldiers and 50 American settlers, whilst the remainder was made up of Russians, Creoles and half-breeds. The company of Russian infantry, which had constituted the garrison, had been sent back to Siberia before my arrival, and the Russians who still remained were a remnant of the officials and workmen of the Company, and had to leave the place within a year. In the Government building an American general had taken the place of the Russian, Prince M.; the club-house was the haunt of officials of the United States; and on the parade ground the orders of American soldiers were heard instead of those of the Russian overseer with his knout. Only in the churches and in the warehouses that were still partly occupied by the Company, and in the barracks of the Russian workmen, was Russian life to be seen going on as usual.

As soon as I felt the firm ground beneath my feet my first enquiry was naturally for a place where I could get a meal and have some sleep, and I gladly accepted the invitation of one of my travelling companions to accompany him to an eating-house whose proprietor he knew and where I should perhaps find a bedroom.

So I handed my small trunk to an obsequious Indian, took up my travelling bag and marched by the side of my Jewish companion, who was evidently not at Sitka for the first time, steadily upwards through the only street of the town, running the gauntlet of inquisitive glances from people who were obviously discussing my business and intentions. A new settlement of this kind consists chiefly of adventurers of every sort, who regard each newcomer with distrust until they have got some idea as to his proceedings.

Making our way toilsomely over carelessly-laid planks, which took the place of a pavement, and were still slippery after a heavy storm of rain, we came to a one-storied wooden house, near the church, which was outwardly in no way different from the other block-houses, except that the part which faced the street served as a dining-saloon whilst

174

the rear portion shut off by a wooden partition contained the kitchen and other dining-rooms. The arrangement of the saloon was very primitive—two long roughly-made wooden tables with forms of the same kind and a few chairs constituted the whole of the furniture.

The proprietor of the hotel came out to us from the kitchen. He was a fair man in the fifties, a German by birth who after many wanderings had settled in Sitka and established the one and only restaurant for American visitors. Henry, as the host was named, received me in a friendly manner on the introduction of my companion and offered me a share in a room with two other men in a hut constructed of unplaned boards near to his restaurant. The offer was not very attractive, for the hut contained absolutely nothing except three roughly-made wooden stands without any overlay except the hard boards which were to serve as beds ; there were no mattresses, no pillows, in fact there was nothing at all. Nevertheless I was forced to accept the offer. Fortunately I had with me my large blanket and a small travelling rug, with which I had to make my bed as well as I could, just as I had to do throughout the voyage. In the hut there was nothing whatever to serve as table, chair or washing apparatus ; for the latter a tub of rain-water stood on a trestle outside the hut and had to suffice for all requirements.

After I had put my trunk under my sleeping-place and had put my travelling-bag to serve as a pillow I returned from my inspection to the dining-room, where a good meal awaited me. Venison, fish and potatoes formed a most satisfactory dinner, at which two of my travelling companions also put in an appearance, and in contrast with our monotonous fare on the boat tasted excellent.

The evening was rainy and after a short walk through the town I retired early on that first evening to a rest which was interrupted by the noisy entrance late at night of my fellow-lodgers. Nevertheless the night passed without incident, though in my unusual situation I was prepared for any contingency. It was not till early morning that

175

I was awakened by my two room-fellows, who were evidently going to their work and were highly surprised at finding me there.

After making an elementary toilet, which was interrupted several times by sudden showers, and taking a breakfast of black coffee and new bread in the saloon, I went with my travelling companion down to the harbour to have our luggage brought on shore from the *Ocean Queen*. Some sturdy Indians were soon found who took the trunks and boxes of provisions (of which a good deal was left) on their shoulders, and we also took ashore the canoe which we had purchased, in order to sell it at the best price we could. Customers for the food supplies were quickly found, the salt meat in particular seemed greatly in request, and we also sold the canoe to an American.

Meanwhile we met a number of Indians clad like their kinsmen in the south in the inevitable blankets and mostly with their faces painted black. They seemed unfriendly and reticent and, as we were told, were allowed inside the settlement only from sunrise to sunset; gun-fire from the fort gave warning for them to leave the town and those who did not do so were sent to prison. Besides these Indians I saw a certain number of people of a Mongolian type, whiter in hue than the copper-coloured aborigines. These were natives of the Aleutian Islands—that chain of islands which extends in the south of the Behring Sea from the western point of the Alaskan peninsula across to the Asiatic coast and serves to-day, as it did in former times, as a bridge between the natives of America and of Asia. Hence comes the Mongolian stamp of these islanders, who have been mostly Russianised and have adopted Christianity (of the Greek Church). The Aleutians are adaptable, good-natured and very contented. They were formerly employed by the Russians partly as hunters and fishermen and partly as seamen, and showed no trace of that resistance to outside influences which characterises the natives of the American mainland and the adjacent islands, whom hitherto it has not been possible to raise to a higher level of civilisation. As hunters and fishers the Aleutians are unsurpassed; in their remarkably light canoes made of seal hide, which barely afford room for one person to sit, they often venture from their island miles out to sea pursuing with the help of two-bladed paddles, which they use with great skill, the inquisitive seal or the timid sea-otter and slaying them by unerring casts of their harpoon-shaped spears. It often happens that the daring hunter in his light craft is capsized by the wounded creature, but he cares little for that since his coat of waterproof sealskin is fastened as a protective cover over the small opening of the canoe, which is so built that it can right itself. The hunting season is, of course, the best time for the easily-contented islanders, and in it they must earn enough to keep themselves for the remainder of the year. In May when the spring gales that rage with great fury in these northern regions have passed, and the ice-fields which enclose the islands in winter like an iron girdle can no longer withstand the warming rays of the sun, the Aleutian villages awake, the " Bajaren " (canoes) are brought out and put in condition, and spears and fishing-tackle are made ready. With child-like faith the men who preparing to go on hunting and fishing expeditions receive the blessing of the Russian priest, and to the sound of the solitary little church bell the flotilla sets out, followed by the good wishes of the women, children and old men who remain behind. Then follow long months of great anxiety for the latter; how great are the dangers which the seafarers must encounter until in August, when the short summer draws to an end, sounds of rejoicing are once more heard in the villages so long silent. Richly laden with their booty, the skins of the valuable sea-otter and the no less prized sea-lion and numerous other kinds of furs, they return bringing plenty and prosperity to their modest homes. Women and children all help to stretch the skins and dry and clean them. The Russian dealers are ready to exchange them at fixed rates for foodstuffs, clothes and the other necessaries with which the Aleutians, who are fairly advanced in civilisation, keep themselves supplied. Many a woman must watch with a heavy heart the welcome given to those who return, for her only support has perchance fallen a victim to his own daring. But even *her* grief will soon be alleviated, for according to the Aleutian custom the widow of a man who has perished thus receives a share of the booty of those who do return. Then come the long months of the northern winter and violent storms which, raging the more furiously in the shallow waters of those regions, make any attempt to put to sea impossible. Then follow snow and ice, the country seems to be petrified and the hapless native buries himself with wife and child in a hut half-underground and spends the next six months in drowsy inactivity, broken only occasionally by the capture of some game.

It should be noted that the Aleutians have held fast to their Russian creed and customs since the transfer of their country to the Government of the United States, and so far have shown no inclination to make use in any way of their newly-acquired American citizenship.

At the very time of my visit to Sitka a proclamation by the former Russian governor was issued in which a free transfer to Siberia or Russia was offered to every Russian, half-caste or Aleutian—an opportunity of which a good many Aleutians and others availed themselves.

SITKA—II.

My experiences in Sitka were so closely bound up with my business there, that I must give an account of its nature before continuing this narrative.

The London business house in whose agency in New York I had been employed for some years had for a long time he'd a contract with the Board of the Russian-American Company, whereby the latter was bound to deliver its whole catch of sealskins each year to the London house at a fixed price. The skins, in quantities large or small according as the season was a productive one or not, were collected at the Aleutian Islands, especially at St. Paul and St. George in the Behring Sea, and were transported at the end of the season by various small vessels to Sitka, the entrepôt for all the goods, whence they were shipped every year at the beginning of December in a large sailing-vessel round Cape Horn to England. All this had gone on smoothly for a number of years and the English company had through the contract obtained the exclusive monopoly in these skins, which were not to be obtained in the same quality from anywhere else, and it had laid out an important factory to treat them. In short no one anticipated any change in the position when suddenly in the autumn of 1867 the sale of the Russian territory to the United States became known.

The Russian-American Company, which held its charter direct from the Russian government, of course lost on the transfer its exclusive trading rights and was compelled to go into liquidation. Our English contract, which was to last till the end of 1868, was thereby jeopardised.

In the late autumn very contradictory rumours reached us. At one time it was reported from St. Petersburg that the Company would not surrender its rights till the end of the year 1868. At another time reports came from San Francisco that the Company had been bought out and that expeditions under American leadership were starting for the newly-acquired territory. It was, of course, of the greatest importance for us that in any event the seal catch of 1867, and, if at all possible, that of the following year also should remain in our hands.

The value of the skins had meanwhile made a marked advance and was far above our contract prices, and consequently there was a risk that the Russian officials, with or without the connivance of the Company, would attempt to take advantage of the confusion caused by its winding-up to sell to speculators a part of the skins which were properly due to us. In order to keep a watch so far as possible on the conduct of the Russian employés in these circumstances, and at least to discover and notify, if not to prevent, a breach of the contract, I was commissioned first to go to San Francisco and collect there all the information that I could.

My business was, therefore, at first rather that of a passive observer than of an active participant, and was, of course, made the more difficult by the fact that all the agents and officers of the Company to whom I had official letters of introduction regarded me with disfavour, as they fully understood that I was sent merely to keep a watch on them.

Immediately on my arrival at San Francisco I learned that the Governor of the Company, Prince M., after selling the whole assets of the company to some American capitalists, had come to San Francisco and was staying there on account of some legal business. At the same time I received information from an independent source that a cargo of sealskins had arrived in San Francisco, a few weeks previously, and been delivered to an American merchant who had shipped it to Europe. No information was given me by the agents of the Company or by the Russian consul or by the princely Governor, with whom I had a personal interview, and of was only from strangers that I ascertained the names of the ship and her captain and the nature of the cargo—facts from which it appeared that the captain, formerly an official of the company, had gone from Sitka to the islands and making use of his position had brought to San Francisco part of the skins which properly belonged to us and sold them there in the presence of the governor or at any rate with his knowledge.

Our fears were therefore justified, only evidence was lacking. Sworn statements of sailors and hunters well acquainted with the northern waters put it beyond doubt that the skins must have been obtained in the course of the summer, that is to say that the Company was not entitled to dispose of them. But to obtain definite and conclusive evidence I was compelled to go myself to Sitka, the more so as I failed, despite all the efforts of the detectives whom we employed, to find any seamen who had been on the particular ship concerned. So I sent all the evidence I had obtained to New York to be forwarded to London and travelled, as inconspicuously as possible so as not to arouse the distrust of my opponents and without saying where I was going, further to the north.

In Victoria my suspicions were strengthened by the fact that people said quite openly, that the cargo of the *Olga* (which was the ship's name, had certainly been brought from the islands to San Francisco with the connivance of the Russian officials, and was not the captain's own catch as he had declared.

On the morning after my arrival in Sitka I prepared my plan of campaign. I had a letter to a Russian official, Mr. L., who had considerable influence with the administration of the Company. The letter had been sent to me from St. Petersburg and was intended to secure the support of this official for the interests which I represented against any improper action by the employés of the Company. Had I obtained the support of this gentleman I should have gained my end, for with it it would have been easy to bring to light the intrigues of the various officials concerned.

Hitherto it had not been possible for anyone to guess my real position with regard to the Company. Before making myself known to Mr. L., I wished to get some information as to his relations with his fellow officials, and so I occupied the first day in learning what I could about his character. The result was not favourable. Mr. L. was not only one of the most influential of the local officials, but he was also closely related to the superintendent of the island by whom the stolen skins had been shipped, so that it was scarcely to be expected that he would give any information which would implicate his kinsman. Nevertheless I decided to make the attempt, relying on my letter of introduction. I had ample funds and wanted at least to know definitely if I should regard Mr. L. as an ally or an enemy.

In one of the Company's houses a small insignificant-looking man introduced himself to me as Mr. L. and conducted me with the usual Russian courtesy to his reception room, a very large apartment furnished in the customary

Russian style with a great number of seats and resembling an audience chamber rather than a private room.

Mr. L., who spoke German and English very well and acted as interpreter for the Company, seemed greatly surprised and confused when I presented my letter. With careful handling I succeeded in obtaining some not unimportant facts as to the voyage of the *Olga* ; but despite all my efforts and veiled promises I failed to get anything that would compromise any one of the Company's officials. But from what he said it was quite clear that immediately on the transfer of the territory some of the Company's officials, under the leadership of Captain H., had gone in the *Olga* (the Company's steamer) from Sitka to the sealing islands, but as to the purpose or result he would say nothing. In his opinion the officials had at that time left the employ of the Company, which had therefore ceased to have any responsibility for them. The worthy gentleman had no idea that I had already made myself acquainted in San Francisco with the arrival there of the cargo and with its nature, so that two of the chief points, namely, the departure and arrival of the expedition, were definitely established and the main task now was to ascertain what had happened during the voyage.

Before I left him he introduced me to his wife, a very pretty Creole who graciously handed me a cup of good tea which apparently was kept always ready in a kettle (the Russian samovar) on the fire. Unfortunately Mrs. L. spoke only Russian.

Somewhat discouraged by my first visit I had an attack of home sickness that night. The outlook was certainly not very promising. I had given up the letter of introduction on which my firm had based great hopes, but it had not had the desired effect. Mr. L. was evidently not inclined to do more for me than ordinary courtesy required ; all that I thought I could expect from him was that he would not betray my incognito to the other officials and would not put any difficulties in the way of further investigations on my part.

So I was entirely thrown on my own resources. Except Mr. L. no one had any suspicion as to my real position, and so I sustained to the best of my ability my rôle as a naturalist and tourist ; I showed great interest in the country and its people, collected curiosities and minerals, and went about sketching as ostentatiously as possible in the settlement, so that my American friends in any event, and possibly many of my Russian acquaintances also, might think me an eccentric person who had chosen this remote region for purposes of study.

SITKA—III.

The first few days passed without any event of importance. As is usual in a small settlement I quickly made the acquaintance of the American officers and soldiers, and the German-speaking Russian officials overwhelmed me with attentions and invitations of every kind. There was, of course, no lack of attempts to find out what I was after, but I succeeded in evading the questions and not giving myself away. I rejected many offers by Russians to provide me with a lodging, since their excessive officiousness seemed suspicious and I preferred to know that my property was in the care of disinterested Americans. In the same way on the occasion of the departure of a Russian vessel for Siberia I refused, perhaps from excessive caution, an invitation to a farewell feast on board, as the opportunity to abduct an awkward witness by that means might have proved too tempting. In Sitka I was reasonably safe on land because of the presence of the Americans, although even there I often believed I was being watched and that probably all my movements were being spied on by the Russians who were perhaps only waiting for a chance to get hold of me. During the whole of my stay I never went outside the settlement and even so I always carried a revolver.

When the weather permitted I devoted myself mainly to sketching, but unfortunately during the first part of my stay in Sitka, the weather was so changeable that one could go out into the open only between the frequent storms. On many days it rained uninterruptedly, as Sitka, according to general report ranks among the wettest places of the earth. Even in summer only a few sunshiny days can be expected and in winter, when the sun is visible only for a few days all told, there is almost unbroken darkness, and snow and rain fall alternately. The climate here is tempered to a marked extent by the neighbouring ocean-currents, so that in Sitka itself even in the depth of winter the thermometer rarely falls below 20° F., and the harbour is never entirely frozen up, in marked contrast with the mainland which is shut off from the sea by a chain of mountains and experiences a real Arctic winter. Curiously enough in Sitka the general health is better in the wet season than in the dry; this is due to the fact that in the latter period the great quantity of decaying vegetable matter gives off noxious emanations which to some extent poison the atmosphere. But at all times the climate is injurious to health, and rheumatism, fever and diseases of the lungs are only too prevalent amongst the white population as well as the Indian.

To this must be added the fact that the nature of the food supply, which as a whole is very monotonous and consists mostly of game and fish (there is no possibility of growing vegetables on the spot, and indeed even fodder for the cattle and sheep is unobtainable), sets up a condition of the body which is conducive to scurvy.

With the utmost difficulty a species of potato has been grown, but it has nothing in common except its name with those which are a product of the more favoured south; the few summer days scarcely suffice to make even this unassuming vegetable fit to eat.

The Russians seem to have acclimatised themselves best of all, though even in their higher ranks few really healthy looking persons were to be seen.

The officials of the Company receive a small salary and get all their subsistence free, and consequently are

184

able to live fairly well. They do not seem to be very hard pressed as the very large number of Russian festivals gives them ample time for recreation even if they did work hard during business hours. Very few days pass without the church bells ringing for hours to summon the faithful to Mass, and there is no official or workman, be he Russian, half-breed or Aleutian, who fails to make his way to the church in his Sunday garb. A bishop and no fewer than ten priests take part in the service, at which the congregation either stands or kneels (there are no seats in the church). A strong smell of incense and innumerable lighted candles

GREEK CATHOLIC CHURCH IN NEW ARCHANGEL, SITKA.   E.T. 1868

have an overpowering effect as one enters the building. In the afternoon the upper class holds small dances when the weather is bad, and have expeditions by sea or land when it is fine—at all these tea and whisky play the chief part. In short, the people seem to have led a *dolce far niente* existence which suddenly had to come to an end. It is not surprising in the circumstances that they sought to get as much as possible for themselves out of the winding-up of the Company, especially as they did not expect to receive a pension or even a lump sum by way of compensation.

In marked contrast with the officials, who lead their lives apart, the workmen dwell with their families in barrack-like buildings where frequently 30-40 persons are herded together. It is impossible to form any conception of the uncleanliness which prevails there ; an Indian hut seemed a paradise in comparison with the abodes of these semi-barbarous people, who lived together with dogs and pigs and whose animal passions were only too plainly marked on their faces. As already noted they were only the remnant of the Russian population, but it appeared as if it were the dregs of it that had been left behind.

The Company paid their workpeople a very small wage and provided them with food, which consisted chiefly of dried fish and bread—the latter prepared in a special way must have been their staple food. As is almost inevitably the case under such a patriarchal system, the men lost in the course of time any sense of responsibility for themselves which they ever had, and their mental forces becoming more and more atrophied they sank into a state of animal apathy, knowing perfectly well that their daily bread was assured and that nothing more was to be hoped for however hard they might work. It was only necessary to compare a number of these workmen, toiling mechanically to the word of command under the supervision of a military overseer, with the Americans who were working perhaps close at hand, to appreciate the difference between slave and free labour.

Every day at noon the workmen could be seen drawn up, in quite the old Muscovite fashion, in a long row in front of the foreman who was distributing their ration of spirits taken from a big copper cask. The quantity of the fiery liquor given to each man depended on the number of persons in his family. The number of rations was increased according to the status of the employé, so that even the higher officials got their whisky in this way unless they preferred to exchange it at the warehouse for other requirements.

Like all Russians these workmen show a respect that almost borders on reverence to any well-dressed person and never pass him with their heads covered. Almost every evening, and especially on festivals, almost the whole community gets drunk and merry, and whilst the higher officials are better able to conceal their condition by drinking in the privacy of their own homes, the noise made by the workmen, maddened by drink, resounds throughout the eerie settlement.

An even worse state of affairs prevailed among the wives of these unfortunates since they (and not only the younger ones among them) gave themselves up openly to prostitution and in their intercourse with the American soldiers disseminated most terrible diseases. In these conditions heaven only knows what happened to the children of the wretched people. If they grew up to a life of crime and immorality what better could be expected of them ?

Very few of the women were of pure Russian origin ; most of them had at least some Indian blood in their veins and had been born in the settlement, and so dark complexions and the Indian type of features were predominant in the children.

If the Russians were to be believed, this sad state of affairs began with the arrival of the American troops. It is possible that this may have aggravated the evil, but it seems quite evident that a very low state of morality reigned in the colony previously. When human beings live together without regard for age or sex, as is the case in the Russian tenements, even the strongest morality must be undermined by the sordid surroundings and eventually give way. In the highest circles there came to light almost every day some scandal not unlike those which have become familiar in the *demi-monde* of Paris. What made matters still worse was that the men not only disregarded the shameful trade plied by their womenfolk but in some cases even openly promoted it in order to gain a profit for themselves.

But it would be a great mistake to suppose that the American population showed greater restraint and propriety than the Russians, for drunkenness and loose living were rampant among both officers and men. The former, who lived in what used to be the Russian club-house, spent all their time, except the few hours they were on duty, sitting round the stove, drinking and gambling till their credit was exhausted; they also carried on the most disreputable intrigues with the wives of the Russian officials and in general behaved so badly that even the Russians, who were by no means irreproachable in this respect, complained of their conduct.

There was a marked lack of discipline, due no doubt to the weakness of the general in command; like so many American officers he had been a civilian and entered the army only at the outbreak of the Civil War, and apparently he did not know his business at all well.

The conduct of the officers was bad enough, but language fails to describe that of the rank and file. Released convicts would not have been more dangerous to the public security than were these men whose task it was to enforce the law. Scarcely a day passed without a robbery, or a case of arson or a violent assault which must be ascribed to the soldiers, and the few respectable people in the town were more on their guard against the soldiers than against the Russians, who were at least good-natured, or even the treacherous Indians.

Although the sale of spirits to the troops was permitted only in special circumstances, they managed to get supplies in one way or another; and drunkenness and debauchery of every kind, together with the unhealthy climate, combined to fill the hospital to overflowing and to increase the number of deaths appallingly.

The situation grew so bad that it became a question at Washington whether it would not be advisable to transfer the troops from Sitka, where they were exposed to the demoralising influence of a loose-living white population and an even more dissolute Indian population, to some smaller and if possible uninhabited station on the coast—a proposal which to the best of my belief was carried out later.

The American civil population fell into three classes, which had little to do with each other.

The most respectable class, and that which was of the best social standing, included the officials of the Quartermaster's Department and of the Customs, the small number of municipal authorities, a military chaplain, and finally the agent of the American Company which, as successor to the Russian Company, was represented in Sitka.

With all these people, some of whom had their families with them, I was in daily intercourse and in their company I was able to some extent, to forget the physical and moral degradation that surrounded me. The agent whom I mentioned above was a German by birth and showed me great hospitality. I was only sorry that my interests and those of his Company were in direct conflict, and that I had to repay much kindness on his part with ingratitude, as I was bound not to let him know my real business, and had later to intrigue against those whom he represented.

The second class, of a much lower standing, comprised the traders, keepers of billiard saloons and dealers in spirits —these were mostly of the Jewish race and carried on a more or less illicit trade with the soldiers and Indians, evaded customs and excise duties, and were liable to prosecution at any moment had the administration of the law not been so lax.

Especial mention should be made of a Polish Jew, who since he had some acquaintance with the Russian language, conducted a disreputable moneylending business between the Americans and the Russians, and under the guise of a spirit dealer carried on a disgraceful traffic in Russian and Indian girls—on both accounts he should have been in prison.

Finally, the background to the picture which I have tried to draw of the population of Sitka was formed by a number of those adventures who were to be found in all new settlements ; but even these were of various grades. Whilst to outward appearance there was no difference between them, with their torn and tattered clothing and general air of being down on their luck, some quite decent people were to be found amongst them—shipwrecked seamen, who were waiting for a chance of returning to the south, and gold-miners who had not been successful in their prospecting and were now without resources in this remote region. But most of them were the so-called " Rowdies," professional loafers, who only waited for an opportunity to take to their evil courses, and looked searchingly at every respectable passer-by. I was always uncomfortable when

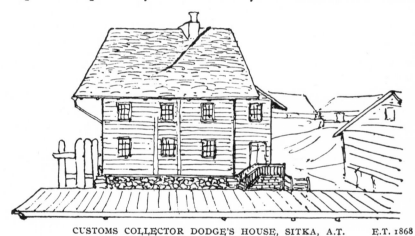

CUSTOMS COLLECTOR DODGE'S HOUSE, SITKA, A.T.   E.T. 1868

any of these fellows were about, the more so as they made a practice of openly displaying their weapons—loaded revolvers. A vain attempt was made to deport some of these undesirables, who simply made their living by terrorising the well-to-do, on a south-bound ship, generous payment being promised to the captain, but despite all the promises made he refused to take the ruffians on board.

Criminal cases were frequent. Scarcely a day passed without a trial by jury being held before the Mayor in the Custom House, which took the place of a town hall ;

the minimum number of jurymen—twelve—could only be got together with great difficulty ; some pettifogging little attorneys, one of whom had travelled with me, supplied counsel for the prosecution and defence, and an honest time-expired soldier, who acted as constable, brought the accused before the Court.

Out of sheer boredom I frequently attended the court. One of the first cases that I heard was the claim made by our steersman against the captain of the *Sweepstakes* who, as I have stated elsewhere, instead of treating him at Fort Simpson as a part owner of the ship, had put him ashore ignominiously ; the captain made a counterclaim in respect of the seduction of his Indian squaw. In the result both parties lost their case. On the same day an Indian who, of course, could only make himself understood through an interpreter—and as there was no one available who could speak English and the Indian dialect the statements had first to be translated into Russian—was accused of theft and sentenced to several days' imprisonment, whilst an American tramp was on the same occasion accused of threatening people with a revolver and was also rendered incapable of doing any harm for several days. On the point as to whether in these cases there was a strict observance of legal procedure and principles I am not able to express an opinion.

A few days after my arrival I had been present at a trial and was about to go from the Custom House to my lodging when I noticed an American soldier who stared hard at me and whose face seemed familiar. Deliberately turning round and looking him full in the face I recognised a young man who had acted as secretary and interpreter to the Prince-Governor during his stay in San Francisco and whom I had frequently met at the audiences given me by the prince. He had attracted my attention, since his slender, almost girlish, figure, pale complexion, long, black curly hair and black moustache betrayed his Russian origin even when he was in American uniform. He seemed to feel that his presence in Sitka as a soldier could not fail

191

to strike me, so he introduced himself to me in quite good English as Mr. P., and explained that having been for a year in the American service on account of his knowledge of Russian, he had been on leave in Sitka and during that leave had accompanied the Prince on his journey to San Francisco as interpreter. With a meaning smile he added that he knew most of the officials of the Company well and during his stay in Sitka had become well-acquainted with all their affairs, and if I so desired he was entirely at my service. Then he looked at me enquiringly with his grey, cat-like eyes and hoped he would see me again shortly.

This chance encounter was of great value to me; Mr. P. must not only have a full knowledge of the secret deals of the officials through his acquaintance in Sitka, but in his capacity of secretary to the governor had been present in San Francisco at the time of the arrival of the ship *Olga* with her cargo of stolen sealskins; and so I could not have wished for a more effective weapon against the Company's officials, provided, of course, that he placed himself entirely at my disposal.

The result of a second meeting was that under a pledge of secrecy and by means of a number of good twenty-dollar pieces I persuaded him to enter my service and furnish me with the necessary evidence. P. made only one condition, that he should delay taking up his new part until the departure of a Russian ship then in harbour, some of whose Russian officers, as he said, were keeping him under observation—a condition to which I could agree the more readily as owing to the lack of travelling facilities I was not yet able to think about my return journey.

Now I had at least made a beginning and had opened a channel of communication with the hostile headquarters. It was, therefore, only necessary to keep my achievement secret and not to compromise my informant in Russian eyes. So with renewed energy I devoted myself to sketching and the collection of all kinds of curiosities, and for this the neighbouring Indian settlement provided a large and fruitful field.

SITKA—V.

INDIAN VILLAGE, SITKA.　　　E.T. 1868

The Indian village lay close by the Russian settlement and was separated from it by the line of fortifications, which consisted here of a double palisade fully 18 feet high and was also defended by a bastion built of strong oak planks and provided with gun casements. Going through a low sally-port and passing the American sentry one came into the open on the shore and found immediately in front the Indian dwellings which lay along the bank. Their construction was in no way characteristic; almost without exception they consisted of huts some 20 feet long, facing the water and constructed of strong deal planks. They were so regularly built as to resemble the block-houses of the white settlers and were all alike, with the exception of the first house which was marked out as the residence of the chief by a staff flying the American flag. Only at the furthest end of the village, which as I have already remarked, stretched very far along the shore, there were some more primitive ones which obviously housed a less important tribe. The number of houses was probably between 80 and 100 and if necessary they could accommodate 150 to 200 Indians.

193

The houses are built so close to the shore and so little above the level of the sea that at high tide it comes quite close to the dwellings, which can then only be reached by a very narrow path. Close in front of each house lie the canoes of its inhabitants. They are of all sizes, from the smallest craft which have just room for one man to the great war canoes which are frequently decked at the prow with carved figures, are built of specially strong wood, and can easily carry 20-30 warriors or even more. These canoes are very carefully looked after by the Indians who

INDIAN CHURCH, SITKA.   E.T. 1868

know only too well how much time and labour is required to hollow out the cedar trunks from which they are made. According to the state of the tide they are drawn up high or low on the fine white sand, thickly strewn with mussels, from time to time water is thrown over them to keep the timber moist, and if there is only a little sunshine the precious craft are covered with sacking or brushwood to prevent them from warping or splitting.

Immediately behind the houses, which stand 30 feet deep, the ground rises gently to a chain of hills covered with low bushes which serve as a burial place for one section of the Indians, as is clearly shown by numerous little wooden huts which serve to guard the ashes of the dead.

The shore presents as a rule, a very lively scene as a large part of the population gathers there. There is always something going on—either a canoe is being launched or a craft comes in from a fishing expedition and is hauled in by the house-mates of the fishermen, whilst the women are busy unloading and preparing the catch and the little naked children watch the proceedings with childish curiosity. The men, as lords of creation, stand about with folded arms and relate their adventures.

Among the Sitka Indians, as with the Indians who dwell further to the south, the women are apparently regarded as much inferior to the men and are forced by the latter to do all the household work.

The Indians who live around Sitka belong to the Galloche tribe, which is one of the seven northern coastal tribes and

GALLOCHE INDIAN CHARM
FROM SITKA, A.T.
E.T. 1868

numbers from 7,000 to 10,000 souls of whom between 1,500 and 2,000 live close to the Russian settlement. In size and strength the Galloches stand pre-eminent amongst the Indians I have seen and are far superior even to those of Fort Simpson. It is not unusual to sec men standing 6 foot high in their bare feet and they are also without exception strongly built and well nourished ; the women, on the other hand, are much smaller than the men and are frequently pretty and almost graceful in their youth, but tend to become corpulent as they grow older.

The clothing of both men and women consists only of the usual blankets, generally blue in colour. Those of the women are as a rule embroidered with beads or mother-of-pearl buttons. A few wear curiously-shaped hats woven of rushes which are waterproof and serve as a protection against both sun and rain, but the majority have their long, straight black hair uncovered or at most bound with a band round the forehead. In winter the Galloches wear garments of leather or fur dressed by themselves, but these are giving way more and more every year to the blankets which are more convenient and more easily obtained.

Frequently, and especially on cold days, they wear cloaks made of fur, particularly that of the lynx, which often become an article of commerce in this form.

During my stay in Sitka I noticed that most of the Indians, both men and women, painted their faces black, thus giving themselves a weird appearance. This was a sign of mourning for relatives fallen in battle or who had died in any other way, and for the same reason a number of the squaws wore their hair cut short.

Many of the Indians have rings and shells pierced through their noses and ears and the older squaws, as a sign that they were no longer unwed, had needles of bone or steel through their lower lips.

Their general health would not be bad were it not for the diseases contracted as a result of their intercourse with the American troops—diseases which have increased rapidly just recently. On the other hand at the time of my visit, cases of smallpox and scarlet fever were rare, but many of the older Indians suffered from rheumatism.

It is worthy of note that any Indian who is ill can obtain advice and medicine free on application to the American hospital, but unfortunately superstition still has a very strong hold over them, so that they prefer to sit patiently and have incantations chanted over them for days by their medicine men rather than have recourse to the help of a white man.

Many of the Sitka Indians can speak a little Russian, and with their usual facility some of the more intelligent men have already added a few English and Chinook words to their vocabulary. Their own language is related to that of the seven kindred tribes, but is more guttural and has fewer vowels than that for instance of the Fort Simpson Indians.

The following words give an idea of the sounds :—

Chief	anchao	what	tasco
Brother	achunoch	ear	kakuk
Sister	achtlakh	to find	judchusché
to steal	aunatshm	soap	usah
secret	klasin	shoe	tilch
to give	hai	light	tsina
to take	na	gun	una
no	klakh	to kill	muna
yes	haunvasa	coat	kenaket
strong	chlidsin	shirt	gudalslch
friend	achakao	rain	sin
axe	schenschoy	snow	gledt
water	klchlitha	fire	chan

The following are numerals :—

1 klach
2 tach
3 natsk
4 tachun
5 chlidschin
6 chliduscho
7 tachaduscho
8 nuskaduscho
9 chuschok
10 tschinkaht
11 tschinkahtkaklach
12 tschinkahtkatach
13 tschinkahtkanatsk
14 tschinkahtkatachun
15 tschinkahtkachlidschin
16 tschinkahtkachleduscho
17 tschinkahtkatachaduscho
18 tschinkahtkanuskkaduscho
19 tschinkahtkachuschok
20 klachka
21 klachkakaklach
30 klachkakatschinkaht
40 klachkakatschinkaht
50 tachka-ka-tschinkaht
60 nutskaka
70 nutskaka-tschinkaht
80 tachunka
90 tachunka-ka-tschinkaht
100 kitschinka

The following are some short sentences :—
    Open the door = chre-dach-schan-tan.
    Shut the door = chre-tschu-tan.
    Sit down, put away, etc. = ganu.
    I want nothing = chlechlatoa andusko.
    Stop talking = katadlché.
    I don't understand = klakh-ra-sa-ko.
    What do you want ? = tasse-it-owa-seko ?
    What's the matter ? = maséjo ?

SITKA—VI.

It would be unjust to accuse the Russians of indifference to bodily cleanliness. Although the provision made for washing in the private houses was of the most primitive kind, there was at least a public bathing-house, which I visited a few days after my arrival (it is open only on Fridays) with some Americans. On knocking at the door of a block-house, of the simplest possible construction and almost hermetically sealed up, we were admitted by a small Russian youth who acted as master of the bath ; he invited us to sit down on the benches in the waiting-room until he had got the bath ready for us. Here we undressed and then walked into the actual bathroom, equipped only with a great vessel of boiling water built round with stone. The temperature was so high that one seemed to be in a vapour bath. The procedure was simply that we dashed hot and cold water over each other, beat one another with whisks woven of bast and fed the steam from time to time by emptying buckets of water over the red hot stones of the boiler—in this way the heat in the small room was raised to such a point that we were compelled against our will to crouch down as low as possible, as the temperature only a few feet above the ground was almost suffocating.

A quarter of an hour's stay in this vapour bath was regarded as sufficient and had a most refreshing effect. After the bath it was customary to spend half-an-hour in the waiting-room, and to have a glass of milk punch and smoke a Russian cigarette there.

On that same Friday evening before going to bed I attended a curious ceremony. Our sleeping quarters, which were built only of planks, abutted on another hut which was used as a warehouse by a Jewish trader. Up to then I had never heard a sound there in the evenings, but on that night my curiosity was aroused by the murmur of several voices in the adjoining room. Looking through a crevice I saw quite an assembly of some twenty men, all of the Jewish persuasion, who were holding their Sabbath service and reading their prayers under the leadership of the oldest man present who took the place of the Rabbi. It was a memorable thing to see this religious gathering in so strange a setting and it said a great deal for the persistence with which the Jews everywhere, even in the most remote countries, practise their devotional exercises. I myself should scarcely have expected it in Sitka among a community which was engaged in such very disreputable occupations.

On the following day, Saturday, there was a service in the Russian church which was attended as usual by all the Russian residents. It was particularly elaborate on this occasion as the Bishop of Sitka and some of the priests were going on a Russian ship for the annual visitation of the settlements on the Aleutian Islands.

At the same time the American warship which had been lying in the harbour sailed for Fort Tongass in order to investigate the sinister reports which were current about the shipwreck of the *Growler*, and if need be, to demand satisfaction from the Indians for their treachery. Our best wishes accompanied the steamer, which though small was strongly manned and well-armed, as it started out to sea with its flags flying and a farewell salute. Only one American warship remained in the harbour; this was a sailing frigate whose guns were directed threateningly towards the Indian village. The other craft were only small coasting vessels with one or two masts.

199

Towards evening a report suddenly spread of the arrival of another steamer, a vessel belonging to the coast defence service, which had on board some customs officers engaged in a coast inspection, but as it had left San Francisco more than a month previously it did not bring any news which was particularly fresh. Nevertheless information as to my intentions in regard to the Company must have been brought to the Director from San Francisco by this vessel, as from that time onward I noticed a certain reticence on the part of the Russian official and a closer watch on my movements.

So the first week passed. Up to now it had rained every single day without interruption and the bad climate, the monotonous food and depressing surroundings seemed already to be affecting my health, and I was feeling far from well when on that Saturday evening I went to my lodging, which was almost soaked with rain, and wrapped myself in my meagre blankets.

I must have been asleep about two hours when a noise woke me up. Sitting up on my couch I listened with bated breath. I heard voices outside the hut; someone was fumbling at the door, which was always unfastened, in an effort to find the lock. Suddenly it yielded and two noisy, swearing ruffians burst in. It was pitch dark and the rain splashed incessantly on the floor. I could see nothing, but I recognised the voices of my room-mates, who had evidently come home very drunk. My anxiety was somewhat allayed as at any rate I did not have to deal with complete strangers, but I was by no means at ease when instead of lying down quietly they continued to rampage about. Apparently they were trying to knock each other down, since they struggled from one corner to another and often stood close to my bed, but fortunately without noticing me. The fracas lasted more than half-an-hour; finally they must both have calmed down. I heard a heavy fall which shook the whole hut, and this was followed by a dead silence. Nothing stirred. At first I thought there had been an accident and was about to get up and give the alarm when a loud snoring convinced me that at least one of the disputants was still alive.

But I got no more sleep that night and lay on my couch with half-closed eyes longing for the dawn. A more repulsive sight than that which met my gaze cannot easily be imagined ; and, in short, despite the repeated excuses and asseverations on the part of my landlord I determined, if possible, not to pass another night under this roof. So I set out forthwith to look for other apartments. In the course of my wanderings I came across a varied assortment of dwellings, some of them so horrible that I should have really been ashamed to be seen there. The best houses that I inspected belonged to Russians and as I had determined in no circumstances to enter a Russian house, my choice was very limited.

I was just returning from one of these room-hunting expeditions when I met a party of American acquaintances who were on their way to the Protestant church, which under the Russian rule was the place of worship of the Finnish-Lutheran officials, of whom there were a fair number. All the important people of Sitka were present ; the front seats were occupied by the general, the chief officers and the mayor with their families ; behind them were the lesser American officials and finally the few non-Jewish traders.

The service was simple but affecting. The military chaplain gave a short address mainly extempore in which he compared great men of various countries—Kossuth of Hungary, Kosciusko of Poland, Alfred the Conqueror (*sic*) of England and Garibaldi of Italy were all great men in their time, but their greatness was only transitory in comparison with that of Our Lord. A good English hymn led by a small but well-trained choir ended the service.

When church was over people paid calls ; even the Russians, who had celebrated their own Sabbath on the preceding day, did the same. On that Sunday the sun showed itself, so that Sitka made a more favourable impression than it usually did, with well-dressed ladies and gentlemen walking about the usually-deserted streets. The fine weather had brought everybody out and in the evening there was a variegated assembly at the landing-stage. Here also there was something to be seen, for our former craft, the *Ocean Queen*, was sailing that Sunday for the south. From the first I had given up all idea of returning on that poor little boat and moreover my task in Sitka had only just begun so I could not think of leaving, but nevertheless I felt homesick when I saw the sloop with its sails outspread drawing near the mouth of the harbour. A Russian official had ventured to take a passage to Victoria on the *Ocean Queen*; a few days afterwards a letter was brought by Indians from him which stated that shortly after the departure from Sitka the mainmast had been carried away in a storm. On my way back I heard in Victoria that the sloop had been six weeks on the voyage and had reached Victoria only after many difficulties and dangers, so I did not envy the poor Russian, who arrived nearly half-dead.

On Sundays and other festivals the Russian officials were in the habit after supper of going towards midnight for a sea-trip; and on several occasions I joined one of these parties which, even if the Russians themselves harboured any evil intentions towards me, were not likely to bring me into any danger owing to the presence of their wives and occasionally of some Americans.

For these trips we provided ourselves with cloaks, blankets and fur coats, also some food and a large wicker bottle of whisky, and thus equipped the nocturnal party, often numbering eight to ten persons, took one of the roomy and fast rowing-boats which are known as " whalers." It is impossible to imagine anything more romantic than one of these excursions, which lasted often for several hours. Sheltered from the breaking waves by the line of islands the water of the bay was as smooth as a mirror, and the sky was covered with light clouds through which from time to time the crescent moon shone out casting her silvery beam athwart the dark water. Thus we made our way slowly along the coast ; before us the settlement lay at rest and only dimly could we distinguish the outlines of the fort. A few lights indicated the town, and now we passed by the Indian village which was entirely in darkness, and only the savage baying of the Indian dogs reminded us that the redskins were there. Turning away from the land we steer across the bay to the small islands. On our left a number of sailing boats lie at anchor, their hulls looking ghost-like in the dark water and their long masts and spars resembling immense outstretched arms. But here people are about for when we come near the flotilla the " Boat ahoy ! " of the watchman warns us that he is at his post. Our " Ay, ay, sir " suffices to convince him that we are not pirates or thieving Indians, and without further question he lets us pass.

During all this time the wicker bottle had been greatly in demand ; both men and women applied themselves to it vigorously. We all became more cheerful ; one of the Russians had his mandoline with him and accompanied the melancholy strains of a Russian folk-song sung by Mrs. L. Meanwhile we had passed by a number of little islands and heard the surging of the open sea ; by this time the party had become courageous and wanted to experience the tossing of the waves. A few powerful strokes of the oars drove the swift boat between two ridges of rock out into the surf—in a moment we were wet through from the spray. The little craft tossed about, the situation became unpleasant and the lady passengers begged us to turn back Happily the sea was quite calm apart from the foam along the shore and the shelter of the bay was reached without mishap. But that outings of this kind at night were not free from peril was demonstrated by some dangerous rocks, half under water, which we encountered on our return and whose nearness we observed just in time to avoid running on them.

It is early morning when we reach the landing-place, the Indian village is already animated, the canoes are being got ready to carry the early hunters to their hunting grounds, the pale light of morning begins to glimmer in the east. In summer the nights here are very short, but I wonder what they are like in winter—so I thought to myself as I sought my lodging!

SITKA—VII.

After a long search for a satisfactory lodging two of my fellow travellers proposed that I should join them. Shortly after reaching Sitka they had rented the cabin of one of the humbler Russian priests, who was obliged to go on a journey with the Bishop, and were ready to place one apartment— if a very small room without furniture of any kind could be called an apartment—at my disposal. The rent for the whole house was 7½ dollars a month, but as I hoped not to remain any length of time in Sitka I paid my share in advance.

MY HOUSE AT SITKA.   E.T. 1868

The hut was made of untrimmed trunks of trees still covered with bark. As regards the interior, which was divided into two parts, a badly-secured door led into a kind of covered front yard, which had apparently served for the storage of wood, straw, hay, etc., and was not floored with planks. The roof was so defective that in wet weather the rain came in steadily and the muddy floor was extremely unpleasant.

From this yard a second door led into the front part of the house which, having at least a roof and a floor, looked more like a human habitation. Of the two rooms which it contained the front one, in which my two house-mates slept in the solitary iron bedstead, was very poorly furnished; from the window there was a view of the Bishop's palace (!) and of the bay beyond.

The second and only other room, which was assigned to me, had at first absolutely nothing more than the bare walls, but as its dimensions were only 6 x 8 feet it was not possible, with the best intentions in the world, to put much there. The little window on one side made it look like a prison cell.

Nevertheless I was very glad to have found this shelter. Above all here I was with Americans, and, more than that, with people as to whose character I had been able to some extent to form an opinion during our adventurous voyage. One of them, the engineer, seemed likely to be a tower of strength to me should any crisis arise, since more than once he had given proof of courage and coolness. I liked him far the better of the two. His room-fellow, an advocate, was much inferior to him in character, morals and personal courage, but he seemed to be friendly towards me, and as in my private enquiries and in the collection of documents and evidence I might well be able to make use of his professional experience, it was worth while having him as a neighbour. A further advantage offered by my new lodging was that I could keep my luggage and private papers as far as possible out of the reach of Russian spies, which was, of course, by no means the case in the sleeping hut of the eating-house, with the door always standing open. So I gave notice to my landlord Henry (a notice which I may remark he quite expected after what had happened in the previous night). An Indian volunteered to take my modest luggage and going on in front of him I sought my new abode.

First of all I busied myself with preparing a sleeping place. Fortunately my comrades had some blankets which they no longer required and seemed to have been used in every possible sleeping place ; with the help of these I made my humble bed in the corner of the small room on the hard ground. My own blankets I put on top ; an old cushion had to serve as a pillow and then my lordly couch was ready.

How I managed for weeks to put up with this wretched accommodation remains a mystery to me even now. During the daytime I naturally stayed in this damp and unhealthy place as little as possible, but at night when I was compelled to remain in I suffered greatly from my surroundings. Often I was awakened by the mice running about on the floor and scampering over my bed and the other vermin, no doubt left behind by my predecessor and with which the house was swarming, were a horrible infliction. I was always glad when the dawn drove these unpleasant room-mates away, but even then my trials were not over. It was impossible to take off one's clothes for the night and consequently I always felt very tired and unnerved by a sleep which instead of being a refreshment was almost a torture. In order to get a wash it was necessary, however bad the weather might be, to go out of the house and seek to fulfil the requirements of cleanliness under an open sky with the help of rain-water collected from the eaves. We considered ourselves fortunate so long as the supply of rain-water used very sparingly held out, but a time came when our stock was not renewed owing to a period of drought, and then one fine morning we were compelled to fetch water for washing purposes in small vessels from a mill-stream that flowed at some five minutes' distance from our hut. The fact that in such circumstances we did not follow in the footsteps of our Russian predecessor says a great deal for the essential cleanliness of our little community. Certainly the old priest who had occupied this place before us had made himself much more comfortable. Our Russian neighbour, a bone turner who was always drunk, assured us that the priest spent the greater part of the day in bed not at his studies but simply drinking whisky and smoking a Turkish pipe. The library which he had left behind in a corner of the house amongst other rubbish consisted of a few books which were by no means of a religious character.

We all three took our meals in the old eating-house kept by Henry, where at breakfast, dinner and supper all the unattached people of standing in Sitka came together. One could not complain of the food ; despite the lack of fresh meat, vegetables, milk, butter, eggs, etc., Henry did all that was humanly possible to give variety to the menu. His coffee was served without milk, but with a large helping of brown sugar. His puddings and pastries, when he was able to supply them, were made entirely of flour and syrup and his home-made bread was so hard and heavy that it had to be eaten quite hot. The soup at dinner-time was made out of a puzzling mixture of various soup extracts, and venison, fish and salt meat appeared so regularly that the necessary variety could only be obtained by changing the order in which they were served up. But despite all these difficulties the meals there were quite good, and only on one occasion when the supply of flour, that essential commodity of the kitchen, was greatly reduced and at the same time trouble amongst the Indians who furnished game and fish threatened to cut off the supply of these food-stuffs which were absolutely vital to us, did our faces grow long. Had it not been for the arrival of a supply ship with a moderate surplus of provisions, the citizens of Sitka might have had to depend on ship's biscuits for their sustenance.

SITKA—VIII.

One of the most striking personalities in Sitka during my visit was Captain F., a man in the early forties, who, despite his rank of captain, was serving as a humble lieutenant in the Artillery. A German by birth he had certainly held a good social position in Germany and had served in the army of his native land. What it was that had brought him to

America I never ascertained, but he had undoubtedly gone through the Civil War there and risen to the rank of captain—most likely in a militia regiment—and at its conclusion he had entered the regular army. In the absence of his wife, who lived in Washington, the captain found himself in a very unenviable position when transferred to Sitka ; a quiet and scientifically-trained man he, of course, kept aloof from the noisy and often rough company of his American colleagues, and consequently had to put up with many jesting or offensive remarks from them, which made his life in the little settlement far from pleasant.

For these reasons the captain had sent in his resignation some months previously, and was waiting only for its formal acceptance by the War Department at Washington. The ample leisure left to him by his military duties was occupied entirely by scientific enquiries as to the country in which he was for the time being an exile, and particularly as to the aboriginal inhabitants, the Indians.

As I, like himself, had almost unlimited time at my disposal and was interested in the same subjects, I gladly sought his company and in it learned much more of the habits and customs of the Red Men than would have been possible had I been alone.

The captain's rooms, which were in the Officers' Club (formerly the Governor's house) contained a whole collection of curiosities. The walls of a quite large room, with an outlook on the sea, were covered with Indian weapons and fishing tackle. Old bows made of whalebone and seal gut, stone battle-axes, short two-edged Indian swords mostly made of copper and with wooden or bone handles, javelins and spears represented the various periods of their war equipment, to which in modern times they had added flint guns generally bearing Russian inscriptions. Amongst these war-like emblems were standing or hanging complete Indian costumes, mostly made of tanned leather and richly embroidered with fringes and beads and in some cases lined inside with warm fur. But even more interesting were the remnants of a still older epoch, cuirasses and

208

jerkins made of thick buffalo-hide and also helmet-shaped headgear and face masks made of hard cedar wood. The latter were, as a rule, painted black with blood-red stripes, which must have given their wearers a fiendish appearance. Some of this headgear was in the shape of complete animal heads, generally of bears or wolves, though eagles' heads were not uncommon. How the Indians thus masked were able to fight is inexplicable to the modern observer. They must have been very strong men to have carried such a burden and yet been able to move about.

When the captain took a particular liking to anyone— and very few people could gain his confidence—then he produced his secret treasures. In well-secured chests and boxes there was a very valuable collection of Indian house-hold utensils, drinking vessels, ornaments, amulets, small images carved in wood or bone, knives, combs, artistically woven mats made of the inner bark of the cedar tree, baskets, hats and numerous head-dresses, etc. In addition, the collection included old Russian coins of silver and copper which had come for the most part from Siberia to America, leather tokens used by the Russian Company instead of money, and finally the drink tokens of the Russian employes, which were already becoming obsolete. There was also a fine collection of specimens of the mineral wealth of Alaska and fossils and plants had not been omitted.

The captain, who proposed to exhibit his collection as an " Alaska Museum " in the United States and, of course, to sell it for the highest price obtainable, had spared neither time, trouble nor money in its formation and in his researches had often run grave risk of being murdered by the suspicious natives.

From the outset the captain had made it his business to get on good terms with the Indians and this he quickly accomplished by means of valuable presents to them, but unfortunately one incident occurred which threatened to nullify all his efforts.

In his character of an officer, particularly concerned with the topographical section of the command, he was entrusted with the duty of surveying the settlement and the surrounding country in order to prepare a map. In carrying out his orders he went outside the fortifications to the Indian village, escorted by only two soldiers, in order to survey that part of the district. The Indians, under the impression that the Americans proposed to extend their territory so as to include the Indian settlement, were greatly mystified by the proceedings of the officer which were quite unintelligible to them. A crowd assembled and before the unsuspecting officer was aware of the danger he was surrounded by the Indians, the two soldiers were deprived of their side-arms, their only weapons, and had not the sentry on the bastion seen what was happening and given the alarm, whereupon a detachment of the guard advanced, it would have gone very badly with the officer, for apparently most of the Indians were armed and had any resistance been made they would have handled the white men very roughly. But they retreated quickly at the sight of the fixed bayonets, and when matters were explained to them later they restored the side-arms they had taken.

On another occasion the captain was in equal danger. One section of the Indians—probably part of the Sitka tribe—had their burial place not like most of them on the hill close behind their settlement, but on a small island lying some distance away which was used only for that purpose and on which the canoes of the deceased could be seen from a distance hanging in the trees. Our indefatigable collector, accompanied by an Indian who was in his employ, went to the island in order to get from the graves Indian relics, of which a large number were buried with the dead—a proceeding which even his strong scientific interests hardly justified and brought the investigator into grave danger.

Considerable spoils had been collected and the captain was just stooping down to pick up an " ash box " containing the incinerated remains of an Indian warrior, when he suddenly felt himself seized by the Indian who was standing behind him and thrown violently down. He believed that he was the victim of treachery and every moment he expected to be stabbed in the back by the broad Indian sword. He was helpless and could not even move, for the sturdy native was lying on him with all his weight. The fear of death lasted only a few minutes but it seemed unending.

As the death stroke did not come, the captain pulled himself together and tried to lift his head from the wet ground and get hold of the revolver which was strapped at his back. The Indian pressed him down again but after

GALLOCHE INDIAN BURYING HOUSE, SITKA, A. T.   E.T. 1868

a few moments allowed him to rise and, hand on mouth, pointed meaningly to a canoe manned by several Indians which had passed close to the island and was just disappearing behind the nearest spit of land. Had these Indians seen the desecration of the graves it would have gone very badly with the captain and his guide, and it is easy to imagine the relief of our explorer thus to escape a dangerous encounter with the Indians. For the guide who had saved his life he always cherished a great regard, but he never interfered with the graves again.

211

SITKA—IX.

The captain's Indian guide and interpreter was in rank a " medicine man," that is, it was his task to heal the sick, and as such he had considerable influence amongst his fellow tribesmen. It was the less excusable therefore for him to enter the service of a white man whose object it was to exploit the Indians for his own purposes. In collecting his curiosities the captain made use of the wily old medicine man as a medium between the Indian village and the white settlement, and did this with great success.

Every morning at a fixed time there was a knock at the collector's door and in response to his loud " Chredach-schantan " (Come in), there appeared the tall thin figure of the old scoundrel, wrapped in the usual blanket. With cat-like steps he glided along the wall to the captain's table, blinking at him dubiously, and only after the captain had offered him his hand in greeting and said, " Yake touthaht, ganu, anchao " (Good morning, sit down, chief) did the Indian become reassured and sit down respectfully, drawing his blanket round him in picturesque folds. Pointing to his mouth and licking his lips he said, " Chradaha nuahu, anchao." (The chief is thirsty.) That was the signal for the collector to produce the usual glass of whisky, which the old sinner emptied with great enjoyment. Evidently he liked it very much, for he rubbed his stomach and said, " Atchra " (Good) and held out his glass for more, which he did not get. Then they proceeded to the real business. The following questions and answers were exchanged regularly every day :—

Captain : Tasse itowaseko ? (What do you want ?)
Indian : Chlechlatoa. (I don't want anything.)

Then followed a few moments silence during which the Indian pulled out an old pipe which he had himself cut from rough wood, begged for tobacco and began to smoke. The uninitiated might believe that the Indian had come only for the spirits and tobacco and had brought nothing with him, but our experienced captain had observed from the first that the Indian was continually feeling under his dirty blanket as if to assure himself that some object was still there. In fact, after a fairly long pause, during which he evidently hoped to get some further attention and be given another drink, but which the experienced collector bore with calm indifference, the crafty old man at last produced, as if by accident, an old piece of carving or some trifle of that kind. The captain apparently took no notice and the Indian, growing bolder, laid it on the table ; the captain just glanced at it, shook his head and indicated that the article was of no use to him. The native looked gloomy and relapsed into his previous silence, but he could not hold out much longer and after a few puffs at his pipe put his hand under his blanket and with a shamefaced grin produced the article about which he had really come, and hoped to sell to the collector. It was an artistically worked braid of Indian hair which, quite apart from its value as human hair, was worth a good deal as a product of the art of this otherwise so uncultivated race of men. The captain, of course, saw at the first glance what a treasure had been put before him, but he took good care to conceal his pleasure from the native who watched him closely and was quite ready to put up his price in proportion to the captain's eagerness. As indifferently as possible the captain now asked, "Chonséo whas ? " (What do you want for it ?) and then ensued a long haggling. Both parties got excited. Several times the old man picked up the plait and threatened to go away. For a long time he would not name a price at all but at last he asked ten dollars and was finally beaten down to 25 cents which was paid him at once ; he then begged for some tobacco and went away saying, " Sakanch." (Till to-morrow.)

This transaction was repeated every day. The old man always pretended that he had brought nothing, then he produced some worthless trifle and finally the real curio, either a valuable plait or an amulet made of walrus ivory or an old weapon. The captain had obtained most of the items in his collection in this way, but he himself also made frequent visits to the Indian settlement and on several occasions I accompanied him.

The first time that he invited me to do so I observed that since the misunderstanding on the occasion of the land survey the Indians had become very friendly towards the captain. As soon as we had passed the American lines and reached the so-called Indian market at the entrance to their village, I noticed that many of the vendors exchanged greetings with him, whereas some American soldiers who had come down to make purchases were regarded with unconcealed hostility.

I was very much interested in seeing this primitive market, as the whole white population of Sitka obtained from it their supplies of fresh game and salt-water fish. As regards the first, every morning several stags were brought in as well as snow-geese, ptarmigan, hazel-hens and other wild game. As to fish there were always large supplies of halibut, a fish peculiar to this coast and often weighing up to 100 lbs. each, and rock cod, a reddish-gold fish which in this region is reckoned a great delicacy.

The white inhabitants are so dependent on the Indians for the supply of fish and game that when there is unrest amongst the Indians—a frequent occurrence—Sitka often gets near to famine, as the first sign of a hostile attitude on the part of the Indians is always their absence from the market.

Marketing is one of the most long-winded performances that can be imagined. It is necessary to be extraordinarily patient until the Indian market-woman makes up her mind to part with her goods. The Sitka Indians readily take American gold and silver as they understand its value and use it for their purchases in the American settlement.

In order to pass the time the Indians form little groups who crouch round fires and gamble. For this purpose they use little shells which are current amongst them for small change. Each takes up a handful in turn and the others guess how many he has in his fist. To a curious chant the gamblers sway to and fro and then all shout out the numbers

214

together. The winner is he who guesses the correct number. It is extraordinary how this simple game, which is greatly in vogue in Italy, has made its way to this distant spot. The Indians may be seen playing this game often for hours together.

After going through the market we visited some Indian huts where we were received with great respect. As a rule we found the whole household camped round a fire in the middle of the hut. The eldest of the group, for each family has a chief of its own, stood up courteously and made room for us by the fire after shaking hands. The captain, who was a master in the art of gaining the goodwill of the

FISHERMAN'S HOUSE.   E.T. 1868

natives, presented the chief with some tobacco and was at once on good terms. If the Indians had anything for sale it was now produced. Trivial objects appeared first, the better things last, and with repeated expressions of friendliness we escaped from the smoke-filled hut into the fresh air. What makes the atmosphere of these huts so particularly unpleasant for Europeans is the smell of fish and oil given out by everything which the Indians touch.

In one hut there was great lamentation. All the inhabitants were groaning and weeping, the men had their faces painted black and the women had their hair cut short. The captain ascertained that a young Indian had met with a fatal accident whilst hunting during the previous night and had been brought home dead. In fact, in a remote corner of the hut we saw a bier, covered with a blanket, on which lay the body of the dead man. The Indians present would not allow the captain to lift the cover to view the corpse and from this we concluded that the face was disfigured, for amongst the Indians a death accompanied by mutilation of this kind is considered a dishonoured one. Laying a small coin at the foot of the bier we left this house of mourning, where we could do nothing more to help, and made our way to a neighbouring hut in which as it happened we could be of much greater use, for there we found quite a young man huddled up in his blanket before the fire and shivering with cold. Evidently he was in a high fever and suffering great pain.

At first he would not let anyone see what was the matter with him, but after repeated questioning he pointed to his foot which was terribly swollen and in such a bad state as to be evidently the cause of the whole trouble. The captain, who seemed prepared for any emergency, examined the foot carefully and ascertained that the Indian had run a nail or some other sharp piece of iron into his foot, that the wound had festered and that he was likely to lose his leg and possibly his life if he continued to rely on the incantations of the medicine men. The captain, who had a lancet with him, made a deep cut and extracted a piece of rusty nail ; then he had the foot washed and bandaged it himself and was warmly thanked by the patient who had borne the painful operation with stoicism. Of course the captain did not show the cause of the trouble to the Indians and so the latter regarded the skilful paleface as a great medicine man and showed him much respect. He was not always able to effect cures so easily, but he had many successes which did him great credit as he was not a trained doctor. On going again through the Indian village a few days later we met the patient quite well again and about to join a hunting expedition, the other members of which had already taken their places in a number of canoes lying along the shore.

SITKA—X.

After I had been a fortnight in Sitka and despite all my efforts my investigations had been quite unsuccessful, I was suddenly given the chance of leaving the settlement. In order not to rouse the suspicions of people who would be hostile to the object which I had in view I had frequently said how disappointed I was in my stay at Sitka and expressed my desire to return to California at the earliest opportunity. Either because these people really believed me or were in doubt as to my real purpose and wanted to get rid of me, anyhow they managed to have a passage to Victoria offered me by the captain of the war frigate.

To everybody's astonishment, however, I declined the offer ; the only excuse I could give for staying on in Sitka was my determination never again to trust myself to a sailing-ship, however large, but rather to wait for a steamer. Glad as I should have been to bid farewell to this very unattractive town I could not go away without rendering futile all that I had accomplished hitherto, and so I was forced to stay on whether I wanted to or not until my informant had furnished me with all the evidence.

With renewed vigour I urged him to spare neither time nor money and in order not to leave any stone unturned I presented him with twelve bottles of red wine which I obtained from what had been the Russian warehouse. The vendor certainly did not imagine that he was selling me a gift for his deadly enemy.

By this time the weather had greatly improved and one could count on at least some fine days in the week. We were now at the beginning of June, that is at the commencement of the period of fine weather which often lasted only eight to ten weeks. There was a hot sun during the day but the short nights were cool and refreshing.

Life became more tolerable, although the doctors assured me that owing to the emanations from the warm moist soil these fine days were also the most unhealthy.

The Russians, who for months past had been greatly enjoying the few fine days we did have, made all the use they could of this warm spell and on practically every bright summer afternoon they went with their wives and children out into the open country, sometimes to an islet in the bay and sometimes to the Indian river which flows into the bay at its north-east end about a mile away from the settlement—as already stated, this walk to the river was the only one along the sea-front. There were no other known ways into the interior of the island; on the other side of the river and in fact all round the settlement there was an unexplored wilderness.

These land excursions were often very animated and cheerful. A shady spot was chosen on the bank of the limpid, rushing mountain stream and everyone set to work to collect dry wood. Under the care of one skilled in such matters a bright fire was soon burning and the inevitable copper samovar boiling over it. Willing hands brought out the supplies, mostly of cold viands; strong tea was passed round in small cups, fiery rum being used as a substitute for milk, and the party soon became very cheerful. The Russians are a very musical race, and usually on an occasion like this many of those present had brought their instruments. The Russian ladies do not require much pressing and readily join in the sometimes cheerful, sometimes sad, melodies of the Russian folk-songs. When the sun begins to go down people amuse themselves usually with round games of various kinds, something like our German ones. It was strange to see how a Russian priest, who was one of the party in his long robe fastened by a cord round the waist, took part in the games of " Captain " and " Hide and Seek " and on one occasion (it was a festival of the Greek Church) he had to allow himself, according to the old Russian custom, to be kissed by any of the women and girls who could manage to throw a wreath over his head.

218

It was usually late when the party returned leisurely to the town in the cool of the evening, but the festivity generally continued, since some member of the party would invite the others to his hospitable house in order to end up the evening in proper style with song and dance. At these middle-class gatherings it was sometimes rather too lively, for the Russians are wont to become very cheerful and even the Russian ladies, nearly every one of whom had a cigarette in her fingers, are not far behind their husbands and lovers in the consumption of strong drink.

Nevertheless these parties formed the few bright spots in the otherwise very dull life of the little colony, and the visitor was much touched by the boundless hospitality of his Russian hosts and gladly draws a veil over certain incidents which took place on these occasions not entirely creditable to this somewhat eccentric gathering.

Despite the monotony of life in Sitka there were some striking episodes.

At one time a report suddenly became current that gold had been found on the Tacon River, close to which we had passed on our journey, and immediately bold adventurers equipped themselves to prospect this new discovery. Two soldiers deserted after making arrangements with two white adventurers to place a boat at their disposal, and they started off for the new gold-field supplied with the barest necessaries and in complete ignorance of the coast. The two soldiers were brought back a few days later by Sitka Indians. One of them had been mortally wounded by a stab in the back and the other was a prisoner bound hand and foot. The Indians declared that as a result of a drunken quarrel the first soldier had been stabbed by his comrade, and that the other white men had given both of them into the charge of the Indians with the request that they would convey the wounded man and his assailant back to Sitka. The Indians had honourably discharged their task and had travelled night and day to get the wounded man to Sitka while still alive. He died soon after their arrival; the murderer, who admitted his guilt so far as he could remember what had happened when he was drunk, was for a time in danger of being lynched by his enraged comrades, but escaping this he was brought to trial before a court-martial and condemned to death. Of the other two adventurers nothing was ever heard, and it may be assumed that venturing along the dangerous coast in an open boat, and ignorant of the topography, they had lost their lives before they could reach the Tacon River.

An expedition undertaken in the neighbourhood of Mount Edgcumbe under the guidance of the American general in command at Sitka passed off more peacefully. It lasted two days and those who took part in it maintained at first a complete silence as to the results. But it was not long before it became known that large coal deposits had been discovered at the foot of the mountain and, as I learned later, these were subsequently exploited under the super-vision of American engineers.

The trade in furs offered another very favourable field for the wild speculation to which the Americans are addicted. Alaska as a whole and Sitka as the headquarters of the Russian Company were reputed not without justice to have great quantities of valuable furs, and all the American immigrants, from the poorest adventurer to the highest ranks in the army and navy, expected to acquire great wealth from this traffic. Each newcomer was ready to deal in furs of any kind and at any price, in the firm con-viction that he would make large profits. The astute Russians, who seemed to have instinctively a first-class knowledge of the value of furs, and had managed to get from the Russian Company by fair or unfair means large quantities of furs of every kind, exploited greatly to their own advantage the eagerness of the quite inexperienced Americans and sold them almost worthless skins at enormous prices.

All the buyers watched one another keenly and even a small purchase was magnified by local gossip into a huge transaction. I myself invested the greater part of my cash which, even after deducting current expenses and gifts to my informant, was a substantial amount, in various furs which I took to New York and sold there at a large profit. Some of these purchases, particularly those made from hunters and trappers who were not experts in furs, were very profitable ; for example, the French captain, " Frank," of the little merchant ship *Sweepstakes* allowed me to choose 250 of the darkest skins out of a stock of 500 mink. A dark skin was worth twice as much as a light one, but for the 250 he charged me scarcely more apiece than he had at first asked for the whole quantity. I bought these furs on board the schooner which was at anchor in the bay, to which I was taken by an Indian canoe from the shore, and there I met Frank's Indian wife, on whose account our former boatman had nearly lost his life. She was quite a young woman, distinctly good-looking, and she cooked dinner for the whole party. When the business was settled an Indian porter carried the furs to my lodging, to which Frank, who was overjoyed at being able to converse in his own language, accompanied me to get his money. Later on I regretted having brought a man who was quite a stranger to me into the hut, as I did not fail to observe with what curiosity and greed he watched me take the shining gold pieces out of my chest. Nothing would have been easier than to break into that badly-secured and lonely hut, and to this day I am surprised that despite the temptation which it offered I was not the victim of robbery. Certainly I put off the purchase of furs as long as possible and increased my vigilance. Nevertheless I often had anxious moments when I was away from the house and thought of my property which was so poorly protected, and had I stayed longer in Sitka I should inevitably have been robbed. But fortune favoured me and I had no losses at all.

A few days after the excitement over the discovery of gold on the Tacon River had subsided, owing to the unfortunate expedition of the two deserters, there was a sudden rumour that a sailing-boat, manned by freebooters, had approached the settlement and tried to land, but had been driven off by the military authorities and consequently had betaken itself to the mouth of the Indian river which was outside the town limits and cast anchor there. The crew of the vessel, which in popular report numbered from twenty to fifty men, had encamped on the shore, posted a regular guard and allowed no one to approach. Of course the whole population of Sitka had nothing more pressing to do than to go and look at this strange camp from a distance, but came back bitterly disappointed, for there was nothing to see except the much-tattered and patched canvas tops of two tents among the trees and the smoke of fires. A savage-looking fellow armed with a Henry rifle, which holds fourteen rounds, defied anyone to approach nearer.

This mysterious aloofness lasted for several days and the strange camp and the unwelcome guests were the talk of the whole settlement. Then suddenly the mystery was cleared up, for one morning two of the men came unarmed into the town to make some purchases, and then everything was explained. It appeared that the sailing-boat was the schooner *Louisa Downes* and came originally from Portland, Oregon. Instead of a supposed crew of fifty there were only fourteen men on board—they were reckless and very greatly incensed because on their arrival in Sitka they had asked for help from the Governor and had been refused, and being consequently very resentful against the authorities preferred to make their lonely camp-fire in the open forest rather than to appeal again to official benevolence. It was impossible to be surprised at the men's anger and defiance on hearing the account of their experiences, and curiosity quickly yielded to sympathy for these unfortunate people, who had been disappointed in all their hopes and found themselves in this strange and remote place without any means of sustenance, except what their rifles could provide.

In the course of conversation with their leader, a stalwart one-eyed man burnt almost black by the sun, I discovered that the whole party came from Oregon and were gold-miners by occupation. Most of them had worked during the past summer at the Cariboo mines, which lie far in the interior, and when the good season was over and the setting-in of the winter, which in those northern regions is very severe, had put an end to the mining they had come down to Portland to wait there for the return of better weather in the spring. In winter all the larger towns of the west coast—San Francisco, Portland, Victoria, etc.— are filled by gold-diggers, many of whom during that season squander in the wildest revelry what they have earned with such toil during the summer. It can be readily imagined that amongst these rough fellows who have nothing to do and are rolling in money for a time, many wild schemes are hatched for the coming year, and that there is no lack of cunning sharpers who beguile the generally sanguine, open-hearted and rarely distrustful miners and exploit them to their own advantage.

The old miner, who took a glass of grog at my invitation, told me that in the previous winter a certain adventurer went round in Portland and made himself the talk of the whole town. His story was that more than five years previously he had been wrecked on the coast of Alaska, rescued by some Indians and sold as a slave from one tribe of coast Indians in the neighbourhood of Sitka to another, and been treated fairly well by the natives until at last he had come to the Tacon Indians who lived on the Tacon River north-east of Sitka. By giving them great help in repelling a hostile attack he had gained their friendship, and in recognition of his service their chief had shown him a place on the river bank where according to his account, gold could be gathered in handfuls only a few inches beneath the soil. The chief allowed him to take as much as he could carry but forbade him ever to give any information about this gold-field to the palefaces.

Becoming thus suddenly the owner of such wealth the man, whose previous position as a slave does not seem to have been altogether unbearable, had at the time no other thought than to escape to Sitka or some other station of the white men and to betray his knowledge of this great store of gold. After incredible efforts and endless perils, and not until he had lost every bit of his gold, he succeeded at last in getting to a small coasting-boat and on board of it in reaching Victoria. For five years this reticent individual had kept his secret to himself, until poverty forced him to sell it.

" We trusted the man implicitly," my informant continued, " and soon fourteen determined men were found to undertake an expedition to this wondrous new Eldorado. The money needed was quickly collected, a schooner was purchased—the *Louisa Downes*—and fitted out for a trip that would last six months. The discoverer of the gold-field was engaged as guide for a high salary, we promised ourselves unheard-of wealth and sailed for Portland on the 10th of March, envied by all the friends we left behind. Four of us had formerly served as seamen on board sailing-ships and could handle the boat well. We had no charts of the coast and relied entirely on our guide's sense of locality. Nothing untoward happened on the voyage from Columbia to Victoria, but on arriving there at the end of March we met with our first adventure. The English colonists who had settled at that place were living then in fear of raids by the Fenians, and the arrival of a vessel with fourteen armed men (including some Irish-Americans) caused great commotion amongst the worthy citizens. As soon as our boat was signalled the alarm was given and the small garrison and the volunteers were called to arms. In vain did we try to explain who we really were, and asserted that we had nothing to do with politics ; our boat was seized, we ourselves were placed under arrest, and we were told that we should be prosecuted as Fenian pirates. Fortunately before matters got as far as that the American consul, to whom we had appealed as American citizens, intervened on our behalf with the British authorities and after much discussion we were allowed to continue our journey, but not without repeated warnings to do nothing which would injure the British colony.

" The journey from Victoria " (by the route I have already described) " to the Stikeen River and from that point to the Tacon River lasted nearly a whole month, and it was the end of April before we came at last in sight of the shores of Tacon after the usual experiences of every traveller along the north-west coast. Our expectations were at their height. After seemingly unending difficulties and dangers we stood at last on the threshold of the promised land of gold. Our guide, who throughout the journey had shown his ignorance of the district and would not have found the Tacon country at all without the Indian pilot whom we had engaged, became more and more uneasy the nearer we drew to our goal. We ascribed this not so much to his uncertainty as to the locality as to his eagerness for the gold which was within our grasp, and we did not imagine there was anything wrong.

" We experienced our first disappointment as we approached the mouth of the river, for we encountered great floes of drifting ice which had no doubt been carried down by the river-current to the sea. The nearer we got to the coast the more numerous became the ice-floes and at last to prevent our boat being crushed by the ice we had to turn back to the open sea. It was impossible to push on towards the river, for the ice-drift blocked the whole estuary in a broad field about a mile wide. So we had to wait until the breaking-up of the ice, for, owing to the unapproachable coasts, it was not possible to reach our destination, which was five miles upstream, by any other route than the river gorge itself. We drifted about at sea for two long weeks ; we were in sight of the promised land and could not reach it. The temper of our party on the boat, which had already displayed itself in various outbursts during the journey, now became very bad ; scarcely a day passed without a quarrel and I had to exert all my authority to prevent open violence.

"At last heavy south-west storms, accompanied by continuous rain, broke the ice-barrier and we made our way to the estuary of the river. The journey upstream against the swollen current was very toilsome and we had much difficulty with floating timber, but the longing to reach the gold deposit overcame all difficulties and on the second evening of our river journey we found ourselves at the spot indicated by the old prospector, which he professed to recognise. It was a wild district—steep rocks scantily clothed with distorted pines in the foreground, snow mountains and glaciers towering in the background. We set up our camp in a little bay and brought our mining tools on land. Then we took an oath to divide the treasure we should get into equal shares, and set to work under the directions of the guide.

"We ought to have found the gold only a few inches below the surface. We dug four feet deep through the river gravel and struck the solid rock. The old man was perspiring with anxiety and at last declared that he must have been mistaken about the place. We dug in two, three, four, five different spots. No one would admit discouragement, but when at the last attempt we found nothing but sand and pebbles, and the hard rock prevented us from digging any deeper all of us, even the calmest, became so angry with the scoundrel who had tricked us in this shameful way that we swore we would hang him on the nearest tree. No sooner said than done. Despite all his protestations of innocence a rope was slung round the neck of the wretched old man and he was dangling lifeless between heaven and earth."

An act of summary justice or of lynch law, as it is called in America, never fails to make a deep impression on all who take part in it, and then those men who had been so enraged seemed suddenly to come to their senses.

"That the swindler had been punished as he deserved for his heartless fraud all of us," continued my informant, "were agreed. The problem now before us was how to get out of our unfortunate plight. Our stock of goods, for exchange with the Indians, and of food would give out very soon, and we did not know at all how far we were from Sitka, the nearest white settlement. We had already given up all hope of finding gold and decided to sail away without losing any time.

"Before we left we received a visit from a chieftain accompanied by a number of Tacon Indians who warned us with tragi-comic gestures to leave his territory without delay. His summons was quite superfluous as we had already put all our tools on board, so we sent him a few shots as a greeting when we were well away.

"That was how we left the golden river which we have often cursed since and none of us ever wants to behold again, and after a repetition of our adventure and toils we came at last on the 6th June, three months after leaving Portland, to the town of Sitka, which gave us so unfriendly a reception.

"Here we are," concluded my informant, "robbed of all our savings of the past year, almost without resources to continue our journey to the south. We have lost the summer which is so important for us gold-diggers, and besides this, when we return we shall be the laughing stock of all our fellow miners."

It is an old story which is repeated over and over again in the life of the gold-digger, but without making him any wiser.

SITKA—XII.

The arrival of the gold prospectors who, though their expedition had been unsuccessful, told many stories of their previous exploits, and the discovery of coal deposits at Mount Edgcumbe revived many of there ports that were current in the early Russian period about the existence of large copper deposits near Sitka. Although I personally attached little importance to the matter and even in the most favourable circumstances could profit little by it on account of my approaching departure, I nevertheless took part in an expedition which was to go some ten miles into the interior of the island and test the existence of the copper deposit. The scheme was prepared by Russian officials, who gave me permission to participate. We met for this purpose at 5 o'clock in the morning at the house of the leader of the party, the former director of the Russian Company. There were six of us all armed and supplied with provisions for one day; a Russian youth accompanied us as porter. It was a dull day and the sky was overcast; the town was sunk in sleep and the only sound was a confused uproar made by Russian workmen in a drinking bar on our route, where they had evidently been soaking themselves all night. Before we left the town we were alarmed by a shot fired close by and then noticed for the first time that our Russian porter was not following us. As we turned back to look for him he came running up and, trembling in every limb, explained that someone had fired at him from the drinking bar and he dared not pass it, so he had made a detour in order to overtake us. Such sorry jests were of such frequent occurrence that no one troubled about them so long as no one was injured, and we continued on our way.

About 6 o'clock we arrived at the Indian river and, after we had breakfasted on the bank, we continued our journey upstream. At first we followed a well-trodden path which was a favourite walk of picnic parties, but gradually the track became fainter and fainter and at the end of a mile it ceased altogether. We now pushed on very slowly, for we had to force our way through the thickets. Sometimes it was a huge tree trunk felled by a storm or old age which blocked our way with its innumerable branches and twigs; sometimes it was thorn bushes growing in wild confusion and rank creeping plants which, though more yielding, clung to us continually and impeded our progress. Besides this the ground was covered a foot deep with loose moss which seemed smooth enough, but woe to the man who carelessly stepped thereon without first testing it. The deceptive covering gave way beneath his feet and often some of the party sank in suddenly and disappeared up to the waist. The tree trunks, which had fallen in the course of time and in these virgin woods had not been cleared out of the way by any human agency lay where they had been wrecked, and it was a long time before they and their branches were completely decayed. But trunks and branches alike were quickly covered with that green carpet-like moss which grows so luxuriantly in the northern forests. The creeping plants that become so rank in the moist air grew over this and in a short time filled up the numerous hollows with a loose veil. When we remember how many thousands and thousands of years this process of decay has been going on without cessation, how generation after generation of trees weakened by old age have sunk back into the ground from which they originally sprang, we can easily understand how from these dead forests the brown and later the hard coal has been formed and slowly but steadily renewed. That in all these primæval woods of the north-west coast coal is to be found and can be exploited when opportunity offers is an established fact, and we should have done better to search for coal than for copper.

We pushed on valiantly, always keeping close to the stream in order to be sure of the way back. Sometimes we found it impossible to keep to one bank and then we boldly plunged through the foaming and ice-cold mountain stream, which, however, was only a foot or two deep in order to try out luck on the other bank. If that side were not practicable then we had to make our way in the stream itself, which, owing to the coldness of the water, was very tiresome and unpleasant. Despite all these difficulties, and without any mischance except a tumble of our leader—which happily had no serious consequences—we arrived about one o'clock at the place where, according to Russian stories the copper deposit ought to be. We may have mistaken the place or we may not have had the patience or the skill to investigate properly, but in any event we found nothing and as not one of us had really expected anything much from the scheme we were not seriously disappointed, and in the enjoyment of our dinner, which was spread out on the soft moss, we soon forgot the original purpose of the expedition. It was very good to have a sleep after our hard tramp and all of us, with the exception of the Russian youth, were soon enjoying a well-earned siesta.

At 3 o'clock in the afternoon we began our return journey, which took much less time as we were now better acquainted with the route, and without seeing an Indian or a single wild animal or any game even from a distance we emerged from the wood, at 6 o'clock, on to the heath which stretched between the wood and the town, and had the towers of Sitka before us. We camped again and quickly lit a fire and in the enjoyment of a cup of tea we soon forgot our toilsome march. It was very pleasant to camp on the scented heather, and the fire crackled and leaped up here and there in tongues from the dry grass so cheerily that we amused ourselves by setting light to small patches of the grass in order to form some conception of what a prairie fire was like.

An hour later we were all back in Sitka and gathered in the house of one of our party when suddenly we heard the alarm given. Hastening into the street we encountered most of the citizens in front of their houses and saw a detachment of soldiers and marines running at the double to the north end of the town. The air was heavy with thick smoke, filling one's eyes and nose, which was evidently being driven from the forest towards the town by the strong north wind. The cause of the commotion was a forest fire and there was danger that the town would be imperiled by the approaching flames. Our folly in lighting a fire on the edge of the forest made us conscience-stricken and we would have given a great deal not to have done it, but it was too late. Thanks to the praiseworthy energy of the commanding general who, well acquainted with the practice of meeting prairie fires with a counter-fire, immediately ordered the soldiers to dig trenches round the town and set fire to a small belt of heath grass on their outer edge, the fire did no damage to the town itself. Later in the night the wind fell and the heavy rain that followed put a stop to the fire in the forest. Nevertheless even in this short time a surprisingly large stretch of the heath and undergrowth was completely destroyed or charred, as we saw next day, and even the lower parts of great old trees had begun to catch fire.

Naturally we did not tell anyone that we had caused the fire, but we vowed that we would never again be guilty of such an act of folly.

SITKA—XIII.

Most of these exploring parties had no particular result and in fact they were really only a pretext for many of the inhabitants of Sitka, who wanted a change, to get away from their business for a day or so. That these trips into the interior of the island were not beneficial to the health of those who took part in them was proved by the various illnesses which ensued, amongst which rheumatic ailments were the most common. Another trouble was caused by a poisonous plant of a thorny nature, the so-called " Devil's Rush," which grew in profusion in the forest. Sufficient precautions could hardly be taken to avoid contact with this plant, for by merely touching it the thorns stuck in one's skin and unless they were immediately cut out they caused violent inflammation which was sometimes fatal, since in this climate even the most trivial wound healed slowly and with difficulty. I myself had my finger violently inflamed in this way and was altogether so unwell as a result of a recurrence of wet weather, that every now and then I retired to my bed feeling very ill and almost gave up hope of the success of my mission. True my informant had obtained answers to a considerable proportion of my questions, but the most important evidence which would have been decisive in any action against the Company he had not yet delivered to me, excusing himself on the ground that access to the archives where the particular documents were deposited was very difficult to obtain and required a great deal of time. But in order to be ready for any eventuality and to put what information I already had in such a form as could be utilised, I employed the long hours when I was unwell and stayed in the house, in putting the evidence I had received in the form of an affidavit, and added to it from time to time any further information supplied by my investigator.

My house-mate, the lawyer, was of course of great use to me in this respect, although I could not acquaint him at the time with the real importance of my mission. Apart from the occasional defence of an accused person, who had in such cases to pay a fee in advance, unless his friends would do this for him, this unfortunate jurist had practically no work to do, and to judge by his general attitude, already regretted that he had ever come to Sitka.

In the only case of importance which was at this time in his hands he obtained by purchase an old document according to which the holder was entitled to claim a large part of the land on which the town of Sitka stood, as his property.

The document in question which, if it were authentic, was by no means dear at the price of 500 dollars paid by the lawyer to a Jewish dealer, originated with the Aleutian who sixty years ago in Baranoff's time was the sole survivor of the Indian attack, and as such received the grant of the property from the Russian officials. From that time the documents had passed through various hands and the present owner was determined to enforce his rights. I never heard if he succeeded in doing so.

Claims of this kind on real property are by no means uncommon in America, and even at the present time there are persons still living, descendants of the first settlers, who claim whole counties with towns, villages and estates, basing their claims on the rights of their ancestors who a hundred years ago and more had settled in these districts when still undeveloped. At that time the boundaries of real estates were not so clearly defined as they are to-day, and each squatter regarded as his own property everything that was not claimed by his neighbour, who often lived many miles away.

One evening we had been talking for a long time by the bright light of the full moon about that valuable deed of gift and I had been lying down for perhaps an hour, when there was a knock at the door. Half-dressed as I was, I cautiously opened the shuttered window by the door and asked who was there and what he wanted so late at night. A young Russian whom I remembered having seen occasionally in the company of the Russian workmen answered in an appalling jargon of English, German and Russian that I was wanted in the house of a Russian captain to take a picture.

Believing the whole matter to be a bad joke I slammed the window, whereupon the Russian went off quietly. Next day the affair was explained. During the night a child had died at the house of a Russian captain who was away on his ship, and as the child was his favourite one, the bereaved mother wanted to have a portrait made immediately after death for her absent husband and had sent for me as she thought I was a professional portrait-painter. I expressed my thanks suitably for such a commission, but excused myself by explaining that I was a landscape painter and did not undertake portraits and in this way I escaped applications for the latter. On the other hand I received many requests that I would allow my sketches of Sitka to be published, and the Mayor of Sitka was willing to certify to the correctness of the sketches which I had made on the spot in order that they might appear in the New York illustrated papers, but I declined the offer with thanks.

During the long and mostly rainy days which followed on the short summer, when the time dragged drearily on, people were glad if the monotony of life was interrupted by anything unusual. Sometimes idle soldiers, in order to pass the time, set a barn on fire. Sometimes a drunken sailor in his excitement challenged the whole male population of the town to a fight. There was a remarkabl person named Rapaport, a German Polish Jew by origin, who spent the greater part of his life in prison and as soon as he came out was again accused. Rapaport was the recognised scapegoat of the whole settlement; whenever anything happened—theft, arson, assault, whatever it might be—he was believed to be the criminal or at any rate to have had a hand in the crime. On one occasion he had a very bad time. He had won heavily when playing cards with three sailors, who accused him, rightly or wrongly, of cheating and assaulted the poor fellow so violently with sticks and knives that next morning he was picked up for dead. Only after long efforts was he brought to. Nothing much happened to the sailors and only one was imprisoned because he was recognised as a deserter. But Rapaport as a result of his injuries was a real picture of misery and had to endure much scoffing.

Almost at the same time in one of the Russian workmen's dwellings a coloured woman was murdered; a young negro who had got into a similar house on amorous intent was thrown out of the window by the enraged husband in defence of his hearth and home; and a half-breed woman, the mother of several young children, eloped with the captain of a coasting vessel.

These incidents constituted the *chronique scandaleuse* of Sitka in a little less than a week, and these are actual facts. Rumours of other events were going about during this same period amongst the idle settlers, but they are not included.

SITKA—XIV.

An event in the neighbouring Indian village with its far-reaching effects threw the quixotic experiences of a Rapaport into the shade.

" Prince Nicholas," an old man of sixty years of age (according to his own statement) who was regarded by the Sitka Indians as their chief and was recognised as such by

234

the Russian officials, had ended his days. For some time past the medicine men of three different tribes had been performing their incantations by his couch, but it was all of no avail. Nicholas became weaker and weaker and after the last resource, namely, the hot springs some 30 miles from Sitka, had been tried without success the old chief's superstitious subjects gave up all hope of his recovery, and without seeking help from the white men the old warrior took to his bed, hovered for a few days between life and death, and at last passed away with true Indian fortitude, an example to his tribesmen.

We received the first news of the old chieftain's death from Russian priests ; for the dead man, like most of the Indians living at Sitka, had been baptised in the way I have previously described and received into the Russian Church.

Either from some real religious belief or because they hoped to obtain some gifts from the church the surviving members of his family notified his death to the priests, who made arrangements for the funeral to be carried out with fitting ceremony.

The day after his death I went to the chief's house, a roomy building made of boards, at the entrance to the Indian village. It differed from the other huts only by its greater size and by the flag flying at half-mast which could be seen from a distance and indicated the death of some important person.

Apparently most of the Indians were keeping in their own huts, for only a few were to be seen ; without exception they were all painted black and the women had their hair cut short. In the chief's house his relatives were crouching over separate little fires at the sides.

In the back of the hut there was a catafalque covered with a black cloth which contained the body of the deceased, and at the head were two lighted wax candles. A general's cocked hat and a Russian sword were laid on the coffin together with some ornaments, chiefly beads and brass chains. At the foot of the catafalque knelt a Russian acolyte in white surplice, who was saying the Prayers for the Dead. New blankets were spread out all around and guns and hunting and fishing tackle, no doubt the property of the deceased chief, were laid out on them ; even his favourite canoe was exhibited—it would never be used again as it must be kept as a memorial. The hut was quite full of incense which the acolyte burned anew from time to time—the whole scene seemed quite unreal. Is it possible to imagine any greater contrast than Greek Catholic funeral rites taking place in the house of an Indian whose conversion was only superficial and whose idols and amulets were hanging on the walls of the hut in evidence of his heathen beliefs ?

The news of the death of the Sitka chief must have spread with great rapidity to the friendly tribes in the neighbourhood, for on the next day but one a great deal of excitement was noticeable in the village. From early morning until dusk there appeared a large number of strange canoes filled with deputations of Indians from the Tacon, Chilcaht, Hennega and all the other tribes friendly to the Sitka Indians, who had come to take part in the ceremonies connected with the death of the former chief and the election of his successor.

As they were supplied by the American officials with liberal rations of the much coveted " fire-water " things soon became very lively in the Indian camp, and when on the afternoon of the same day I happened to be at the harbour, which was not far from the camp, I heard a most remarkable noise of cymbals, drums and fifes. Although some of my friends advised me not to go near the Indians, who would all be more or less worked up, I could not resist the temptation to try and see how the savages conducted their ceremonies and so I went down to the camp in company with one other white man—we had our revolvers ready for any emergency. The sentry on the bastion, though he did not attempt to prevent us from going out, warned us not to mingle with the excited natives as the many Indians who had come from elsewhere could not be relied on ; but now that we had started we were ashamed to go back without having seen something.

In front of the chief's house there was a dense throng of Indians gesticulating wildly and just making way for a medicine man who was making a dreadful din by rattling his medicine box. After this the crowd of Indians pressed through the low door by which only one person could enter at a time, stooping as he went. We thought this was a favourable opportunity and although we encountered many a hostile glance from the lynx-eyed natives, we managed to get into the hut along with the crowd before the little door was shut. When, however, we did get in we regretted that we had gone so far, and we reluctantly realised how very difficult it would be to get out again should any unpleasantness occur. If the Indians wanted to do us any harm it would be very easy for them. The whole interior of the roomy hut was packed full of natives who all stood on a gradual slope to the exit, forming a strange spectacle, and showed their approval by making animal-like cries and their disapproval by yelling and stamping.

At the back of the hut near the body, which to-day was not surrounded by Christian emblems, but was simply covered with skins and blankets, a kind of platform had been erected a few feet above the ground. On it there was an Indian dressed in skins, with a hideous mask over his face, and his head decked with feathers, who executed a series of the wildest leaps and bounds. This he did at first slowly, then more and more rapidly rising to a frenzy that bordered on madness until the poor wretch at last sank down exhausted and was carried away by his comrades who were prepared for this to happen. The whole performance was accompanied by an orchestra of Indian cymbals, fifes and clappers, the noise of which grew louder and louder as the dancing quickened until when the half-maddened performer collapsed it suddenly stopped with a deafening crash, whereon the spectators broke out into a tremendous noise of their own.

If one of the candidates for the chieftainship (for that was what the performance appeared to be) were carried away unconscious another was immediately ready to go on with the interrupted performance. Each tried to excel the others in his devil dance ; the longer a performer could hold out and the greater the applause, the better prospect had he probably of being chosen as chief.

After we had seen no fewer than three candidates dance till they were half-dead we began to think seriously of getting out, for the whole scene in the semi-darkness of the hut, which had only the poor light from two fires, the faces of the Indians which though mostly painted black were reddened by the fire light, the horrible noise and the atmosphere, which was thick with the smoke and the odour of such a crowd of natives, made our stay there a real torture. In order not to attract the attention of the Indians we had kept as much as possible in the shadow of the walls, but that meant that we were forced by the press of the natives away from the door towards the side and did not see how we could get out, for several times when we attempted to push our way through we were driven violently back by some broad-shouldered Indian.

In this uncertainty we had a piece of good fortune for I noticed near me the old medicine man whose acquaintance I had made through his traffic with the collector of curios. I tapped him cautiously on the shoulder and made him understand that I wanted to get to the door. The wily old man pretended at first that he did not understand me, but a roll of tobacco, which my companion fortunately had with him and which I pressed unobtrusively into the Indian's hand, had the desired effect. He stood near us and signed to us to keep close to him and without taking any notice of the objections and occasional shoves of unfriendly Indians, the skilful old man manœuvred us quickly towards the door. We waited until some other Indians went out and then made our way through the open door into the fresh air, breathing freely when we saw the clear sky over us once more and had no half-drunken natives near us.

For three days the dead chief lay in state in his house, then the solemn burial was to take place ; this the pro-selytising Russian clergy had been able to arrange in such a way as to give the dead chief Christian burial, although the Indians from other tribes who were not friendly to the Russian Church had strongly opposed it. The dull and rainy day which was early heralded by the bell from the Russian church was a fitting one for the sad ceremony which was to take place in honour of the deceased. The Russian priests hastened earlier still to the church in which the body of old Nicholas was to be blessed and the whole Russian population was out in its Sunday raiment to attend the ceremony.

On the stroke of eleven the funeral procession started from the Indian camp. At its head there walked with military bearing the solitary town policeman, accompanied by three bandsmen who played a funeral march. Behind these, borne by six Indians, came the coffin with the hat and sword of the dead chieftain on it. The pall-bearers, relatives of the chief dressed in European clothes, followed close behind the coffin and some twenty Indians, mostly women, brought up the rear of the simple procession. The great majority of the Sitka Indians and all the men of the other tribes had apparently stayed away.

On entering the church, which was quickly filled with Russians, the coffin was set down and a Russian " Pope " gave a short address in which he set out the merits of the dead chief and at the end to show that his sins were forgiven he made the sign of the cross over him. A prayer repeated by the kneeling congregation ended the service, during which the Russians present—all without exception—held lighted wax candles and a number of choir boys continually burnt incense.

The six Indian bearers, who had knelt throughout the service, took the coffin again on their shoulders and the burial procession, accompanied now by three priests and a large number of Russians, moved towards the burial place, which lay beyond the fortifications and behind the Indian camp.

The place was reached amid torrents of rain, and the mourners assembled amidst the burial huts that held the ashes of the chieftain's subjects. Here a very deep grave had been dug and after a short prayer the coffin was let down into it. The American flag, which had hitherto covered the coffin, was drawn away, but in its place the deceased's umbrella and walking stick were laid there. Some matting was put on next, then food and a bottle of wine, and finally everything was covered with an old sail. Amidst the lamentations of the Indian women who served as professional mourners the grave was filled up, and the bystanders went away in silence.

I am bound to say that I was not very favourably impressed with the whole proceeding, and I was actually glad to hear from a Russian, who was well acquainted with Indian conditions, that the funeral ceremony was merely a pretence intended to uphold the dignity of the church amongst the natives, and that after a few hours the latter would take up the body of the chief and conduct the funeral in their own way.

This statement explained the absence of the uncivilised Indian, from the Christian ceremony and, as foreseen, the mortal remains of old Nicholas did not rest for long in the cold earth and the great pieces of timber which the natives had collected denoted that the funeral would, as usual, be completed by burning the body.

Whilst we were eagerly watching the movements of the Indians from a distance (a near approach was prevented by a native who was stationed as a sentry) an extraordinary event occurred.

Suddenly an Indian youth broke out of the undergrowth which reached up to the palisade ; at the same instant a shot rang out behind him and a second one followed. Like a hunted deer the youth ran along the palisade towards the little sallyport, which he reached uninjured though a third shot struck it at that moment close above his head. But the guard had now taken him in and the door was closed, and the poor fellow was in safety, though he fell senseless from the strain.

Through an interpreter we learned what had happened. It appeared that, according to the custom of the Sitka Indians—which however was kept secret lest the white men should intervene—when an important Indian died a slave was sacrificed to appease the evil spirits, who amongst these natives seemed to play a more important part than the good spirits. This youth, barely fifteen years old, had been taken prisoner in a war with the Kaigh Indians and consequently made a slave; now he had been chosen as the victim and was about to be sacrificed when he had cleverly eluded the vigilance of his guards and made a successful attempt to escape in order to put himself under the protection of the white men. Whatever happened he was safe there, but the Indians were greatly enraged at the escape of their intended victim and prepared quite openly to revolt.

As if at a command the natives who during the day had been wandering about a good deal inside the palisade suddenly vanished. The Indian market, usually so busy, was absolutely deserted and an eerie silence reigned in the settlement. The commander of the American troops realised immediately what the behaviour of the natives meant and prepared to repel them vigorously if they should take the offensive. The guards were strengthened, two 12-pounders were directed against the Indian camp, and a strict watch was kept throughout the night.

At dawn next day from 600-800 Indians, all armed with guns, were to be seen assembled on the shore; and one of them waved a small piece of white sail-cloth as a sign that they wished for a parley. In order to avoid a conflict the American general agreed to receive their proposals. The determined attitude of the garrison had apparently already impressed them, for they were willing to make a compromise. Their actual offer was to give up to the American commander four male Indian slaves if he would

241

return the youth who was under his protection but in their view had been condemned to death.

Of course the general rejected this proposal firmly, and at the same time gave them twenty-four hours in which to make complete submission. During that time a gun-boat which was lying opposite the Indian village had orders not to allow any canoe to pass to or from the shore.

Either because of this measure which struck the Indians in their most vulnerable spot, as they earned their livelihood entirely by means of their canoes, or because wiser counsels prevailed, anyhow when the time allowed them had

MILITARY H.Q., SITKA, A.T.   E.T. 1868

expired they sent a deputation which abandoned the demand for the surrender of the boy and asked for peace and an amnesty. This was readily granted, for the white population would have suffered severely from a dispute with the Indians and the lack of the game and fish which the natives brought to market was already beginning to make itself felt.

Unfortunately the dispute did not pass off without bloodshed. During the blockade by sea a canoe manned by Indians contravened the prohibition by setting out from the shore; the American sentries fired on it, killing one and wounding two of the crew. This unfortunate incident, perhaps due to a misunderstanding, had an unhappy result when shortly afterwards two white men who had started before this on an expedition to the Chatham Straits, about thirty miles from Sitka, for barter with the

242

Indians, met a relative of the native who had been killed. He, as it appeared later, had sworn to avenge the death of his kinsman on the first white man he met, and so he killed one of the traders. The other escaped with great difficulty and hardship and brought the news to Sitka. Thus an entirely innocent person had lost his life. I do not know if the murderer was ever brought to justice. Nor do I know what became of the fugitive slave. The American commandant intended to return him to his tribe, the Kaigh Indians, when opportunity offered, since if he remained near the Sitkas he might have fallen a secret victim to their fanaticism.

SITKA—XVI.

Owing to the excitement in Sitka caused by these events in the Indian encampment the arrival of two ships, which would have been of great interest in ordinary times, passed almost unnoticed.

One of them was the warship *Saginaw*, which for the second time had visited the scene of the wreck of the *Growler* in order to investigate that catastrophe, and on this occasion brought back with it conclusive evidence that the crew of the schooner had been slain, when they landed, by the piratical natives. A number of Hyder Indians were prisoners on board the warship and were to be brought for trial before the general in command. In course of the investigations it had already been proved that practically the whole cargo of the *Growler* had been salvaged by the Indians and part of it had been sold to other tribes ; in fact, a mass of goods and provisions had been found in the camps of the Cape Chacoum and Georgina Indians which must have come from the ill-fated ship. A compass and sextant and some other nautical instruments which were of course of no value to the natives, had been recovered from the Indians by the captain of the war-ship. One of the life-boats of the *Growler* in an absolutely seaworthy state was found in a camp, and obviously, if the crew of the wrecked vessel had been able to save themselves in it, they would not have been attacked by the Indians.

Besides this an Indian squaw who had been brought by the warship as a witness seemed to have declared when she was drunk that the schooner had run aground near the coast during a violent storm ; that the crew had tried to reach the shore in their boats but had been received with gun-fire from the natives and been driven back. Some were drowned in the breakers and the few who managed to get ashore were killed by the Indians.

It is difficult to say whether this story was entirely reliable, but the general opinion was that the squaw had told the truth while she was half-stupefied even though, when being examined later, she tried to contradict her previous statement.

The second ship which entered the harbour at almost the same time was a two-masted sailing-ship, the schooner *Black Diamond*, which came from the Nanaimo mines near Victoria with a cargo of coal. This vessel had been fourteen days on the way, having come by the so-called Outer Passage westward of Vancouver and Queen Charlotte Islands. I at once got into communication with the captain in order to ascertain if the ship brought any news from California and heard from him nothing new except, what was very important for me, that he proposed to start on the return journey to Victoria in eight days. He was not fitted out for carrying passengers but nevertheless offered to make room for me if I was disposed to travel with him. Henceforth I thought of nothing else than of finishing my business as quickly as possible and not to let slip this opportunity. In consequence of my constant urging I had already received a large amount of important evidence from my informant, but it seemed to me that he was intentionally delaying matters and so, being driven to extremes, I had recourse to threats and gave him to understand that he had delivered himself into my hands by the evidence which he had already supplied, and now it rested with him to decide whether I should give him the promised reward or expose him to his fellow countrymen as a spy and a traitor.

There was a violent scene, but where entreaties failed threats were successful, and much as he hated me his cupidity drove him at last to complete what he had undertaken. I then obtained information which could not possibly be controverted, not only as to the earlier trickery of the officials in selling dishonestly to third persons part of the sealskins to which my firm was entitled and putting the proceeds in their own pockets, but also as to the intention of these unscrupulous individuals to sell a large part of this year's catch at high prices to American dealers and thereby defraud my firm, which, according to the contract, was entitled to the whole catch.

The various pieces of evidence which had been contained in the archives of the Company, I had carefully arranged in order, with the help of my house-mate, and when armed with this document I sent for the last time for my informant, I am bound to confess that I felt somewhat nervous at being alone with this shifty fellow in my lonely dwelling on the shore. I read the document to him slowly and carefully and as I had adhered very closely to his verbal and written statements there was nothing to which he could object seriously. But when I wanted him to come with me to the Town Hall in order to complete his statement by an affidavit made in the presence of the Mayor, the coward tried to raise new difficulties and to excuse himself by saying that his signature on such a document would stamp him for ever as a criminal in the eyes of the Russian Company.

I explained curtly that even if he did not do what I now wanted he had put himself in my power, but that should there be any legal proceedings I would protect him as much as possible and only reveal his name as a last resort. After prolonged hesitation he at last accompanied me to the registry. It was a usual custom when statements were sworn to, to read the declaration out loud before the oath was administered. I was well aware of that, and also that publicity of this kind would betray to the inquisitive officials not only the name of my informant but also the whole character of my mission.

To avoid both these difficulties I had chosen a time when the official who administered oaths was particularly busy. I laid the complete documents before him with as little show of concern as possible. My plan succeeded. Without even looking at the statement the official administered the short oath to my witness. The old and dirty Bible which had been touched by so many lying lips was kissed and the document was signed. He himself added his own name and the official seal and both of these I then had certified by the commanding general, who at the time was taking statements through two interpreters from a number of Hyder Indians, and with a light heart and the important documents in my pocket I left the Government building and handed over to my witness the gold dollars which were the price of his treachery.

All this took place on the day before the *Black Diamond* was to sail. My acquaintances, to whom I had said nothing as to my intention of going back on that ship and who remembered only too clearly the determination which I had formally avowed never again to travel by a sailing-vessel, could, of course, not understand what it was that had suddenly induced me to rush off on a sailing-ship which was not fitted up for passengers.

I packed my goods that same evening and sent them on board and very early next morning I went on the ship accompanied by one of my house-mates. The absence of wind compelled the captain to remain at anchor some hours longer and during that time I made a mental picture of the homely town with its Russian cupolas and spires, the picturesquely-situated Indian camp, and the mountain ranges in the background.

The sun rose full over the nearest mountain tops, the deep blue sea was smooth as a mirror, the white sailing-ships in the harbour lay asleep in the still water, light columns of smoke rose from the Indian huts and a few canoes were putting out from the shore.

Soon the melancholy peal from the Cathedral began the summons to early Mass and the ship showed signs of life. The deck had to be washed and the mast and the yards rubbed down. Then the town began to wake up ; many of my acquaintances came to say good-bye. About 9 o'clock a breeze sprang up, the anchor was weighed, the wind caught the sails, there was a loud greeting from the shore, hats and handkerchiefs were waved and amidst loud cheers our vessel glided slowly towards the mouth of the bay.

It was not altogether without regret that I looked back on that place which to-day lay so peacefully in the golden sunlight and I should be hardly likely ever to see again. Anxious as I had been during my six weeks' stay to get away from the town, my departure now caused me a pang, and with the deepest sympathy I thought of the many good fellows whom I, coming as a stranger there, had made my friends and who were condemned to lead, heaven only knows how long, a life full of hardship in that barren spot shut off from the rest of the world.

ON BOARD THE "BLACK DIAMOND"—I.

Whilst our ship was tacking against the light breeze and making its way cautiously between the many rocky islands, we met at a considerable distance from Sitka many canoes with Indians engaged in fishing who, with their conical rush hats as their only clothing, pressed round the ship and offered to sell us fish.

" Halibut " (a kind of perch), " haju halibut " (large halibut), was shouted on all sides and it was very difficult for our steersman to avoid running down the poor devils, who crowded round the bows and held on to every rope that hung down. At last we shook them all off. Mount Edgcumbe with its Vesuvius-like outlines lay almost to our right, apparently at no great distance, and as we steered to the south the land soon lay behind us in a blue mist.

SITKA. 1868.

About 6 o'clock in the evening we were on the open sea with a good north-west wind blowing, and I began to take notice of my fellow-travellers.

The crew of our ship consisted of the Scotch captain, whose personality and seamanship I cannot sufficiently praise, the steersman called " Ned " (a seaman of the good old English type in the prime of life) and two sailors, one of whom had to serve at the same time as cook, and a young Indian youth, a Stikeen.

Besides the crew there were as passengers five members of the unsuccessful gold prospecting party ; they were rough-looking fellows somewhat of the adventurer class. These were berthed with the sailors in the forecastle and had to supply their own provisions, whilst I shared with the captain and steersman a small cabin erected on the quarter-deck. This was, as a matter of fact, provided with only two bunks, but as the captain and the steersman shared the night watch they also had in turn one of the bunks while I made myself comfortable in the other.

Even though I had again to live in very rough company the conduct of the captain and the steersman inspired me with such complete confidence from the first, that I had not the least hesitation in putting myself in their hands.

Moreover I had the careless and slipshod navigation of the *Ocean Queen* so constantly in my mind that I could not but be very pleased with the seaman-like order that was maintained on this ship, which apparently was due to the supervision and ability of the captain.

With conscientious regularity two men took the watch on deck and kept at their posts until relieved by two others at the end of four hours. The captain or steersman was always one of the watch and often when I was lying peacefully in my bunk I heard the alert captain get up to see if all was well.

Our ship had originally been designed as a tug for the carriage of coal between the Nanaimo mines and the town of Victoria, and as on this passage it had to make use of more or less narrow channels its design was particularly long and narrow. It was only a comparatively short time previous that the mines administration had taken over the ship, provided it with two masts and assigned it to sea transport. Captain MacCulloch, who had formerly been in command of a steamer in the service of the Company which had been wrecked, was given the command of the newly-fitted-out schooner and was now making his third journey to and from Sitka.

It will be readily understood that he was not particularly pleased at the transfer from the command of a steamer to that of a sailing-vessel, but he appeared to regard this as a kind of punishment for the accident which was in no way his fault, and he adapted himself to the change as well as he could. He was not particularly impressed by the sea-worthiness of the *Black Diamond* since, as he explained to me in the course of conversation, the ship in proportion to its size and length was too narrow and consequently was in danger of being capsized if struck broadside and so, he commented with a sailor's coolness, he must keep the ship as much as possible before the wind and hope for the best.

This conversation caused me some apprehension when I remembered that the vessel, though 81 feet long and 7 in depth, was only 17 feet broad and that we were in the North Pacific which was often very dangerous. Her carrying capacity was 63 tons but we were actually sailing only in ballast. Still the weather on that first evening gave promise of remaining fine and at any rate I had begun the journey and I must put up with whatever fate had in store.

I have so far not spoken of the meals which I took in the cabin in the company of the captain or steersman. They consisted of simple but wholesome and sustaining food and were quite excellent. We had regularly break-fast, dinner and supper with good tea and I could not fail to draw a comparison between this and our old mode of life on the *Ocean Queen*—the thought of what we had undergone there made me shudder.

My first night on board the *Black Diamond* was never-theless not undisturbed. I had only been lying down for a short time and had blown out the lamp when I felt something crawling over my face and hands. I sprang up in dismay, got a light and to my horror saw that my whole body was covered with black beetles which, as soon as they saw the light, disappeared in the wainscotting of the cabin. So long as I kept the lamp burning these vermin left me alone, but as soon as I put it out they appeared again *en masse* and finally I was compelled to keep a light burning all night, although the captain assured me that this kind of beetle was quite harmless. I don't know if there were any other kinds of creatures and I prefer to keep silent on the point.

The next two days followed each other almost without incident; there was no land in sight, only sea and sky. The north-west wind, usually light, carried us forward slowly but surely.

When one is on the open sea one certainly feels drawn to one's fellow passengers who are the only possible company and even when, as in the present case, they were not very attractive they were better than no company at all, and so I made an effort to get into conversation with the rough-looking gold prospectors. At first they were sulky and reticent, probably because they were not sure whether I wanted to listen to them simply out of curiosity and not because I was really interested. I treated them, however, quite frankly and by a few neighbourly acts soon brought them to the point of talking quite openly and, strange as it may sound, in the course of our thirteen days' voyage we developed such friendly relations that these men who seemed so rough and hardened would scarcely refuse me anything and fell in with all that I suggested.

There were some interesting personalities, amongst them particularly the leader of the party—who had been in command of the *Louisa Downes*. This Wilmer, a one-eyed, strongly-built person, was a man of a type that is only to be found amongst the adventurous population of the West Coast. Sometimes favoured by fortune, sometimes deserted by it, this fellow who was now over fifty, had passed through all the stages of Californian adventure. In his youth he had served in Mexico in the United States army; after the campaign was over he went to the Mormon City at Salt Lake and then had to guide the caravans of emigrants over the Sierra Nevada to California. At that time the whole district was swarming with hostile Indians. After many a hard fight with the marauding natives, in one of which he owed the loss of his eye to a hostile arrow, the service became too strenuous. Moreover he had saved some money and resolved to use it to go to the gold-mines of California which were then so flourishing. Here he had the same experience as the majority of those who were fired by the gold-fever. He was often the owner of considerable property but could never bring himself to give up this kind of life, and then lost all he had got together with so much toil.

Whenever there was a rumour of a fresh discovery of gold anywhere Henry Wilmer was certain to be one of the foremost amongst the adventurers who rushed to the spot, and only too often the over-hasty hunt for gold ended in disappointment. Thus he had let himself be drawn into the ill-fated expedition to the Stikeen River, and now found himself with the pitiable remnant of what had once been a substantial property on the way to Oregon to commence life over again.

It appeared that Wilmer was the only one of the prospectors that had come to Sitka who had managed to save something from the almost utter ruin of the expedition, and he had given it all up in order to secure the return of at any rate four of his companions. The latter were evidently in great poverty and bore all the marks of bitter disappointment.

We were not to complete our journey, without a storm for on the evening of the fourth day dark clouds heralded rough weather during the night and our steersman felt these weather signs confirmed by rheumatism in the left arm, which since he had been bitten by a poisonous snake in East India had become a reliable barometer.

Immediately all possible precautions were taken. The deck was cleared, the sails furled and two men ordered to take the rudder. I felt rather sea-sick and at dusk retired to the cabin after a searching glance at the sea which was as black as ink.

The captain and steersman were both on deck and I was alone in the cabin. I may have been lying awake for about two hours, the atmosphere was heavy and stifling, and I could hear the roaring of the wind through the open companion. At first I heard the sound of the wind only over the water, then suddenly it began to whistle in the sails and rigging. Quick and heavy steps sounded on the deck over my head and then the storm broke out. Our poor little ship was tossed mercilessly about—a more appalling sight it was impossible to imagine. The tempest sighed in high shrill tones through the spars, sometimes moaning lightly, sometimes raging furiously. Then the rain pelted on the deck, lightning flashed and lit up the cabin with glaring light and was followed by rolling thunder amid which I could hear from time to time the orders of the captain and the " Aye, aye " of the seamen. Now the sea began to swell and I could feel our little ship rise and fall ; how she creaked and groaned as the powerful strain of the rudder turned her against the waves, and how she trembled in every limb when a specially-powerful wave swept over her. My lantern had long since been blown out, so, crawling on all fours, in the darkness I made my way to the ship's ladder which led to the companion and cautiously put my head out.

I shall never forget the sight. The night was pitch dark and so was the sea except where the white foam showed the breaking of the ceaseless waves. Our ship was running like a hunted beast ; the foam of the waves combined with the torrential rain to soak me to the skin in a few minutes. As if from the clouds above I heard the cries of the seamen who were up in the yards. At first I could not see them, but then there was a glaring flash of lightning and by its light I could make out three men up on the spars struggling with a sail that had broken loose and seemed every moment, as they strove to master it as if it, would hurl them into the sea.

I had seen enough—shivering with cold I climbed back into my bunk and prayed for those poor fellows who in such a deadly struggle were exposed to the rage of the elements. In that hour I did not think of myself, for I felt so insignificant and helpless in comparison with those heroic men that I forgot everything else.

It was only after two hours' desperate battle that they mastered the storm and it was midnight before the captain came into the cabin for a few minutes to get a drink. Without thinking of sleep that conscientious man stayed on deck the whole night, encouraging his men and himself lending a hand when they hesitated.

The next morning when I came on deck the sky was free of clouds, there was hardly any wind, and only the sea which was still running strong showed how violent the storm had been during the night.

The ship was not seriously damaged ; true there were many gaps in the bulwarks caused by the violent sea, our sails were badly tattered, but that damage could all be easily repaired and in a short time was made good by the industry of the sailors. Some water had got into the hold but two hours' pumping sufficed to force it all out.

Then the captain called his men together on the afterdeck and in simple words praised their courage and endurance during the night and ordered extra rations to be served out. The gold prospectors with Wilmer at their head, who seemed to be quite at home on the sea, also got their share since, as the captain told me, they had placed themselves at his disposal when the storm broke out and had done particularly good service in taking in the sails.

I could not refrain from comparing my sensations during this storm with my feelings during the many dangers we underwent on board the *Ocean Queen*. It may be that our present ship was never in such peril as our former one, but in any event during the past night I never lost heart for I knew that everything in human power was being done to save us, and that thought alone inspired me with unshaken courage and confidence, whereas in the hours of danger on board the *Ocean Queen* I felt our condition to be so desperate that I gave myself up to what can only be called the most arrant fatalism.

ON BOARD THE " BLACK DIAMOND "—II.

After the storm there was an absence of wind for days and with it a period of monotony such as can be experienced only on sailing-ships.

It is pleasant enough when the slender ship with, outspread sails, cuts through the waves and glides merrily along like a swan. Then the log is cast out in order to measure the speed of the ship, at one time a sail is furled, at another a rope is hauled to change the yards, and all goes well. In such conditions it is much more pleasant to be on a sailing-vessel than on a steamer, for the movement of the former is quieter, more graceful and comfortable and more natural. The boat rises and falls with the waves and therefore causes much less sea-sickness than the strong motion and constant shaking of a steamer.

But it is quite different when a sailing-ship is becalmed. The general good humour disappears, the captain and crew become irritable ; the little work to be done seems too much, and the crew lie about idly on the fore-deck. Only those who have experienced a calm can realise what it means when, day after day, the boundless sea remains the same, unruffled by any breath of wind, when the captain scans the heavens in every direction but sees not the slightest trace of wind—even a contrary wind would be welcome as some progress, however slow, could be made by tacking. He calls, he whistles for a wind in the customary sailor fashion but it does not come. The sails hang limp and flap from one side to another as the ship sways about— even the steersman is useless since the helm does not answer when there is no breeze, and he can scarcely hold the ship to her course. This was our lot now and, though this may seem a mere idle boast, even a storm would have been more welcome to us than this monotonous death-like stillness.

Certainly at first we tried to pass the time with tales of our adventures, but when people are together all day long subjects of conversation give out at last and had it not been that now and then the impudent head of a seal emerged from the water or one of those great sea-birds, called albatrosses, came in sight we could scarcely have endured it. Of course the seals were fired at immediately, but the intelligent creatures were so quick in their movement, and seemed to watch our actions so closely, that they always dived before we could take aim at them and reappeared in a quite different place.

The hunt for the sea-birds was more successful. With the help of a piece of bacon fastened to a cord, which we threw out and on which they cast themselves voraciously, we pulled a number of these creatures on board and were greatly amused by their comical behaviour. They weigh about 30 lbs. each and are the size of a full-grown swan, are usually striped black and white and have remarkably long and narrow wings. The strength of these wings is amazing and one of the sailors had his arm quite lamed through getting in the way of the angry, struggling birds. The helpless movements of the terrified creatures on the deck was an extraordinary sight as they rolled from one side to another and shuffled laboriously forward, and their wings seemed to be so constructed that they could not rise directly from the ground, but had to mount on to something higher before they could take flight. There is an old tradition amongst sailors that the albatross brings luck to a ship and that to kill one brings misfortune, and so after keeping them prisoners for a short time we set them free again. Another thing that helped to pass the time was the occasional appearance some distance away of whales, which are to be seen fairly often on this coast. They were usually brought to our notice by an upright jet of water and when we looked more closely we could clearly distinguish the black, ungainly bulk of these giant denizens of the deep. There were often three or four of them together and they seemed to be swimming round carelessly, not troubling in the least about us.

On the fourth day of the calm, when there was still no sign of a change in the weather, the captain called us together and told us that our situation was beginning to cause him some anxiety. According to his reckoning we were about 400 miles from our starting-point, that is, scarcely half-way between Sitka and Victoria and therefore had a long stretch still before us, but our water supply was only enough for six more days and if no wind sprang up within the next twenty-four hours we must put ourselves on short rations. In fact, on the following day only a small amount of water was measured out to us which we had to conserve as much as possible. For washing purposes, of course, we could now only use sea-water, which was by no means good for the skin and could be used only with a special kind of salt-water soap.

The crew and passengers put up with the new regulation without complaint, as we realised that our lives might depend on its observance. As I had always been accustomed to an unlimited use of fresh water I suffered the most from this restriction, and it was really touching to see how the gold-diggers, who seemed so rough and hardened, readily gave up part of their own ration in order that I might not suffer any deprivation. Fortunately I had brought some extra provisions on board at Sitka and I distributed part of these to my fellow-travellers in return for their kindness.

At last towards evening on the fifth day of the calm we noticed a light breath of wind stirring the water; it came nearer and nearer and finally our sails began to fill out. Gradually the breeze increased and at dusk we moved south-eastwards at about five miles an hour.

For two days we made slow but steady progress in this way and our spirits began to rise. The captain alone seemed rather uneasy. I took him aside and asked what it was that was troubling him when all was going on so well. He told me straightforwardly that he must have made a mistake in his reckoning; according to his calculations we ought to have reached the coast of Vancouver long before this, but there was no sign of it. Unfortunately he had only a sextant and no chronometer and consequently could only determine our latitude. According to his last observation we were in the latitude of Vancouver, but without a chronometer it was totally impossible for him to determine the longitude. Therefore, so far as he could estimate, we were just as likely to be off the Chinese as the American coast—a pleasant outlook for us with a short supply of water As appeared later we had in fact been carried by the ocean-currents some hundreds of miles away from the coast and driven right out of our proper course, for we sailed for three whole days with a strong westerly wind direct towards the east before, on the evening of the twelfth day after our departure from Sitka, shortly before sunset, we saw the heights of Vancouver and soon after, the rays from the lighthouse on Cape Flattery. As darkness fell thick clouds of mist swept out towards us from the land and soon we were enveloped in thicker and thicker fog which dripped cold and damp upon the deck.

It was an uncomfortable night and none of us slept much. I lay in my bunk and saw the captain come down from time to time, bend over the chart and with compass and parallels make his reckoning. Apparently the sudden descent of the fog had made him uncertain as to the position of the land for I heard him several times order the ship's direction to be changed. Great care was certainly necessary. Not only were we dangerously near to the coasts of Vancouver with their outlying reefs—and could not tell where the strong cross-currents might drive us—but we were in the course of the large number of steamers and sailing-ships which went in and out of the Fuca Straits and there might be a collision in the thick fog. So at night both at bow and stern a sharp watch was kept and we listened carefully for the noise of the breakers along the coast or the sound of a ship's approach.

The night passed without accident and when next morning the sun dispelled the heavy mist, to our surprise and delight we saw about a quarter of a mile away Cape Flattery lighthouse, which stands on a steep bare promontory and marks the entrance to the channel. With a light-westerly breeze we sailed up the sound and greeted cheerily a number of ships which passed us loaded with timber. During the whole of our journey these were always the first signs that a harbour was at hand. At 4 o'clock in the afternoon we reached Sook Bay, about 15 miles from Victoria, and were confident that we should be able to make the harbour before dark; but the breeze suddenly died away and we had to undergo another test of our patience which was not free from danger.

The Fuca Straits are swept by unusually strong currents, chiefly caused by the tide streaming in and out between numerous islands. Safe enough as the channel is for steamers in calm weather it often becomes dangerous for sailing-vessels which are becalmed. As they do not then answer their helms, these craft are easily driven by the cross-currents on to the coast and wrecked on the rocks by which it is studded. In just this way the ship on which our captain had come for the first time to the West Coast, a stately three-master had been wrecked almost on this spot in calm weather and so lost close to harbour when it had accomplished in safety a voyage half round the world.

We ourselves narrowly escaped a similar fate, for to our dismay we realised that our ship had been caught in the current and was rapidly nearing the dangerous reefs. Never had we longed so eagerly for a rescuing breeze than we did at that moment, and strangely enough we saw at that instant a ripple on the surface of the water and our ship answering again to the helm we passed the dangerous spot. But the wind was so light, and it died away so often, that we made scarcely three miles an hour and it was not until about 11 o'clock that we entered the harbour of Victoria. To our left and right we saw in the darkness the ghostly outlines of two steamers and without being hailed by them we tacked cautiously towards the inner bay. It was striking midnight when we came alongside the wharf of the Hudson Bay Company's warehouse and at daybreak the next morning, on the 3rd July, on the thirteenth day after leaving Sitka, we were once more on dry land.

THE RETURN JOURNEY TO SAN FRANCISCO.

My first business when I had settled myself comfortably in the French hotel, where I had previously stayed, was to get into telegraphic communication with my firm in New York and to inform my friends there of the success of my expedition. This was the longest telegram that I had ever sent—it consisted of 147 words and cost 120 gold dollars. Then I sought out my former acquaintances and was unpleasantly surprised to hear that our ship had been given up as lost and they had not expected to see me again. It is a strange experience when one's death has been reported to appear suddenly in the flesh, and I shall never forget the glad surprise of my English hotel acquaintance when, scarcely trusting his eyes, he saw before him a man whom he believed to have perished.

So far as I could make out, the report of our loss had already been sent to San Francisco and naturally I was very much distressed at the thought that the news might have been sent on from San Francisco to New York and thence to my relatives. The tidings must have been brought to Victoria by one of the northern coasting steamers and it was the more readily believed because just at that time two trading-vessels, the *Red Rover* and the *Thornton*, both of which we had encountered on our outward journey, had been attacked by Indians. The former had been lost with all hands, whilst the *Thornton* had had a very narrow escape.

Precise details of the loss of the *Red Rover*, with which it will be remembered we had voyaged for some days, were never known. It was certain, however, that the ship had been attacked by Indians, had been run on the rocks by the crew in their efforts to escape pursuit and gone down with all hands on board. The disaster must have taken place shortly after we had left them, somewhere between Fort Simpson and Fort Tongass. On the other hand, the *Thornton* which had been the first to tell us of the loss of the *Growler*, and had even obtained some fragments of the wreck, had on its way back to Victoria been near the settlement of the Nukletah Indians, that small cluster of islands in Queen Charlotte Sound where we had spent a night and been well received by the natives. Whether the Indians had some particular grudge against the crew of the *Thornton*, or wanted to avenge themselves in their usual way for some wrong done to them by the white men, was never cleared up. Perhaps they knew that the trading-ship, which was returning from a long voyage, had a valuable cargo of furs. Anyhow when the ship, which had no intention of going to their settlement, which lay deep in the island labyrinth, was coming from Nervitty and wanted to pass by them, a canoe manned by three Indians came out and called on the ship to come to their camp and do trade with them. The captain of the *Thornton* declined the request but was becalmed and so compelled to remain in that neighbourhood much against his will, for the Indian pilot from the neighbouring Nervitty settlement warned him that the Nukletahs were not to be trusted, as in his opinion they had evil designs and probably only wanted the ship to stay in the narrow channel in order that they might be able to capture it more easily.

In fact something seemed to be going on on the adjacent bank. When the first canoe had returned nearly to the shore, suddenly three large war-canoes appeared round the next headland, behind which they had evidently been lying hidden, and paddled down towards the sailing-ship. Meantime the two white men had not been idle and everything had been put in a state of defence. A number of empty casks were rolled on deck to serve as a barricade; the captain placed himself with his Henry rifle, which held fourteen rounds, behind the mast, the sailor posted himself behind the life-boat armed with two revolvers, the Indian pilot stationed himself at the helm protected as much as possible by a rampart improvised from mattresses. A young Indian, who was on board as cabin-boy, lay down in the hatchway armed with an old-fashioned carbine with wide mouth like a funnel, which was capable of keeping up a destructive fire at a short range. Two squaws, who would not venture outside the cabin, volunteered at any rate to help with the loading, so everything was ready when the three canoes approached.

" We counted," so the captain, who still seemed to be suffering from his wound, told me, " twenty-three Indian warriors all painted with red-and-black stripes, which clearly showed that they had hostile intentions. As they came up to the ship, which was now feeling a light breeze, the three canoes, which had hitherto kept close together, separated and tried to get alongside, so that the Indians could jump on board. I called to them twice to keep back but when despite this, one of the Indians at the bow of our boat seized a rope which was hanging there and tried to swing himself on board, I shot him down. The poor wretch, wounded in the breast, fell overboard and sank. At the same moment the other Indians had thrown off the cedar-bark mats, which covered the bottoms of the canoes and revealed an extraordinary number of guns which they had kept hidden. Instantly each seized one and from three different directions the fire of the assailants broke out. Fortunately for us, though there was little wind, the sea was rather rough so that the canoes were very unsteady and the Indians could not aim straight. Most of the shots flew over our heads but others struck, and after a few moments all of us had got our share of the hail of shot which they poured on us. Each Indian appeared to have three or four loaded guns, mostly double-barrelled ones, for they fired without interruption, though we did not see them reload. They thought that by this means they would offset the deadly revolvers.

"But meantime we had also been busy. Almost every shot from my Henry rifle was a hit; the sailor fired only when he was certain of hitting his man; and the fire of the cabin-boy was quite remarkably effective, for he used his carbine untiringly and once emptied the whole charge into one of the well-manned canoes. Against a fire of this kind the Indians, who had only small shot, could not make a stand. Two canoes were literally riddled and sank; fourteen Indians in them were either killed or mortally wounded, and the remainder saved themselves on the other canoe in miserable flight.

"The retreat of our foes did not take place a minute too soon, for with the exception of the pilot, who must have protected himself in a remarkable way, we were all wounded though only by small shot. The Indian youth seemed to be in the worst plight, for as soon as the excitement of the repelled attack was over he suddenly collapsed and came to himself only after a few minutes under the care of the Indian women. The whole upper part of his body was literally full of shot but happily his face was not injured. The sailor too had many of the small shot in his arms and shoulders, and I myself felt a stinging pain in the abdomen where, as I discovered later, I had received a whole charge at the range of only a few feet.

"Wounded and exhausted though we were we took to the oars and tried to get away from that dangerous place as quickly as possible for the Indians might be reinforced and renew the attack and we could scarcely have withstood a second onslaught.

"A breeze now came to our help and in the evening we reached Fort Rupert, where we were looked after until we were able to resume our journey to the south. Our pilot, however, begged for permission to return immediately to his own tribe that he might call on them to prepare for the conflict with the Nukletahs, who were enraged by the defeat they had sustained and would also know that it was he who had played the part of informer.

" It was only five days ago " concluded my informant, " that we reached this harbour and the state of our sails, which are as full of holes as a sieve, as well as my own ruined health will be sufficient to convince you of the terrible time we passed through."

The crime committed by the Nukletah Indians, formerly so peaceable, and thus brought to the notice of the authorities at Victoria naturally caused a great stir. One of the gun-boats which served to guard the coast was immediately despatched to the Nukletah settlement with orders to raze the whole camp to the ground and if possible to bring back some of the chiefs as hostages for future good behaviour. The order was doubtless carried out, so far as concerns the first part ; but, as always happens, the gun-boat on its arrival must have found the birds flown, so it fired on and completely destroyed the miserable huts, whilst the wily Indians, having received timely warning, watched this useless destruction from a secure hiding-place, and when the warship had gone merely built a new camp a short distance away.

The small effect of such reprisals is shown by the fact that a few weeks later, when our old ship, the *Black Diamond*, was returning from her next voyage to Sitka and on that occasion was taking the inner passage by Queen Charlotte Island, she was herself attacked in the neighbourhood of the Nukletah settlement and entirely plundered. The captain and crew escaped with their bare lives only because another ship happened just then to come into sight.

It may be imagined that we esteemed ourselves fortunate to have come off unscathed from so many dangers and had no desire for a repetition of our experiences.

After several days' stay in Victoria, which I utilised in repairing the ravages in my neglected wardrobe, I took a passage on board a ship bound for Portland and disembarked at Astoria in order to catch the steamer which was starting for San Francisco the next morning and thus avoid the long journey up the Columbia River. At Astoria I parted from my old friends, the gold-diggers, after wishing them a cordial farewell and good luck on the way. Before that I had to supply them with my address so that they could liquidate their debt to me should they chance to strike a " vein." I had advanced them their passage money to Oregon and may possibly some day, get the money back, though I do not expect it.

From Astoria we reached the Golden Gate of San Francisco in two and a half days and on the 14th July at 4 o'clock in the afternoon I was once again in my old quarters, which I had left on the 4th April, more than three months previously.

PART IV.

The following is extracted from the rough notes which constitute the original English Diary.—O. T.

CONCLUSION.

After remaining about two months in San Francisco (during which time I made several excursions in the neighbourhood, including one of 280 miles to Virginia City and its silver mines), I purchased my ticket from Wells Fargo

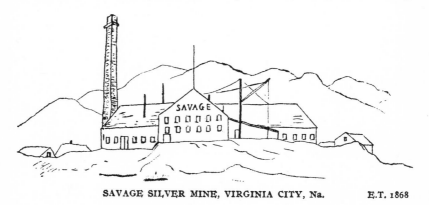

SAVAGE SILVER MINE, VIRGINIA CITY, Na.   E.T. 1868

& Co., costing 290 dollars, for the journey (3,491 miles) to New York. Leaving San Francisco at 4 p.m. on the 25th September, the steamer reached Sacramento at 2 a.m. on the following day. A few hours later I boarded the C.P.R.R. train, which was very crowded on account of the State Fair which was being held at Sacramento. The country was flat and fertile at first, but at Rocklyn the ascent commenced, and after passing Trukee station and Donner Lake, near the summit of the Sierra Nevada, the track followed the Trukee River valley. After changing trains at Reno-Virginia station, which was crowded with

Negroes, Chinamen, miners, desperadoes and fast women, the journey was continued through sage brush country along the Trukee River valley as far as Wadsworth station ; the latter, situated at the crossing of the Trukee River, is at present railhead, and consists of some 50 irregular shanties and a number of tents. About 1,500 men are at work some distance ahead and another 5,000 behind. Owing to the overland stage coach being too crowded, three other passengers and I decided to stay until the next day : we managed to get a bedroom in the boarding-house with 20 other rough-looking men, who, however, behaved very decently. Close to the house was a large camp in which numbers of Chinamen were working by torchlight.

BONNER SHAFT GOULD & CURRY SILVER MINE, VIRGINIA CITY, Na. E.T. 1868

We were informed that quite recently 70 white men from Virginia had been massacred by Indians in the vicinity. There is excellent trout spearing in the Trukee River in this district, also a large Piute reservation.

At 2 p.m. on 27th September, the stage coach left Wadsworth, and arrived at Coffinwood some four hours later. The scenery now changed, and our route lay through a great alkali desert, containing enormous deposits of pure salt ; this desert basin partly surrounded by mountains, on the sides of which one could still see the " watermark," had evidently been connected with the sea in olden days, and at " high tide " it is even now occasionally flooded with salt water.

As we drove along in the moonlight, the effect of the latter on the glistening white salt was most striking.

After passing Ragtown, the place where the emigrants threw off their clothing, Still Water, at the confluence of the Trukee, Humboldt and Carson rivers, was reached at midnight. We had driven 105 miles since 2 p.m.

28th September.—After an hour's halt the stage was on the move again ; at dawn we passed Fairview, where a number of roading Indians and mule-trains were encountered. At Westgate one noticed that the houses

STATION, OVERLAND ROUTE, NEVADA.   E.T. 1868

were built of mud, and not boarded. A little later our route crossed a range of bare rocky mountains, past deserted ranches,—more Indians, this time mounted on fiery mustangs. After passing White Rock and Butterfield we entered the famous New Pass Cañon between the high steep bluffs of picturesque rocks : at Jacobsville there is a very large team station. Austin, a town of some 4,000 inhabitants, situated in the Rees River valley, and famous for its silver mines and sulphur springs, was our next halting place, soon after sunset. At 11 p.m. our journey recommenced ; it was bitterly cold on the driver's seat, but this was preferable to the stuffy atmosphere inside the coach. By midnight we had accomplished 120 miles since 1 a.m.

29th September.—As the sun rose we passed through Cape Horn and a little later changed horses at Dry Creek ;

after halting again at Cropp Wells, we reached the White Pine Mountains, famous for their silver mines. Our company now consisted of Moody (President of the Silver Mine Company in Austin), Freedenburg (a Dutchman from Japan), a Baptist Minister, two ladies from Austin, and two young miners from White Pine Mountains going East. After passing through Diamond Valley, Crystal Springs and Ruby Valley, the country became less sterile, and we occasionally saw hay and milk ranches : also large camps of Suschone Indians, and many roading Indians

NEW PASS STATION, NEVADA.   F.T. 1868

wherever we halted. The outstanding feature of the landscape was a range of mountains running N.E. and S.E. with broad valleys intervening ; sage brush predominated again, there being very little pasture-land, and loghouses took the place of stone huts. 107 miles run at 7 p.m.

30th September.—After changing coaches we set out again at 1 a.m. This time very uncomfortable and crowded, which made sleep impossible. We passed Piute Station at 5 a.m. and an hour later reached Eagan's Valley and Home Station. Here we saw another silver mine, and very savage-looking Indians, who, however, did not molest us : thence through curious-looking rock formation and narrow passes to Shell Creek, at mid-day. At sunset we reached Silver Springs, and a little later Deep Creek, where we made our evening halt. There were some large alkali flats in the neighbourhood and a few silver and copper mines. Three years ago when the westward bound stage was approaching Deep Creek Station, it was ambushed by Suschone Indians, who shot (and killed) the driver, station-keeper and ostler, but a passenger seizing the reins, the coach reached Silver Springs safely, though closely pressed by the Indians. This was followed by severe fighting, after which there were only about 100 Suschone Indians left. By midnight our day's run amounted to 140 miles.

1st October.—At 3 a.m. we reached Fish Spring, the track through alkali flats was very bad, making sleep quite impossible. At 1.30 p.m. we entered Utah territory, and noticed that the country began to look more fertile.

HAY RANCH—UTAH TERRITORY.
(OVERLAND ROUTE.)   R.T. 1868

After passing an emigrant camp and several ranches we crossed the last mountain range at 3 p.m., and descended into Rush Valley station, in sight of several Mormon settlements and Stockton Lake. We were now in a grass country dotted with cedar bushes, and a few hours later the Great Salt Lake came into view—114 miles run.

2nd October.—A few hours halt was made at Salt Lake City, and as soon as it was light, the Dutchman and I seized the opportunity of seeing as much as possible of this remarkable place. The town covers an area of about nine miles, and is a beautifully-laid-out city. The streets are wide, with water running down the side of each ; every block of houses is surrounded by shady trees, and nearly every house has its own orchard of apple, peach, apricot and cherry trees. The chief buildings are the Tabernacle, the Temple and Brigham Young's residence, the latter consisting of the Beehive House and Lion House enclosed within a high stone wall. We were told that Brigham Young has 60 women, 75 children and is 65 years of age. There were several other large houses, which were the residences of the Mormon Bishops and Elders.

On leaving Salt Lake City our route lay through the wonderful valleys of the Wahsatch Mountains, beautiful foliage and mountain streams. Passing through Parley's Cañon we reached Parley's ranch at mid-day, where a company of U.S. soldiers, en route for Camp Douglas, was resting. Thence through fertile valleys into East Echo Cañon, past Silver Creek and the Mormon settlements of Moschip and Colville to Choak Creek, and entered the famous Echo Cañon at sunset. Here timber was being collected for the new railroad, and the beautiful scenery was somewhat spoilt by the drunken desperadoes who were encamped in the vicinity. Day's run—107 miles.

3rd October.—During the night we passed through Echo Cañon, and at 3 a.m. reached Quaking Asp Bridge, the summit of the Western Rocky Mountains ; here we saw Yellow and Sulphur Creek which flow into the Salt Lake, and Muddy Creek which joins Hamps Fork and thus reaches the Pacific. Descending to Pioneer Hollow we passed through a comparatively level plateau, without much timber, and reached Fort Bridger at 8 a.m. This is a pleasant spot, a fresh stream runs through the camp-yard, the Valley is green and fertile, and in the background are the beautiful and always snow-covered mountains. 300 soldiers are stationed in the Fort, where also stores for the supply of the Suschone and Pawnee Indians are kept ; this spring, 5,000 Indians came to get supplies. The civilian population of this station appeared to consist of the most evil-looking desperadoes. Soon after leaving this fertile valley, we entered a desert and sage brush district, punctuated here and there by earth heaps resembling tumuli. The day was hot and we saw numerous mirages. Towards sunset we reached Bryant City, where the construction of the track for the U.P.R.R. was in progress. After passing Green River City, our coach forded that river by moonlight, a somewhat dangerous passage. Thence through a series of narrow cañons, the sides of which were studded with castle-like rocks, until midnight.

October 4th.—During the night our route lay through a continuous series of cañons, along bad alkali roads, on which we met numerous herds of horses and cattle. We passed the spot where our coach had been robbed a month ago of 48,000 dollars bullion. This highway robbery had been organised by a blacksmith, formerly employed by the Wells Fargo Company, aided by a number of desperadoes with blackened faces; the surrounding country is still being scoured for the miscreants. After passing the Devil's Post Office (a big rock full of holes) where we shot an antelope and a wolf; Rock Point, the terminus of the U.P.R.R. was reached at 6 a.m. Here I boarded the train, and travelling via Omaha, Chicago, Niagara (where a day was spent) and Palmyra, reached New York on 11th October; the distance from San Francisco is 3,491 miles, and I had accomplished this in 17 days.

On 22nd October I sailed on the *Deutschland*, and on board made the acquaintance of Nathaniel Hawthorne and his family, arriving, after an uneventful voyage, at Southampton on 1st November.

MILITARY POST, U.P.R.R.   E.T. 1868

THE END.